Meeting the Standards in Primary Science

A Guide to the ITT NC

Lynn D. Newton

London and New York

First published 2000
by RoutledgeFalmer
11 New Fetter Lane, London EC4P 4EE

Simultaneously published in the USA and Canada
by RoutledgeFalmer
29 West 35th Street, New York, NY 10001

RoutledgeFalmer is an imprint of the Taylor & Francis Group

© 2000 Lynn D. Newton

Typeset in Bembo by Graphicraft Limited, Hong Kong
Printed and bound in Great Britain by TJ International Ltd,
Padstow, Cornwall

British Library Cataloguing in Publication Data
A catalogue record for this book is available from the British Library.

Library of Congress Cataloging in Publication Data
Newton, Lynn D., 1953–
    Meeting the standards in primary science: a guide to the ITT NC /
Lynn D. Newton.
        p.   cm. – (Meeting the standards series)
    Includes bibliographical references and index.
    1. Science–Study and teaching (Elementary)–Standards–Great Britain.
    I. Title.   II. Series.
    LB1585.5.G7 N498 2000
    372.3'5044'0941–dc21   99-087404

ISBN 0-750-70991-X

Meeting the Standards in Primary Science

There is increasing pressure on students training to be primary teachers to develop their subject expertise and classroom competence in a short space of time. All students on primary initial teacher training programmes must meet the requirements of Circular 4/98, *Teaching: High Status, High Standards* (DfEE, 1998) relating to science subject knowledge and subject application. **Lynn Newton** guides students through what they need to know, using clear explanations and drawing on students' own knowledge of science.

Meeting the Standards in Primary Science provides:

- the pedagogical knowledge needed to teach science in primary schools;
- chapters explicitly linked to blocks of curriculum requirements;
- support activities for work in schools and self-study;
- information on professional development for primary teachers.

This practical, comprehensive and accessible book should prove invaluable for students on primary initial teacher training courses, PGCE students, lecturers on science education programmes and newly qualified primary teachers. It is one of a series of books that provide subject knowledge and application in English, maths, science and ICT for primary and secondary students and teachers.

Lynn D. Newton is Senior Lecturer and Director of Primary Programmes in the School of Education, University of Durham. She has extensive experience researching and writing on science issues for primary teachers and she is the author of *Coordinating Science Across the Primary School*, also published by RoutledgeFalmer.

Meeting the Standards Series

Series Editor:
Lynn D. Newton, School of Education, University of Durham, Leazes Road, Durham, DH1 1TA

Meeting the Standards in Primary English
Angel Scott

Meeting the Standards in Primary Mathematics
Ann MacNamara

Meeting the Standards in Primary Science
Lynn D. Newton

Meeting the Standards in Primary ICT
Steve Higgins and Jen Miller

Meeting the Standards in Secondary English
Frank Hardman, John Williamson, Mike Fleming and David Stevens

Meeting the Standards in Secondary Science
Marion Jones and Ros Roberts

Meeting the Standards in Secondary ICT
John Halocha and John Ingram

Contents

Illustrations

FIGURES

TABLES

TASKS

Series Editor's Preface

This book has been prepared for students training to be primary teachers who face the challenge of meeting the many requirements for science specified in Circular 4/98, the Teacher Training Agency's framework for initial teacher training, *Teaching: High Status, High Standards* (TTA, 1998). The book forms part of a new series of publications that sets out to guide students on initial teacher training programmes, both primary and secondary, through the complex package of subject requirements they will be expected to meet before they can be awarded Qualified Teacher Status.

Why is there a need for such a series? Teaching has always been a demanding profession, requiring of its members enthusiasm, dedication and commitment. In addition, it is common sense that teachers need to know not only what they teach but how to teach it most effectively. Current trends in education highlight the raising of standards (particularly in the areas of numeracy and literacy), the use of new technologies across the curriculum and the development of key skills for lifelong learning. These run alongside Early Learning Goals, Baseline Assessment, the requirements of the National Curriculum, Standard Assessment Tasks (SATs), interim tasks, GCSE examinations, new post-16 examination structures, BTEC qualifications. . . . The list seems endless. Such demands increase the pressure on teachers generally and teachers in training in particular.

At the primary school level, since the introduction of the National Curriculum there is an even greater emphasis now than ever before on teachers' own subject knowledge and subject application. Trainees have to become Jacks and Jills of all trades – developing the competence and confidence to plan, organize, manage, monitor and assess all ten areas of the National Curriculum plus religious education. The increasing complexity of the primary curriculum and ever more demanding societal expectations makes it very difficult for trainees and their mentors (be they tutors in the training institutions or teachers in schools) to cover everything that is necessary in what feels like a very short space of time. Four of the books in this series are aimed specifically at the trainee primary teacher and those who are helping to train them:

- *Meeting the Standards in . . . Primary English*
- *Meeting the Standards in . . . Primary Mathematics*
- *Meeting the Standards in . . . Primary Science*
- *Meeting the Standards in . . . Primary Information and Communications Technology*

For those training to be secondary school teachers, the pressures are just as great. They will probably bring with them knowledge and expertise of their specialist subject, taken to degree level at least. However, content studied to degree level in universities is unlikely to match closely the needs of the National Curriculum. A degree in medieval English, applied mathematics or biochemistry will not be sufficient in itself to enable a trainee to walk into a classroom of 13- or 16-year-olds and teach English, mathematics or science. Each subject at school level is likely to be broader. For example, science must include physics, chemistry, biology, astronomy and aspects of geology. In addition, there is the 'how to teach it' dimension – subject application. Furthermore, secondary school teachers are often expected to be able to offer more than one subject. Thus, four of the books in the series are aimed specifically at the secondary school level:

- *Meeting the Standards in . . . Secondary English*
- *Meeting the Standards in . . . Secondary Mathematics*
- *Meeting the Standards in . . . Secondary Science*
- *Meeting the Standards in . . . Secondary Information and Communications Technology*

All the books deal with the specific issues which underpin the relevant TTA requirements identified in Circular 4/98. The very nature of the subject areas covered and the teaching phases focused upon means that each book will, of necessity, be presented in different ways. However, each will cover the relevant subject Annex from Circular 4/98. Thus, the books will deal with:

- subject knowledge – an overview of what to teach, the relevant subject knowledge that the trainees need to know and understand in order to interpret and teach the National Curriculum requirements for that subject;
- subject application – an overview of how to interpret the subject knowledge so as to design appropriate learning experiences for pupils, organize and manage those experiences and monitor pupils' progress within them.

The former is not presented in the form of a text book. There are plenty of good quality GCSE and A-level textbooks on the market for those who feel the need to acquire that level of knowledge. Rather, the subject knowledge is related to identifying what is needed for the trainee to take the National Curriculum for the subject and translate it into a meaningful package for teaching and learning. The latter is structured in such a way as to identify the generic skills of planning, organizing, managing, monitoring and assessing the teaching and learning. The content is related to the specific requirements of Circular 4/98. The trainee's continuing professional development needs are also considered.

The purpose of the series is to give practical guidance and support to trainee teachers, in particular focusing on what to do and how to do it. Throughout each book there are directed tasks and activities which can be completed in the training institution, in school or independently at home. They serve to elicit and support the trainee's development of skills, knowledge and understanding needed to become an effective teacher.

Dr Lynn Newton
University of Durham,
February 2000

1 Welcome to Your Teaching Career

Teaching is without doubt the most important profession; without teaching there would be no other professions. It is also the most rewarding. What role in society can be more crucial than that which shapes children's lives and prepares them for adulthood?

(TTA, 1998, p. 1)

So, you have decided to become a primary teacher. You will, no doubt, have heard stories about teaching as a profession. Some will have been positive, encouraging, even stimulating. Others will have been negative. Nevertheless, you are still here, on the doorstep of a rewarding and worthwhile career. Without doubt teaching *is* a demanding and challenging profession. No two days are the same. Children are never the same. The curriculum seldom stays the same for very long. But these are all part of the challenge. Teaching as a career requires dedication, commitment, imagination and no small amount of energy. Despite this, when things go well, when you feel your efforts to help this child or these children learn have been successful, you will feel wonderful. Welcome to teaching.

RECENT DEVELOPMENTS IN PRIMARY TEACHING

As with most things, the teaching profession is constantly buffeted by the winds of change. In particular, the last decade or so has been a time of great change for all involved in primary education. At the heart has been the Education Reform Act (ERA) of 1988. The Act introduced a number of changes, the most significant of which was probably the creation of a National Curriculum and its related requirements for monitoring and assessment.

Although in the past there have been guidelines on curricula from professional bodies (such as teachers' unions), local authorities and official government publications, until

1988 teachers generally had freedom to decide for themselves *what* to teach and *how* to teach. Different approaches to curriculum planning and delivery proved influential at different times. As far as primary education is concerned, the most influential event before the ERA was probably the publication of the Plowden Report (Central Advisory Council for England, 1967), with its now quite famous phrase, 'At the heart of the education process lies the child'. Children were viewed as participants in the learning process, not passive recipients of it. Active involvement, a consideration of their needs and interests, the matching of curricula and support to the needs of individuals and groups were all seen as significant developments in the education of primary children. However, by the 1980s, there were those in education and in government who believed that the 'post-Plowden progressivism' had gone too far. There was a need to redress the balance, restore a structured curriculum and bring back traditional approaches to the classroom. Blyth suggests that as a consequence over the last decade or so:

> The relation between subjects and children's learning has preoccupied thinking about the primary curriculum especially since Plowden, and has unsurprisingly generated a very substantial body of professional literature.
>
> (Blyth, 1998, p. 11)

This preoccupation not only with the primary curriculum, but with progression in pupils' learning throughout the period of compulsory schooling and in all subjects, has resulted in the development of the idea of an official curriculum for England, Wales and Northern Ireland. Many other countries already had national curricula, so the idea was not new and there were models to draw upon.

In the second half of the 1980s, the government introduced the idea of a *Basic Curriculum* for all pupils of compulsory school age. At the heart of this is the *National Curriculum*, which is underpinned by a subject-led approach to areas of experience and their assessment. The focus of the National Curriculum was a 'core curriculum' of English, mathematics and science. This core was supported by a framework of 'foundation' subjects: art, design and technology, geography, history, information technology, music and physical education. In Welsh-speaking areas of Wales, Welsh was also included as a core subject and as a foundation subject in other parts of Wales. Outside the National Curriculum, but still embedded within the broader framework of the Basic Curriculum, were areas of experience such as religious education and a range of cross-curricular dimensions, themes and skills which allowed topic and thematic approaches in the primary classroom. This curriculum structure is summarized in Figure 1.1.

Initially grossly overloaded, the National Curriculum underwent a sequence of judicious prunings. The most drastic was in 1995, when Sir Ron Dearing reduced and reorganized the content, placed more emphasis on the key skills which all pupils should acquire and allowed the cross-curricular dimensions, themes and skills to disappear into the background. This generated a slimmed-down document which addressed some of the criticisms and concerns of primary teachers, and was accompanied by a promise that teachers would have a five-year period of calm. Revisions of the current National Curriculum are underway and will see Information and Communications Technology (ICT) introduced as the fourth core area.

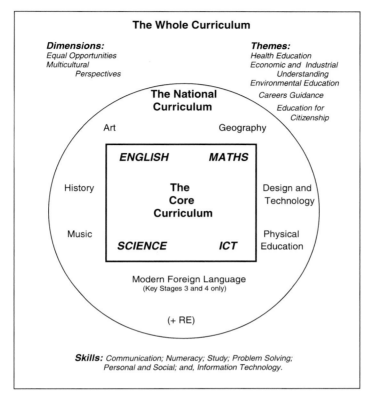

Figure 1.1 A representation of the primary school curriculum
(At the heart of the basic curriculum is a core of English, mathematics, science and ICT,
supported by the foundation subjects, such as art and history, plus religious education.
The National Curriculum is embedded in the broader framework of the Whole Curriculum,
which incorporates a range of cross-curricular dimensions, themes and skills.)

THE STANDARDS DEBATE

Parallel to the changing perspectives on curriculum has been an increasing emphasis on
standards. There has, in essence, been a shift in perspective from *equality in education*
(as reflected in the post-war legislation of the late 1940s) to the *quality of education*.

The term *standard* is emotive and value-laden. According to the Oxford English
Dictionary, it is: '(i) a weight or measure to which others conform or by which the
accuracy of others is judged; and (ii) a degree of excellence required for a particular
purpose'. Both definitions sit well with the educational use of the term, where it
translates as acceptable levels of performance by schools and teachers in the eyes of
public and politicians alike.

Over the last decade, the media have reported numerous apparent instances of falling
standards. This, in part, was a major force behind the introduction of the National

Curriculum and its related assessment procedures. In 1989, when the National Curriculum was first introduced, it was claimed that:

> There is every reason for optimism that in providing a sound, sufficiently detailed framework over the next decade, the National Curriculum will give children and teachers much needed help in achieving higher standards.
>
> (DES, 1989, p. 2)

Underpinning these forces of change in primary education have been two major emphases. The first is to do with the curriculum itself and the experiences we offer pupils in primary schools. The second, and not unrelated, is to do with how we measure and judge the outcomes of the teaching and learning enterprise. To achieve the appropriately educated citizens of the future, schools of the present must not only achieve universal literacy and numeracy but must be measurably and accountably seen to be doing so, hence the introduction of league tables as performance indicators.

David Blunkett, the Secretary of State for Education and Employment, said in 1997:

> Poor standards of literacy and numeracy are unacceptable. If our growing economic success is to be maintained we must get the basics right for everyone. Countries will only keep investing here at record levels if they see that the workforce is up to the job.
>
> (DfEE, 1997, p. 2)

While the economic arguments are strong, we need to balance the needs of the economy with the needs of the child. Few teachers are likely to disagree with the need to get the 'basics' right. After all, literacy and numeracy skills underpin much that we do with children in science and in other areas of the curriculum. However, the increased focus on the 'basics' should not be at the expense of these other areas of experience. Children need access to a broad and balanced curriculum if they are to develop as broad, balanced individuals.

All primary schools are now ranked each year on the basis of their Key Stage 2 pupils' performances in the standardized tests (Standard Assessment Tasks (SATs)) for English, mathematics and science. The performances of individual children are conveyed only to their parents, although the school's collective results are discussed with school governors and also given to the local education authority (LEA). The latter then informs the Department of Education and Employment (DfEE), who publish the national figures on a school/LEA basis. This gives parents the opportunity to compare, judge and choose schools in their area. The figures indicate, for each school within the LEA, the percentage above and below the expected level, that is, the schools which are or are not meeting the standard. This, inevitably, results in debate about whether standards are rising or falling. Such crude measures as SATs for comparing attainment have been widely criticized. Fitz-Gibbon (1995) emphasized that such measures ignore the 'value added elements', the factors which influence teaching and learning such as the catchment area of the school, the proportion of pupils for whom English is an additional language, and the quality and quantity of educational enrichment a child receives in the home. Davies (1998) suggests that,

Dissatisfaction [with standards] is expressed spasmodically throughout the year but reaches fever pitch when the annual national test results are published. Whatever the results, they are rarely deemed satisfactory and targets are set which expect future cohorts of children to achieve even higher standards than their predecessors.

(Davies, 1998, p. 162)

Targets to be achieved by schools by the year 2002 include, for example, those to do with raising the standard of literacy and numeracy and improving standards of class management and control.

There are also targets for initial teacher training, to redress the perceived inadequacies in existing course provision. These centre on a National Curriculum for initial teacher training, prescribing the skills, knowledge and understanding which all trainees must achieve before they can be awarded Qualified Teacher Status (QTS). As a trainee for the teaching profession you must be equipped to deal with these demanding situations as well as meeting all the required standards. How will you be prepared for this?

ROUTES INTO A CAREER IN TEACHING

Let us first consider the routes into teaching open to anyone wanting to become a teacher. Teaching is now an all-graduate profession, although this has not always been the case. For most primary teachers in the United Kingdom, this has usually been via an undergraduate pathway, reading for a degree at a university (or a college affiliated to a university) which resulted in the award of Bachelor of Education (BEd) with Qualified Teacher Status (QTS). Such a route has usually taken at least three and sometimes four years. More recently, such degrees have become more linked to subject specialisms and some universities offer Bachelor of Arts in Education (BA(Ed)) with QTS and Bachelor of Science in Education (BSc(Ed)) with QTS. A smaller proportion of primary teachers choose to gain a degree from a university first, and then train to teach through the postgraduate route. This usually takes one year, at the end of which the successful trainee is awarded a Postgraduate Certificate in Education (PGCE) with QTS. In all cases, the degree or postgraduate certificate is awarded by the training institution but QTS is awarded by the DfEE as a consequence of success-ful completion of the course and on the recommendation of the training institution. Whichever route is followed, there are rigorous government requirements which must be met by both the institutions providing the training and the trainees following the training programme before QTS can be awarded.

During the late 1980s and early 1990s, a number of government initiatives have moved initial teacher training in the direction of partnership with schools. This has meant school staff take greater responsibility for supporting and assessing students on placements. A transfer of funds (either as money or as in-service provision) is made to the schools by the universities in payment for this increased responsibility. Alongside this, school staff have increasingly become involved in the selection and interviewing of prospective students, the planning and delivery of the courses and the overall quality assurance process.

More recent legislation established the Teacher Training Agency (TTA), a government body which, as its name suggests, has control over the nature and funding of initial teacher training courses. This legislation is important to you as a trainee teacher, since the associated documentation defines your preparation for and induction into the teaching profession. How will the legislation affect you?

TTA REQUIREMENTS ON COURSES OF INITIAL TEACHER TRAINING

In 1997, a government circular number 10/97 introduced the idea of a national curriculum for initial teacher training (ITT), to parallel that already being used in schools. This major focus in the training of teachers is on the development of your all-round professionalism. It implied:

> more than meeting a series of discrete standards. It is necessary to consider the standards as a whole to appreciate the creativity, commitment, energy and enthusiasm which teaching demands, and the intellectual and managerial skills required of the effective professional.
>
> (DfEE, 1997, p. 2)

At the heart of this is the aim of raising standards. Circular 10/97 had specified:

1   the standards which *all* trainees must meet for the award of QTS;
2   the initial teacher training curricula for English and mathematics; and,
3   the requirements on teacher training institutions providing courses of initial teacher training.

Subsumed under (1) were groups of standards relating to the personal subject knowledge of the trainee, criteria related to his or her abilities to apply the skills, knowledge and understanding to the teaching and learning situation, and criteria related to the planning, management and assessment of learning and behaviour.

In May 1998, the DfEE issued circular number 4/98, *Teaching: High Status, High Standards*. In it, the Secretary of State's earlier criteria were revised and extended. As well as generic standards for the award of QTS, the new document specified separate national curricula for initial teacher training not only in English and mathematics, but also in science and the use of information and communications technology in subject teaching. The fundamental aim of this new National Curriculum for ITT was to:

> equip all new teachers with the knowledge, understanding and skills needed to play their part in raising pupil performance across the education system.
>
> (DfEE, 1998, p. 3)

Circular 4/98 included the following sections:

> Annex A: Standards for the award of Qualified Teacher Status;
> Annex B: Initial Teacher Training Curriculum for the Use of Information
>   and Communications Technology in subject teaching;
> Annex C: Initial Teacher Training Curriculum for Primary English;
> Annex D: Initial Teacher Training Curriculum for Primary Mathematics;
> Annex E: Initial Teacher Training Curriculum for Primary Science;
> Annex F: Initial Teacher Training Curriculum for Secondary English;
> Annex G: Initial Teacher Training Curriculum for Secondary Mathematics;
> Annex H: Initial Teacher Training Curriculum for Secondary Science; and,
> Annex I: Requirements for all courses of Initial Teacher Training.

How does this affect you as a student teacher? In essence, it means that you must 'meet the standards' before you can be awarded QTS. One of the major tasks facing you as an entrant to the teaching profession is that of showing competence in not dozens but hundreds of standards and statements relating to your skills, knowledge and understanding. As a trainee, you must show that you have met these standards by the end of your training programme so as to be eligible for the award of QTS. Courses in universities and other higher education institutions are designed to help you do so, both in schools and in the institution, but the onus is likely to be on you to provide the evidence to show how you have met the requirements. This series of books, *Meeting the Standards in . . .* , is designed to help you with this task. This particular book focuses on those skills and competences you will need to acquire to show that you have met the requirements for science.

There is more to teaching primary science than simply having a good knowledge and understanding of the subject. One of the major tasks ahead of you is to develop the ability to translate what you know and understand about science into worthwhile teaching and learning experiences for your pupils. You need to develop your *pedagogical skills, knowledge and understanding*. This is as important as your knowledge and understanding of the National Curriculum Order for Science. The latter provides you with a framework of what to teach in primary science. It does not tell you how to teach it – how to plan, organize, manage and assess the learning of the thirty or so children in your class, each with varied and changing needs. This is left to your own professionalism. This book is designed to help you to make a start on this.

OVERVIEW OF THIS BOOK

Few students on primary initial teacher training programmes begin their courses as experts in science. You are unlikely to have expertise in the teaching and learning process although you will have experienced it in some shape or form. While such experience and expertise does vary from person to person, all trainees have one thing in common, *potential*. You have successfully cleared the hurdles of application forms and interview procedures and have a place on a primary initial teacher training course.

It has been decided that you have the personal qualities which indicate that you are capable of acquiring the skills, knowledge and understanding needed to become an effective primary teacher. In other words, you have shown evidence that you have the potential to *meet the standards*.

This book is designed to help you do this, but it is only a part of the picture. It will be most useful to you if you read it in conjunction with the other experiences offered to you on your training programme. These will range from the theoretical to practical in the following way.

- *Directed reading:* reading might be handouts related to lectures, books and articles for assignments or professional newspapers and magazines simply to broaden your own professional base;
- *Taught sessions:* these could take the form of formal lectures, informal practical workshops or combinations of either, whether in schools or in the institution;
- *Talks/discussions:* again, these could be held in school or in the institution and can range from formal structured seminars with a group to more informal one-to-one discussions, usually with the aim of integrating theory and practice;
- *Tutorial advice:* one-to-one sessions with a tutor, mentor or teacher to plan for and reflect upon your practical experiences;
- *Observations:* opportunities to watch your class teacher and other experienced primary teachers at work in their classrooms;
- *Restricted experience:* opportunities to try out, under the guidance of your teacher or mentor, limited teaching activities with a small group of children, perhaps building up to a whole class session;
- *Teaching practice:* a block placement where you take responsibility for the planning, teaching and assessment of a class of children, under the guidance of your class teacher, school mentor and tutor and usually within defined parameters.

What is important about all of these is the amount of effort you put into them. No one can do the work for you. Your tutors, mentors in school and class teachers may all offer you advice, guidance and even criticism. How you respond is up to you. This, once again, is a reflection of your professionalism.

The book is written with the aim of giving you a general introduction to teaching science in primary schools. It is set out in such a way that the sections and chapters link explicitly to the clusters of standards in Annex E of the DfEE Circular 4/98. You will probably be given copies of the relevant sections of DfEE Circular 4/98 on your ITT training course. The book will also link indirectly into the more generic standards specified in Annex A, to be met by all trainees regardless of phase or subject specialism. Each chapter can stand alone. Each has clear sub-headings, so you can relate them directly to your institution's training programme for science and to the experiences you have in school. Throughout, whenever appropriate, there is reference to recent research into topics and issues in primary science and suggestions for further reading.

This should be particularly useful for you if you hope to become a science co-ordinator. The structure of each chapter generally follows, as far as is possible, the sections and sub-sections of Annex E, reflecting the clusters of requirements in science which you will need to think about.

Some of the skills and competences that you are expected to acquire are best done in the practical context of the schools in which you will be placed for your school experiences. To this end, there are a number of tasks and activities for you to complete while on these school placements. Obviously, these will have to be interpreted flexibly by you, as schools and access to children will vary. Other tasks are suggested to encourage you to think about how theory and practice work together, in other words to begin the process of reflection.

SUGGESTIONS FOR FURTHER READING

If you would like to explore further some of the issues touched upon in this introduction, the following books might be of interest to you.

Cashdan, A. and Overall, L. (eds) (1998) *Teaching in Primary Schools*, London: Cassell
In their book, Cashdan and Overall bring together a collection of views on a range of issues to do with primary education. The book is useful for the trainee in that it provides the background from the perspective of government's requirements on new entrants into teaching, in particular the generic skills, knowledge and understanding underpinning Annex A of Circular 4/98.

Edwards, A. and Collison, J. (1996) *Mentoring and Developing Practice in Primary Schools: Supporting Student Teacher Learning in Schools*, Milton Keynes: Open University Press
For trainees interested in the role of schools and teachers in the process of initial teacher training, this book provides a detailed discussion. Written primarily for the primary teacher taking on this role, it considers the different aspects of the role and how the trainee can best be supported and developed.

Moon, B. (1996) *A Guide to the National Curriculum*, Oxford: OUP
This third edition of Moon's book expands upon the discussion in the light of the 1995 revisions and provides an excellent overview of the National Curriculum, its nature and evolution.

PART 1

Your Science Skills and Knowledge Base

Introduction

In science, there are a number of skills which you must develop and practise and a large body of knowledge and understanding you must acquire as a trainee teacher. These are specified in Circular 4/98. Before being awarded QTS your training institution will have to verify in various ways that you have demonstrated these successfully and can teach primary science effectively.

You are not coming to your teacher training course with absolutely no experience of science. You will have formed some ideas of what it is all about based on your encounters with science in school, through the media and through other adults. All of these experiences will have resulted in your own personal feelings and perceptions of science. We will begin with these. How do you feel about science?

Task P1.1 Feelings about science	For each pair of words, decide where you fit on the scale. Put a tick in the boxes which most closely match your feelings. The middle column is neutral. It means you are at neither one extreme nor the other.					
			Science is . . .			
Easy						Hard
Boring						Fun
Theoretical						Practical
Relevant						Irrelevant
Concrete						Abstract
Masculine						Feminine
Facts						Procedures
Problems						Solutions
Words						Calculations
Good						Evil

There are no right or wrong answers. This is just to let you see how your own experiences have coloured your views about science. Children are just the same. According to Nissani (1996),

> Educators are concerned . . . with widespread misconceptions about science itself . . . students [pupils] often believe that science is dull, irrelevant, incomprehensible, authoritarian, or purely descriptive.
>
> (p. 166)

A major influence on our perceptions of science is the experience we had at school, particularly secondary school. What is it that switches some children on to science? Why are others switched off? What happens at school to make such a difference?

Task P1.2 What do you remember about science?

What are your own memories of school science?

1 Make a list of about twenty things that you can remember from your science experiences.

2 Sort your list into two columns: those which are mainly positive and those which are mainly negative.

What does your list tell you about the things that you are going to have to think about as a teacher?

Evidence from educational research and school inspections indicates that one of the characteristics of effective teachers of science is that they have control over the science material being taught. In other words, they have a sound knowledge and understanding of science as a subject. The security that comes from this means teachers can plan carefully, have clear targets for lessons, organize and manage activities efficiently, deal with questions and queries without becoming confused and monitor progress. Let us begin with what you need to know and understand about science.

The scientific enterprise is usually described as having two major aspects:

- science is a *product* – a body of knowledge which requires you to understand the facts, laws, principles and generalizations that the scientific community call 'science'; and,
- science is a *process* – a way of thinking and working which requires the development and practice of skills in various contexts.

There is also a third aspect, often overlooked, which is equally important for you to think about:

- science involves *people* – it is human enterprise which is of direct relevance to all our lives and this relevance needs to be made explicit.

Think of these as the three Ps of science – Products, Processes and People. As you develop and expand your science skills, knowledge and understanding base into the realms of teaching and learning science, it is upon these three Ps that we shall be focusing.

In Part 1, you will consider your own knowledge and understanding of science, both as a process (a way of thinking and working) and as a product (a body of knowledge). We shall place these products and processes in the context of people (science as a human enterprise and its relevance to our lives). This is your *Science Skills and Knowledge Base*. It will support you in teaching science effectively at the primary school level. Obviously, this is not all you need to know and understand to be an effective teacher of primary science. You need to understand about matters such as how to plan science, organize resources and manage children. We will come to these and other related issues in Part 2.

What you are expected to know and understand about science is closely linked to the requirements of the National Curriculum Order for Science (DfEE, 1999). Although the Order covers the requirements for pupils between the ages of 5 and 16, that is, of compulsory school age, we will consider only the requirements which apply to Key Stages 1 and 2 (5 to 11-year-old pupils).

The summary in Table P1.1 compares the main elements of the National Curriculum for schools with the main elements of the requirements in Circular 4/98 (Annex E) relating to science.

Task P1.3 The National Curriculum Order for Science and the Science Requirements of Circular 4/98	Study the summaries of the two documents provided in Table P1.1. Compare the main features of the two. (a) What parallels do you notice between the documents? (b) How are they different?

Evaluate your own experiences of science in the light of these two sets of requirements. Consider the extent to which your own experiences provided you with a preparation for meeting these requirements, both as a learner and as a teacher.

Think of some strategies you might use to move forward with the development of your skills, knowledge and understanding of science. (Using this book is a starting point!)

When you first arrive at your college or university you may find that your science tutors will carry out an *audit* of your knowledge and understanding of science content. Where you have gaps you will be expected, usually with some form of support, to acquire the missing knowledge and understanding so that by the time you complete your training programme you can demonstrate that you have the necessary skills, knowledge and understanding to teach primary science effectively.

What is it that you, as an adult, must know and understand about science, both as a process and as a product? An important point to make is that even if you want to specialize in a particular phase of education you must still be trained to teach primary science right across the primary school at both key stages. This means that there is a lot to cover.

Table P1.1 The National Curriculum Order for Science (1995) at KS1 and KS2 compared with Circular 4/98 (Annex E) – Primary Science in Initial Teacher Training

National Curriculum Order for Science at KS1 and KS2	*DfEE Circular 4/98 – Annex E: Primary Science in ITT*

Common Teaching Requirements:
Inclusion: schools have a responsibility to provide a broad and balanced curriculum for all pupils, encapsulated in three principles:
  (a) setting suitable learning challenges;
  (b) responding to pupils' diverse learning needs;
  (c) overcoming potential barriers to learning and assessment for individuals and groups.
Use of language across the curriculum: pupils should be taught to express themselves correctly and appropriately and to read accurately and with understanding, and recognise and use standard English.
Use of information and communication technology: pupils should be given opportunities to develop their ICT ability through the use of ICT tools to support their learning in all subjects.
Health and Safety: in the context of science pupils should be taught about hazards and risks, how to make assessments and manage their environment to ensure the health and safety of themselves and others.
	General Requirements:
	Opportunities to enjoy science: so that you can teach science with enthusiasm.
	Use of technology: so that you can recognise the opportunities and strengths and weaknesses of technology like calculators and computers, and can use them appropriately.
	Access information sources: so that you can support your teaching by reference to appropriate research, inspection and other evidence.
	Use of language: you must understand and use correctly scientific and technical vocabulary in various contexts.
	Unifying overview: you must be able to identify how the different areas of the subject relate to each other, make conceptual links across science and be able to present a coherent perspective to pupils.
	Understanding of scientific ideas: you must be able to articulate and review your own understandings of the key ideas in science.

The Programmes of Study for Key Stages One and Two:
There are a number of requirements which apply across the four programmes of study:
  • promoting pupils' spiritual, moral, social and cultural development through science;
  • promoting key skills through science; and,
  • promoting other aspects of the curriculum.
	Trainees' scientific knowledge and understanding:
	This is the scientific knowledge and understanding which all trainees must demonstrate by the end of their course. *Trainees must demonstrate that they know and understand:*
	
	a. **the nature of science;**
	b. **the processes** of planning, carrying out and evaluating scientific investigations;

Table P1.1   *(cont'd)*

National Curriculum Order for Science at KS1 and KS2	DfEE Circular 4/98 – Annex E: Primary Science in ITT
Sc1: Scientific Enquiry ***1. Ideas and evidence in science:*** *Pupils should be taught that it is important to collect evidence by making observations and measurements when trying to answer a question.*	c. **the methods employed** in scientific investigation and how to use them in order to collect, record, analyse and interpret evidence;
2. Investigative skills: Pupils should be taught about: • Planning • Obtaining and presenting evidence • Considering evidence and evaluating	d. **the need for** clear and precise forms of communication in science; e. **health and safety requirements** and how to implement them;
Sc2: Life Processes and Living Things *Pupils should be taught about:* 1 Life processes 2 Humans and other animals 3 Green plants 4 Variation and classification 5 Living things in their environment	f. **life processes**, including functioning organisms, continuity and change and ecosystems;
Sc3: Materials and their Properties *Pupils should be taught about:* 1 Grouping materials (and classifying materials at KS2 only) 2 Changing materials 3 Separating mixtures of materials (at KS2 only).	g. **materials and their structure**, including particle theory and the conservation of mass;
Sc4: Physical Processes *Pupils should be taught about:* 1 Electricity 2 Forces and motion 3 Light and sound 4 The Earth and beyond (at KS2 only).	h. **physical processes**, including electricity and magnetism, energy, forces and motion, light, sound, and the Earth and beyond.
Breadth of Study: *Pupils' skills, knowledge and understanding should be extended through:* relevant *contexts* the role of science in *technology* the use of a range of *ICT*-based sources the use of appropriate *communication* skills a consideration of *health and safety* issues	

From your examination of the overview of the National Curriculum Programmes of Study for Key Stages 1 and 2 and the requirements of Circular 4/98, you will see that the curriculum for primary science in initial teacher training programmes generally incorporates the National Curriculum requirements. Your training programme is likely to be designed to ensure you cover all that you need to know. The chapters in this section make a start on this process. Each chapter has been deliberately structured to reflect a major cluster of standards from Circular 4/98, for example, *The Nature of Science* or *Life Processes*. Within each chapter, strands of the documents will also be picked out as sub-sections, so you can be clear about what you are covering (for example, *Humans as organisms* in the National Curriculum within *Life Processes* in Circular 4/98). These are elaborated upon appropriately. However, it is important to point out that the aim of this book is not to provide you with a GCSE level biology, physics or chemistry textbook. If you need this level of detail you are advised to turn to the many excellent textbooks available for this purpose. The aim of this book is to cover the key areas that meet the standards. Because this includes a large number of teaching and learning standards as well as subject knowledge standards, space is limited. Consequently, only the main ideas can be provided in a broad way. It is these ideas that are explained in the subsequent chapters.

SUGGESTIONS FOR FURTHER READING

If you would like to explore more fully some of the issues covered in this section, the following books might be of interest to you.

Carey, J. (ed.) (1995) *The Faber Book of Science*, London: Faber and Faber
This collected anthology of scientific writings captures the flavour and excitement of science while at the same time showing scientists to be human beings. Carey brings together a collection of readings that spans time and areas of science, but he has chosen them with care to be enjoyable and easy to read.

Farrow, S. (1999) *The Really Useful Science Book: A Framework of Knowledge for Primary Teachers*, London: Falmer Press
This second edition of *The Really Useful Science Book* has been written with primary classroom teachers and teachers-in-training in mind. It is designed to support and extend teachers' and students' own subject knowledge and understanding of science, particularly those who see themselves as 'non-specialists'.

Wenham, M. (1995) *Understanding Primary Science: Ideas, Concepts and Explanations*, London: Paul Chapman Publishing Limited
This book is written with the needs of primary teachers and their pupils in mind. It is based on the National Curriculum requirements and presents the facts, develops the key concepts and explains the theories underpinning them so that teachers and pupils will be able to understand the outcomes of the observations and investigations they are likely to be involved in. The text does not assume a great deal of scientific knowledge.

Wolpert, L. (1993) *The Unnatural Nature of Science*, London: Faber and Faber
Intended for the layman, this book sets out to de-mystify the nature of science and explain in clear and enjoyable terms what science is all about and, perhaps more thought-provokingly, what it is not.

2 What Do We Mean by the Nature of Science?

What is science? According to Wolpert (1993), it is:

> . . . arguably the defining feature of our age; it characterizes Western civilization. Science has never been more successful nor its impact on our lives greater, yet the ideas of science are alien to most people's thoughts.
>
> (p. ix)

Research would seem to indicate that the general public have only a vague idea of either what science is all about, or of what the scientific method involves (Fuller, 1997). To most non-scientists, science consists of discovering new facts about the world (Dunbar, 1995). Indeed, scientists themselves seldom seem to stop to ask what it is that characterizes their work.

> Being pragmatic people, they [scientists] have simply got on and done it. Philosophers, on the other hand, have spent a great deal of time worrying about how we should define science . . . Both groups have, in the end, been concerned with the same central issue, namely the certainty of our knowledge about the world, but their perspectives have been very different.
>
> (Dunbar, 1995, p. 12)

What is more, while such surveys confirm that there is both interest in and admiration for science, this goes hand in hand with a deep-seated fear of and hostility towards it (Wolpert, 1993).

So, to return to the earlier question, *What is science?* More accurately, we could ask, *What is involved in understanding the nature of science and the scientific enterprise?* There is not an easy answer, as Wolpert (1993) indicates:

> . . . defining the nature of science and scientific method with rigour and consistency turns out to be extremely difficult.
>
> (p. 101)

Let us first consider some of the various attempts to define the nature of science.

EARLY IDEAS ABOUT THE NATURE OF SCIENCE

Philosophers of science have attempted for centuries to capture the nature of science to answer the question, *What is science?* They have produced many different ideas. Over two thousand years ago, Aristotle tried to explain science based on his observations of the world. He put forward the idea that science was based on common sense and intuition, what we might call *intuitive science*. The problem is that, as Wolpert argues in his book, the world is not constructed according to the rules of common sense, so using common sense and intuition to explain the nature of science seldom works. Science is often *counter-intuitive*. Simple observations of the world and the development of lay theories using common sense are usually inaccurate and unreliable. Later philosophers, like Socrates, built on this idea and emphasized *logical deduction*, the importance of applying logic to argument. Science was worked out logically, from first principles.

By the Middle Ages, people like Roger Bacon, William of Occam and Robert Grosseteste were stressing the need to avoid theories with too many assertions and unproved assumptions and recommended the *empirical testing* of ideas. This was not a totally new idea. It had been considered by Aristotle. Grosseteste, in the thirteenth century, actually began a debate on the problems of *induction* and the validity of knowledge. At the same time, the great Arab alchemists and philosophers like Muhammad ibn Musa al-Khwarizimi and Haytham, were developing and refining *experimentation* in science.

Francis Bacon, in the late sixteenth and early seventeenth century, turned his attention to the nature of science. For him, science was a matter of proving something to be true. His view of science was that of an *empiricist*. He argued that you observe the world and this gives you an idea or theory about why things are the way they are. You then prove your theory by carrying out formal experiments to test it and show it to hold true. Bacon's ideas, and his criticisms of the earlier philosophers, were extremely influential in the seventeenth century. Galileo, around this time, returned to the idea of intuition, or rather, counter-intuition. He challenged theories based on common sense and intuition which placed the Earth at the centre of our solar system. Galileo put forward a counter-intuitive theory, in which Earth was just one of several bodies moving around the Sun. At the time, his theory was rejected although he was later shown to be correct, but the views of common sense science held sway for many years. Indeed, even in Victorian times such great men of science as Thomas Huxley, a friend and colleague of Darwin, spoke of science as being nothing more than trained and organized common sense.

Unfortunately, until the end of the nineteenth century, both scientists and philosophers generally concluded that the ideas and theories of science are simple *generalizations* derived from observations and experiments. Science was viewed as a process comprising three distinct stages:

- *Description*   – the scientist describes a phenomenon observed, perhaps one observed repeatedly;
- *Induction*   – the scientist generalizes from the phenomenon, putting forward a theory;
- *Experimentation* – the theory is tested to see if it holds true against new observations of the phenomenon.

According to Dunbar (1995), this view dominated biology and the social sciences well into the twentieth century. However, even as far back as the seventeenth century, views were changing in the physical sciences. Gathering empirical generalizations was proving inadequate to cope with the emerging scientific revolution. Explanations of *why* things happened the way they did were needed, rather than straightforward generalized descriptions of *how* they happened. Attempts to justify the physical sciences based on logic and induction were proving inadequate.

A further point about experimentation is that it cannot be carried out in a vacuum. When we experiment we are finding out about *something*. That something begins with the existing knowledge base. Experiments on electricity, genetics or quantum mechanics begin from whatever is already known in those fields. This returns us to questions about the accumulation of knowledge and ideas in science. We do not simply add on new knowledge to the existing stock, like adding bricks to a pile. Rather, the new knowledge and ideas are integrated with and often change the shape of the pile. Science is about the interaction of the existing body of knowledge with the new ideas and evidence to construct new understandings and perspectives.

'TRUTH' AND 'CERTAINTY'

Albert Einstein is reported to have once said:

> No amount of experimentation can ever prove me right: A single experiment can prove me wrong.
>
> (Wynn and Wiggins, 1997, p. 107)

In the early twentieth century, the Austrian philosopher Karl Popper explored this idea. He put forward the notion of the *testability* of theories and explanations and argued that, logically, you can never prove or verify a theory; you can only ever *disprove* it. So, investigations and experiments serve the purpose of testing the idea but not to prove it to be true. As attempts to disprove a theory fail, the case in support of it is strengthened. This means that whether or not a theory is acceptable is always open to debate. Is there ever enough evidence to claim truth? What is enough for the theory to be acceptable to the scientific community? On this basis, all theories are tentative. This aspect is sometimes over-emphasized to the point of absurdity, where the learners of science might begin to believe that the scientific body of knowledge is very shaky. In practice, many of the ideas have stood the test of time – some over hundreds of years. Archimedes' explanation of why objects float or sink has still not been proven false, even after several thousand years. Is it likely to change now? In reality,

> . . . much of science consists not in trying to prove theories wrong but in trying to define their limits of application by identifying the points at which the theories do not work (i.e. the areas in which they make incorrect predictions).

(Dunbar, 1995, p. 20)

This is sometimes put forward as a weakness of Popper's theory. A second weakness sometimes cited is that his view of cause-and-effect relationships in the biophysical world seem to be overly simplistic, with one cause resulting in one effect. In reality, there are often a number of factors (variables) at work, leading to a range of possible outcomes. It is only in very carefully controlled experimental situations, as in the world of Newtonian mechanics, that Popper's theory is absolutely valid. Dunbar (1995) suggests that

> Strictly speaking, Newtonian physics must rank as the biggest confidence trick in the history of human learning: it makes all kinds of totally unrealistic assumptions about the existence of perfect vacuums, ideal gases and frictionless processes, none of which ever occur in nature. Every experiment has to be carefully contrived to get it to work, otherwise extraneous variables are likely to produce results that bear no relationship to what the theory predicts.

(p. 98)

Another view was put forward by the American physicist, Thomas Kuhn, working in the 1950s and 1960s. From his studies of the history of science, he concluded that science proceeds in fits and starts (Kuhn, 1970). He pointed out that at any one time scientists tend to work within a particular conceptual framework or *paradigm*. So, in Newton's time (the mid-1600s) the paradigm was that of classical mechanics, to do with forces, mass and motion. But nature, or rather the biophysical world in which we live, can always be viewed in different ways. Einstein's view of some aspects of nature was very different to Newton's. Einstein developed a view (or theory) based on relativity. It still included references to mass and motion, but he introduced new ideas to do with changes in mass relative to motion, energy and space and time. This is a very different paradigm to Newton's. When such a view of the natural world is generally adopted by the scientific community, this amounts to a *scientific revolution* and a *paradigm shift* has taken place. This does not mean that the earlier paradigms are necessarily wrong. Within their contexts and the available knowledge and understanding of the time, they were quite appropriate. However, the new perspectives and ideas now explain other or additional aspects of the world. At any one time, 99.9 per cent

how it is conducted. In particular, it sometimes makes it look like a very neat and tidy process, starting with A (an idea) and progressing through B, C and D to E (the conclusion) which, if there are no logical faults in the argument, must be accepted by the scientific community. It is seldom so simple. In *The Five Biggest Ideas in Science*, the authors sum up this problem in their discussion of a scientific method.

> Some people argue that there is no such thing as one, singular method of science. They argue that discussions such as this make it appear that one could simply apply these steps in sequence to make discoveries and to solve any scientific problem. Undoubtedly, the actual work of the scientist is much less formal. It is not always done in a clearly logical and systematic way. It involves intellectual inventiveness, the creation of mental images of what has never been actually experienced, and even the devising and testing of strong intuitive feelings. So please do not get the idea that this scientific method is some sort of automatic procedure.
>
> (Wynn and Wiggins, 1997, p. 5)

Rigorous experimentation is only one aspect of a scientific method. Ideas can be tested in other equally valid ways, for example through the use of mathematics. In particular in the nineteenth and twentieth centuries with the development of mathematical statistics, scientists have an array of powerful techniques to identify and isolate influential factors using purely observational data. As we move into the twenty-first century, computers not only allow this mathematical processing to be carried out with ease and speed, they also allow scientists to model phenomena and make predictions and hypotheses within the modelling process. From these, explanations can be constructed. The use of sophisticated information and communications technology (such as electron microscopes and radio telescopes) also allows the exploration of realms previously unvisited, like the micro-worlds of cells or the macro-worlds of deep space. However, there are still many gaps in our knowledge and understanding, questions we cannot begin to answer or phenomena we cannot explain *in terms of our present paradigm*. In the future, who knows?

Very few people are professional scientists. Although we live in a biophysical world in which a scientific method is a 'natural' approach to explaining things, there is a tendency to resort to simple rules of thumb based on experiences and generalizations that work well enough to get by (Dunbar, 1995). What is more, there is a reluctance to give up an idea that seems to have worked well enough in the past when only one piece of evidence is against it. Only when these rules of thumb no longer work at all do we resort to the empirical approach of *a* scientific method. Children are no different to adults in this respect. They bring with them to the classroom their own 'rules of thumb' about the world in which they live. These ideas (or conceptions) can be quite accurate, fitting in with those of the scientific community. They are as likely to be misconceptions – incomplete, partly wrong or even totally wrong. As their teacher, it then becomes one of your tasks to help them to construct new ideas and theories about the world, to teach them science. This issue is returned to in Part 2.

TEACHING ABOUT THE NATURE OF SCIENCE

In an interesting paper in the ASE *Guide to Secondary Science Education*, Jonathan Osborne argued that:

> . . . individuals do not require an extensive knowledge of science, nor even the ability to make practical use of it. Rather, what they need is an understanding of the nature of science – the ability to assess the level of certainty of scientists' claims; to appraise risks; to understand how scientists produce reliable knowledge; to distinguish correlations from causes; and an ability to translate and interpret common scientific reports presented by the media.
>
> (Osborne, 1998, p. 100)

He suggested that such an understanding would help us to face and respond to the various scientifically-loaded choices that increasingly confront us as individuals and as a society as a consequence of the 'relentless advance of science and technology'.

The National Curriculum for England and Wales (DfEE, 1999) has a distinctly Popperian flavour in that experiments are carried out to see if ideas are invalid. While it is true that all explanations of the biophysical world are, in the final analysis, tentative there is a risk that children undervalue scientific knowledge and understanding because of this. Science *is* a very successful enterprise. It owes its success to the robustness of its explanations. It is the best explanation of our world that we have. Although teaching about the nature of science is not an explicit requirement of the National Curriculum at Key Stages 1 or 2, there are aspects of the nature of science which permeate work in science at these levels. The nature of science can be used to support the teaching of KS1 and KS2 Programmes of Study, for example:

- the way in which scientific evidence relates to familiar phenomena including personal health and the environment;
- ways of treating living things and the environment with care and sensitivity;
- the importance and value of science as a way of explaining many phenomena.

(Circular 4/98, page 78)

How can we include the nature of science in our primary science teaching?

THE 3PS OF SCIENCE – PROCESSES, PRODUCTS AND PEOPLE

The structure of the National Curriculum for Science tends to force you to focus your attention on science as a way of thinking and working (Sc1) and as a body of knowledge (Sc2, 3 and 4). These are what we might describe as the processes and the products which make science what it is. As such, you will be thinking about what children should be able to do and what they should know and understand. But you also need to think about what science has in common with other human enterprises: people. It is easy for you as a teacher to see the relevance of what you want the children to learn but it is not always so easy for the children to do so. Science is relevant to all of us throughout our lives. This relevance needs to be made explicit for children. These are the 3Ps of science teaching: processes, products and people. When you are planning for teaching and learning in science, these 3Ps should be carefully balanced.

When teachers introduce a new topic in science, the first thing they usually do is establish immediate relevance. They capture children's attention by using pictorial or videorecorded materials, an artefact, a story or a poem, or a visitor to the classroom (human or otherwise). The aim is not only to set the scene for the lesson but also to motivate the children.

However, there is another kind of relevance in science education which is longer term and this depends very much on your children's stage of development and their previous experiences. Younger children need to explore and experience things which are both concrete and meaningful to them. These are situations which are close to them both physically and emotionally: themselves, their families and friends, their homes and the immediate and local environment. Older children, who have more experience to fall back on, are more able to stand back from situations, empathize with others and use their imaginations to 'travel' to more remote situations. Therefore, wider and more distant issues can be considered.

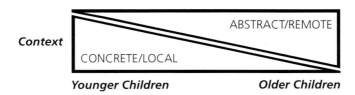

Figure 2.2   Making science education relevant

Task 2.2 Making science education relevant	During your visits to school in preparation for school placements, arrange to observe your class teacher teaching a science lesson. If possible, observe several different teachers or your class teacher teaching several different science lessons.

Note how the teacher introduces the lesson. How does he or she make the topic or focus of the lesson explicitly relevant to the interests and abilities of the children? Does he/she use any visual or other aids? How does he/she link the science to the real world of the child? Does relevance occur later in the lesson? If so, how?

Keep a record of any strategies you notice and ask the teacher about them later.

With primary school children, activities and situations need to be designed to enable them to participate actively in the process of science. They 'do' science, that is, they work on matters related to the real world around them in their immediate and local environment. The children need to experience for themselves the satisfaction that 'working like a scientist' can offer. The child's awareness of this can be increased by asking them if they enjoyed it and using happy-face self-evaluation sheets. Such relevance has the added bonus of helping to break down stereotypical images of science and the scientist. These images of scientists as male, bald and bearded, with spectacles and a white coat and working alone in a laboratory surrounded by an assortment of chemical apparatus, form about 6 years of age and, once established, they are very difficult to change (Newton and Newton, 1998a).

Real-world contexts can be provided by taking as the starting point current events or situations with which the children are familiar. A new baby leads to investigating *Growth and Change*. The supermarket allows *Materials, Foods* and *Packaging* to be investigated, not necessarily all at the same time. Some commercially produced schemes take this approach, providing stories about common events like *Washing Day* or *Bonfire Night*. Teacher-designed science trails around the school can also usefully emphasize the impact of science on all of our lives.

Introducing older children to the history of science by studying the lives of scientists, past and present, can help to address some of the stereotypes they hold. Showing them scientists who are both male and female, international, who work out of doors as well as in laboratories, with plants and animals as well as machines and glassware, all can help to provide alternative role models and show the great diversity of science as an activity.

SOCIAL, MORAL AND ETHICAL ISSUES

Science, through technology, enables us to manipulate ourselves and our world. Biotechnology, genetic engineering, and similar advances all have potential advantages, but they also have potential disadvantages. Just because we *can* do these things does not mean we necessarily *should* do them. Science generates opportunities. It also produces dilemmas which lead to choices having to be made. Values and ethics help us to face and make those choices. As Osborne (1998) suggests,

> . . . scientific issues are now increasingly permeating our daily lives. Whether it is the disposal of nuclear waste, the beef we eat, the warming of the climate, the effects of pollution or the cloning of humans, the relentless advance of science and technology has implications for the choices that confront us both personally and as a society.
>
> (p. 100)

Children need to understand this and their science education needs to prepare them to make these choices. The introduction of this social, moral and ethical dimension is one often left until secondary school, although even then it may be ignored. Lock and

Ratcliffe (1998) suggest that opportunties to raise such issues in secondary science are often ignored for several reasons:

1   Perceived dominance of acquiring knowledge or abstract facts and concepts, encouraged by the assessment system.
2   Lack of confidence or ability in handling discussions where there may be no 'correct' answers but a range of value judgements.
3   Lack of clear teaching strategies to cope with controversial, social issues.
4   Views that social applications of science should not be a part of the science curriculum.

(p. 109)

While all of these obstacles might also face primary teachers, they are not justifications for not trying.

As primary children mature and gain experience, wider social and ethical issues can be introduced. Older KS2 children can very sensibly and sensitively debate the issues related to the importance of the rainforest or the most recent oil tanker disaster. Children's books, stories and poetry can aid such debate, and as a result of the discussion ideas for experimentation and investigation can arise, for example, for work on *Polluting Our Environment*. As primary teachers, we can help children to understand an argument and judge the validity of the evidence. Looking at sources of evidence, allowing discussion in which individuals feel sufficiently confident to put forward their perspectives, and sharing ideas can all lead to recognizing values and beliefs of others and making choices between differing values.

SUGGESTIONS FOR FURTHER READING

If you would like to explore further some of the issues touched upon in this chapter, the following books should be of interest to you.

Dunbar, R. (1995) *The Trouble with Science*, London: Faber and Faber Ltd
    Dunbar provides a very thorough but easy to read account of the nature of science and the importance of establishing a public understanding of science. In particular, in Chapter 2, 'What is this thing called science?', he gives an overview of the changing views of science over time and the theories of the key philosophers.

Newton, D.P. (1989) *Making Science Education Relevant*, London: Kogan Page
    In this book for teachers, what is meant by relevance at both primary and secondary level is considered and a range of strategies which teachers can use to support relevant science teaching are described.

Wynn, C.M. and Wiggins, A.W. (1997) *The Five Biggest Ideas in Science*, New York: John Wiley & Sons, Inc
    Of particular interest in the context of the nature of science is the *Prologue* (pp. v–vii) and *Chapter One: The Road to Discovery* (pp. 1–12). The whole book is, in essence, an exploration of the nature of science and how our ideas have developed and changed over time, all presented in an entertaining way with anecdotes and cartoon illustrations.

3 What Do We Mean by Science Investigation?

Science involves more than just knowing the scientific facts about the world in which we live. It is an active mental and physical process through which we gather evidence and make sense of data to extend our understandings and explanations. This is what Wynn and Wiggins (1997) call the road to discovery. Nor, according to Wynn and Wiggins, does thinking and working like a scientist, 'require incredibly precise, highly sophisticated, other-worldly logic' (p. 2).

In this chapter we shall be focusing on this road to discovery. We shall explore what is meant by a scientific method and the skills and procedures of science which underpin such a method. We shall also consider how you can introduce these ways of thinking and working in science to your pupils. This is the essence of Sc1: *Experimental and Investigative Science* in the National Curriculum Order for Science (DFE, 1995) and will underpin the new Sc1: *Scientific Enquiry* in the year 2000 (DfEE, 1999).

A SCIENTIFIC METHOD?

In science, ideas which explain what we see in the world around us are not merely discussed and either rejected or accepted. Scientists try to put the ideas to the test. This procedure is a key feature of scientific investigation and underpins thinking and working methodically in science.

In Chapter 2, I indicated that some people argue that there is no such thing as *the* scientific method. They suggest that scientific problem solving and discovery is just too complex to be described by any single, recipe-like method or procedure, carried out in a logical and systematic way. It is undoubtedly true that scientists are all different and have their unique ways of thinking and working. These are sometimes neither formal nor systematic, and emotion and intuition can play a part. There are, however, some common elements to *how* they work, which can be identified on reflection. It is these common elements that have given rise to the idea of *a* scientific method.

If you look in any book on teaching science, you will come across descriptions of such methods and procedures which can be used to put ideas to the test as we try to explain events in the world around us. They are usually in the form of flow diagrams, showing a sequence of stages or actions, and they have certain features in common:

1 something is noticed or *observed*;
2 a tentative *hypothesis* is created to explain what is observed;
3 the hypothesis is used to make a *prediction* about the event;
4 an *experiment* is carried out to test the prediction;
5 a *conclusion* is reached as to whether or not the hypothesis is valid;
6 if not, then a *re-test* is carried out to check a revised hypothesis.

Figure 3.1 shows an example of a flow diagram representing this type of scientific method. (It is important to emphasise that it is *a* method and not *the* method, since it must, of necessity, be flexible. In practice, scientists probably do not work through such steps precisely in this order. Rather, it summarizes what they do in total.)

The procedure (or 'method') is often shown as a cyclical one, since testing ideas and collecting evidence does not always lead to an acceptable or clear-cut solution. Sometimes more questions are raised for investigation or new phenomena are noticed. According to Wynn and Wiggins (1997),

> Observation and experimentation are the 'facts' upon which scientific hypotheses are based. Although observation precedes hypothesis formation and experimentation follows prediction, when a hypothesis needs to be recycled, the experiments are included as observations leading to the recycled hypothesis.
>
> (page 107–108)

CLARIFYING THE TERMINOLOGY – THE PROCESS SKILLS OF SCIENCE

Underpinning a scientific method are a number of skills and processes. Few of them are unique to science. Many are drawn from other areas of experience, such as mathematics and language, or could be described as general manipulative skills. What is unique to science is the way they are brought together and used to investigate and explain phenomena. To understand the idea of a scientific method, it is necessary to understand what each of these skills and processes involves and what each contributes to the method as a whole.

How do you define a skill? If you look in a dictionary you will come across statements such as:

> **skill**, n. Expertness, practised ability, facility in doing something, dexterity, tact.
>
> (*The Concise Oxford Dictionary*, p. 1195)

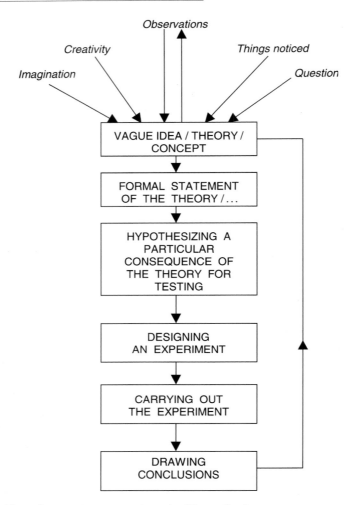

Figure 3.1 Flow diagram to represent a scientific method

Task 3.1 Skills and processes in science	Thinking and working scientifically involves a number of skills and processes. Some have already been mentioned (for example, observing, predicting, and drawing conclusions).

Make a list of twenty skills and processes that you think will be used in science investigation.

Beside each, write 'S' for skill or 'P' for process.

Was this easy to do? Construct your own definition of a skill or a process for your classification.

In the context of science, a skill would be an ability to do something in connection with thinking and working scientifically. In other words, carrying out, with facility and some degree of expertise, some of those steps in a scientific procedure. How is this different from a process? Again turning to the dictionary,

> **process**, n., & v.t. 1. Progress, course, esp. in ~ of construction, etc., being constructed etc., in ~ of time, as time goes on; course of action, proceeding, esp. method of operation in manufacture, printing, photography, etc.; natural or involuntary operation, series of changes.
>
> (ibid., p. 974)

So, underpinning a scientific process is the idea of a course of action or procedure – a scientific method. What about a method? The dictionary tells us:

> **method**, n. Special form of procedure esp. in any branch of mental activity, whence ~OLOGY n.; orderly arrangement of ideas; orderliness, regular habits;
>
> (ibid., p. 764)

If you look in books to do with teaching science you will find that some authors refer to skills, others to processes and some to process skills. The terms are very often used rather loosely, in an interchangeable and confusing way. Figure 3.2 makes a somewhat arbitrary division between the two but serves the purpose of illustrating that processes tend to involve clusters of mental skills. It provides a list of some of the skills and processes you might have thought of for Task 6. This is not, however, an exhaustive list. It is intended to give you a feel for the range of skills, some mental, some physical, that you might use in scientific activity.

These different skills and processes come together in different types of activity in science. What does each involve? In the remainder of this sub-section we will consider the main ones which you will need to be familiar with as a primary teacher. For convenience, they have been listed alphabetically.

- *Controlling variables:* a process (or procedure) in which you keep the same or change particular aspects of an *experiment*. The *independent variable* is what you change, and the *dependent variable* is what changes as a consequence. In order that you ensure the experiment is a *fair test*, other aspects may have to be kept the same (constant).
- *Drawing conclusions:* deciding what the evidence, usually in the form of data, has to tell you.
- *Experimenting:* a process (or procedure) through which you carry out a controlled test of an idea or *hypothesis* to see if there is any evidence to support it.
- *Exploring:* a process (or procedure) in which you use your various senses to notice situations and events and make appropriate *observations*.
- *Fair testing:* a process (or procedure) in which *variables* are controlled to reduce doubt about the cause of an effect.

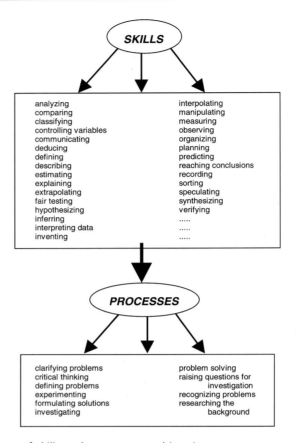

Figure 3.2 A range of skills and processes used in science

- *Hypothesising:* putting forward a tentative idea or explanation to be tested in an experiment.
- *Investigating:* a process (or procedure) in which you search systematically for evidence to test an idea or explanation, usually through an experiment.
- *Measuring:* Using a range of skills from areas such as mathematics to record evidence accurately and in a standardized format.
- *Observing:* Using the senses to collect information. In investigative work, observation becomes more systematic and focused; simply 'looking' at things tends to be less focused, but may help to generate questions and ideas.
- *Predicting:* Forecasting what will happen, drawing on your prior knowledge and experience.
- *Problem solving:* a process (or procedure) in which a range of skills and processes, both mental and physical, are brought together to answer a question or solve a problem.
- *Questioning:* asking or raising questions about something you have been thinking about or something you have noticed or observed, in a form which will allow a tentative idea or explanation to be generated and tested.

- *Variables:* the factors which you manage in an investigation; they can be *categoric* (e.g. eye colour, favourite pet, . . .), *discrete* (number in family, shoe size, . . .) or *continuous* (height, time, . . .).

These skills and processes can be developed and practised separately through directed activities. However, in the context of investigations and experiments, they are brought together and used as needed in an holistic way.

CAUSES, EFFECTS AND PATTERNS

To think and work like a scientist requires us to have something to think about and to work with. In the world around us there are any number of phenomena which would lend themselves to scientific investigation.

Although we are observing things all the time, some things are more noticeable and more easily explained than others. We remember them better because they seem to fit with something we already know, understand or have noticed before. In other words, there is a pattern to the situations or events. The apparent pattern can be used to generate the explanations for the *Why . . .? Because . . .* questions that are fundamental to science. What causes a particular effect? How can we explain it?

Explanations of these events and phenomena often serve the purpose of accounting for why something behaves the way it does. Sometimes we cannot actually generate a complete explanation, we can only describe the phenomenon and its relationship to other similar events. These could be called *descriptive explanations*, and they are fairly common in the world of biology, astronomy and geology. However, through investigation and experimentation we can go some way towards explaining some events in the world around us, particularly those that are causally related in the world of chemistry and physics. These can be called *causal explanations*.

EVIDENCE IN SCIENCE

> Understanding evidence is a central part of science and of informed decision-making in everyday life. As technology advances and more 'critical thinkers' are required, science education has a duty to enable students to examine the quality of scientific evidence.
>
> (Gott and Duggan, 1998, p. 98)

Understanding evidence has been emphasized in the National Curriculum for science. Yet, one of the major difficulties in experimental and investigative work in science is planning an investigation which will yield worthwhile evidence. This is probably because, as Gott and Duggan comment, there has been no attempt at defining what exactly constitutes an understanding of evidence. They suggest that there are two aspects of evidence to be considered. First, there is an understanding of the *quality* of the evidence to be considered. Second, there are factors which influence making decisions *about* evidence to be taken into account.

Evidence can take a variety of forms, from descriptive notes (which rely on subject-ive observations, guesses and estimates) to tabulated data (which rely on standardized measures and formats). How valid and reliable the evidence is, and how acceptable it will be to others in the scientific community, will depend upon the care, control and accuracy used in collecting the evidence. Validity refers to the extent to which you can answer 'yes' to the question, *Is the evidence really answering the question I think it is answering?* Reliability relates to the extent to which you feel sure you can answer 'yes' to questions like, *Is the evidence to be trusted? If I do it again will I get the same results?*

To this end, carefully planned procedures (which include controlling variables and fair testing), the use of appropriate measuring instruments both to observe and gather data, and the use of standardized units for recording results, can all help with the process of obtaining evidence.

How the evidence is recorded and presented is also important. Skills in the use of recording sheets, designing suitable tables for recording data, and constructing graphs and charts (perhaps with the help of a computer package) are all relevant. They enable patterns and trends to be seen more easily when the evidence is being considered. As much time should be spent considering evidence and explaining the findings as in collecting it, as this is the essential precursor to reaching a conclusion. The aim is to demonstrate whether or not the evidence supports the original idea and the predictions made from it. In the National Curriculum for Science these two aspects – obtaining and considering evidence – constitute the second and third strand of scientific investigation.

WHAT CAN CHILDREN DO?

We now know that the perceptual world of very young children is quite sophistic-ated. A 2-year-old has an understanding of cause and effect. If shown a broken toy, the child may ask, *Who broke it?* The child recognizes the effect and attributes a causal link. Children know that symbols in the form of words and pictures can represent things, so they recognize the word 'dog' or 'tree' and pictures of dogs or trees. They also recognize colour and size as important features and will begin to put things into groups, like favourite colours or 'bigger than, smaller than'. Finally, as any parent or teacher knows, young children ask questions. These abilities develop as they grow through direct experience of the world. By the time they start school, children have constructed their own common-sense views of the world, based on limited experi-ence but rarely on science. As they grow older they pass through several stages in their competence to perform particular tasks and show an intuitive sense of what is fair, but they cling to their personally satisfactory explanations for their own actions based on these common-sense creations. Their world is filled with living forces, spontan-eous movement and animism. Objects have free will; things move because they want to; there is even a possibility of magic in some of their explanations. We can see these kinds of explanations in some of their ideas which will be discussed in this and later chapters.

WHAT DO THE CHILDREN NEED TO BE ABLE TO DO?

One of the fundamental aims of primary science education is for children to investigate. In the 1995 National Curriculum Order for Science, the first attainment target, *Science 1: Scientific Enquiry*, is concerned with those practical skills and mental processes which enable children to think and work scientifically. For assessment purposes, being able to carry out investigative work (Sc1) is equal in weight to the three knowledge-based attainment targets put together (Sc2, Sc3 and Sc4). Sc1 is summarized for you in Table 3.1. However, Sc1 does not stand alone. Children cannot practise skills and carry out investigations in a vacuum. The National Curriculum requires that the children be taught about experimental and investigative methods in science using contexts derived from *Sc2: Life Processes and Living Things, Sc3: Materials and their Properties* and *Sc4: Physical Processes.*

In a recent study of the kind of science investigations being carried out in schools, Watson (1997) found that effective investigations in science have two characteristics:

- first, the children have to make their own decisions about how to carry out the investigation;
- second, they must use processes (or procedures) such as planning, observing, measuring, analysing data and drawing conclusions.

Teachers involved in the project indicated that pupil motivation, skills in collaborative working and opportunities for discussion were all positive outcomes of successful scientific investigations. As a consequence the children learn new scientific concepts and procedures (Watson and Wood-Robinson, 1998). However, the same research also showed that there was a mismatch in perceptions of the aims of the investigative work between the teachers and their pupils. Over 50 per cent of the teachers specified the learning of procedures such as how to develop hypotheses or plan a fair test, while only 20 per cent of the pupils identified these as what they had learned. Of the latter, 74 per cent emphasized the learning of concepts, the aim of only 33 per cent of their teachers. Watson and Wood-Robinson (1998) concluded that this is because pupils concentrate only on the more obvious features of investigative activity – they see what it is about as being the cognitive content (dissolving or photosynthesis, for example) rather than the skills and processes being developed and practised.

This suggests that as a teacher you need to make explicit to your pupils the educational aims of the investigative activities. These include:

> . . . opportunities for learners to: enquire, predict and hypothesise; explore, investigate and discover; solve problems; and to discriminate, judge and evaluate.
>
> (ASE, 1997, p. 2)

From their work with teachers, Watson and Wood-Robinson (1998) identify nine stages common to most investigations:

Table 3.1 Overview of Sc1 of the National Curriculum Order for Science for Key Stages 1 and 2

◆ *Scientific Enquiry* ◆

Ideas and Evidence in Science

KS1: 1 – *know that it is important to collect evidence when trying to answer a question;*
KS2: 1a – *know that science is about thinking creatively to try to explain how things work and establish links between causes and effects;*
KS2: 1b – *know that it is important to test ideas using evidence from observation and measurement.*

Investigative Skills: Planning

KS1: 2a – *ask questions and decide how they might find answers to them;*
KS1: 2b – *use first-hand experience and simple information sources to answer questions;*
KS1: 2c – *think about what might happen before deciding what to do;*
KS1: 2d – *recognise and unfair test or comparison;*
KS2: 2a – *ask questions that can be investigated scientifically and decide how to find answers;*
KS2: 2b – *consider what sources of information will be used to answer questions;*
KS2: 2c – *think about what might happen, what kind of evidence to collect equipment and materials to use;*
KS2: 2d – *make tests and comparisons fair by changing one factor and noting effects while keeping the rest the same;*

Obtaining & Presenting Evidence ——— Considering Evidence

KS1: 2e – *follow simple instructions to control risks;*
KS1: 2f – *explore using the senses and make records of observations and measurements;*
KS1: 2g – *communicate what happened in a variety of ways, including ICT;*
KS2: 2e – *use simple equipment and materials appropriately and act to control risks;*
KS2: 2f – *make systematic observations and measurements, including the use of ICT;*
KS2: 2g – *repeat observations and measurements to check them;*
KS2: 2h – *use a wide range of methods to record and communicate data appropriately;*

KS1: 2h – *make simple comparisons and identify simple patterns or associations;*
KS1: 2i – *compare what happened with what was expected and try to explain it;*
KS1: 2j – *review work and explain what was done to others;*
KS2: 2i – *make comparisons and identify simple patterns and trends;*
KS2: 2j – *use observations, measurements and other data to draw conclusions;*
KS2: 2k – *decide whether conclusions support predictions;*
KS2: 2l – *use scientific knowledge to explain observations, measurements or other data or conclusions;*
KS2: 2m – *review work and the work of others and describe its significance and limitations.*

1   *Focusing*: recalling prior knowledge, understanding and experience and estab-
      lishing relevant contexts;

2   *Defining the problem* – clarifying what is being investigated;

3   *Planning*: deciding what they are going to do and planning it;

4   *Doing/obtaining evidence*: carrying out the activity and collecting the evidence/
      data;

5   *Describing method*: reporting on what was done;

6   *Recording and describing results*: examining and describing results and searching
      for patterns and regularities; displaying results in an appropriate way;

7   *Interpreting evidence*: drawing conclusions from the results and making links
      with existing knowledge and understanding to explain findings;

8   *Evaluating methods used*: critically evaluating the data and the way it was collected;

9   *Reflecting on learning*: recognizing what knowledge has been acquired or
      skills and procedures used and developed.   (Adapted from p. 88)

You will see that these are very similar to the steps in Figure 3.1, which exemplified
a scientific method. In other words, by carrying out investigations in this way the
children are using a scientific method. They are thinking and working like a scientist.
Through such activity a second aim can be achieved, that of developing children's
scientific knowledge and understanding.

TYPES OF ACTIVITY UNDERPINNING THINKING AND WORKING SCIENTIFICALLY

Scientific investigation is only one type of activity through which children develop
their abilities to think and work scientifically. They cannot carry out effective investigation if the ground has not been prepared for them beforehand. Nor will every
investigation allow for every kind of skill and procedure to be used. On many
occasions, you will focus on particular skills and key aspects of an investigation. The
children should also be given opportunities, from time to time, to be involved in the
whole process of investigation. For you to be able to provide such opportunities, you
must be able to recognize which ideas are fruitful for investigation, and identify the
skills which will be practised and the knowledge base which will be drawn on.

Studies over the last decade or so have indicated that some primary teachers have
difficulty in doing this. Following the introduction of the National Curriculum in
1989, HMI collected evidence on the quality of science teaching in primary classrooms (DES, 1991). Their data indicated that primary teachers were generally good at
providing experiences in which the children observed, noticed and described. However, they encountered difficulties with other aspects of scientific activity. A research
study evaluating the implementation of the National Curriculum for Science in 1991
indicated that while many teachers were very good at planning activities which
involve the children in observing scientific situations and phenomena and describing and
communicating their observations, few were competent at providing opportunities for

children to develop skills like predicting, hypothesizing, or developing opportunities for whole investigations (Newton, 1992).

One cause of this problem is a lack of clarity as to what terms like predicting and hypothesizing mean when they are used in relation to experimental and investigative science. A second problem arises from the processes of *exploring, investigating* and *experimenting* themselves. These are slightly different kinds of activity, often used synonymously but serving different purposes. A final problem is the distinction between *know what* (conceptual knowledge) and *know how* (procedural knowledge). There is also confusion about how to relate Sc1 to the other, knowledge-based attainment targets. For example, HMI in their first evaluation report on National Curriculum for Science, found that although process skill development was given a high priority, the work was insufficiently linked to subject knowledge (DES, 1991).

A possible reason why some teachers neglect certain aspects of science as a process may be due to a failure on their part to distinguish between the various kinds of activity which constitute Sc1. As a teacher, you need to be aware of the kinds of activity which are possible to meet the requirements of the National Curriculum Order for Science. Goldsworthy (1998) elaborates on this, providing details of six different types of investigation identified by the AKSIS team working with Watson (1997). These were:

- *Fair testing:* investigations concerned with relationships between variables or factors.
  (For example, What do plants need to grow? What will affect how quickly sherbet lemons dissolve? Which toilet paper is the 'best buy'?)
- *Classifying and identifying:* investigations which involve the children in arranging a range of objects or events into manageable groups or sets (classifying) and then using the characteristics of those groups or sets to recognize objects and events as members of them (identifying).
  (For example, What materials are attracted or not attracted to a magnet? What is that minibeast? What does a cow have or do that makes it a cow?)
- *Pattern seeking:* investigations involving the observation and recording of natural phenomena, or the collection of data in a systematic way (like a survey) and then looking for patterns and regularities in the data.
  (For example, Do tall people have bigger feet? Do cows always lie down before it rains? Do plants growing in the shade have bigger leaves than the same type of plants growing in sunshine?)
- *Exploring:* investigations in which children use their senses to make careful observations of situations and events in the world around them, some of which occur over time.
  (For example, What happens if you hold an ice cube in your hand for five minutes? How do the cress seeds change when you put them on damp cotton wool? Write down ten interesting things about the goldfish.)
- *Investigating models:* investigations, usually more appropriate to KS3 or 4, which use a modelling process to explain scientific phenomena.
  (For example, What happens to the mass of a substance when heated? Use an analogy to explain current flow. How is a plant like an energetic machine?)

- *Making things or developing systems:* investigations which give children an opportunity to apply their scientific skills, knowledge and understanding in a new context, often technological.

  (For example, Can you design and make a burglar alarm system for a doll's house? How can you make a plant water for while you are on holiday? How can you build a bridge to carry the toy truck using just paper?)

From their data, Watson and Wood-Robinson (1998) suggested that the first type of activity, fair testing, was over-emphasized by teachers to the detriment of the other types.

Although Sc1 is concerned mainly with experimentation and investigation, it rests very firmly on a foundation of exploration. The latter is especially important with younger children or when introducing new or more difficult ideas. However, an overemphasis of activities associated with exploration will result in the children having a restricted diet of skills. So what is the difference between the three kinds of activity in the context of primary science? This is summed up diagrammatically in Figure 3.3.

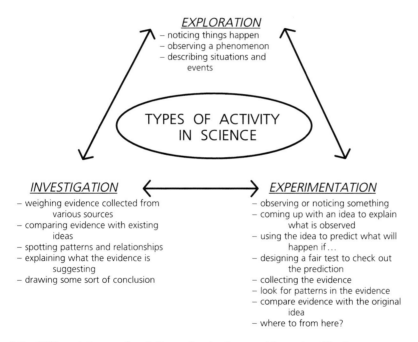

Figure 3.3 Different types of activity underpinning working scientifically

Exploration

Some activities serve mainly to demonstrate the existence and nature of a scientific phenomenon, property or relationship. Such activities inevitably emphasize observation and communication. When teachers do provide activities to exercise such skills and processes there is evidence that they overestimate the children's abilities in them. Even when they understand the terms, there is a danger that they will stick with the

safe and comfortable, rather than stretch the children and themselves with real prediction, hypothesis testing and scientific explanations (Newton, 1992). One of the things
which you will need to guard against is offering your children a rich diet of exploration, in the belief that other skills and processes are being developed as well.

Investigation

Some activities are intended to provide opportunities to find out more about the
particular aspects of phenomena, practising and using a variety of other skills in
addition to observation and communication while doing so. In the process, evidence
collected from different sources can be compared and used to explain the observations
and events and to reach some sort of conclusion.

Experimentation

By this stage, the steps of exploration and investigation have been refined and the
various skills are brought together to raise a question based on what has been noticed
or observed and to put forward a tentative theory or hypothesis to explain this
generally. This is then used to predict future effects in specific situations, which are
then tested to see if the prediction is working. This is the experimental stage. The aim
of experiments is to find occasions which test predictions, theories or hypotheses. We
can never prove them to be true, but we can test them to their limits.

You should be able to see from this how the three groups of activity relate to
Goldsworthy's six types of investigation mentioned earlier. Sometimes teachers confuse
exploratory, investigative and experimental activities. Further, they fail to see the value
of other kinds of activity, such as teacher–demonstrations or the use of secondary
source materials, both of which can usefully underpin Sc1. There are many kinds of
science activity which children might usefully participate in to develop their knowledge, understanding, skills and procedures. Not all activities are necessarily experiments
or even investigative activities. Indeed, not everything in science can be investigated
by children in an experimental way. For example, to investigate Earth in Space, the
children would need to develop and use a range of information research skills so that
they can draw on library and other resources, such as the use of information technology hardware and software. This does not constitute scientific experimentation but is
investigation as used by an investigative journalist who finds out more about things.
As such, it is a form of investigation in which the evidence is collected, weighed and
conclusions reached.

Underpinning the different activities are different skills. Indeed, the activities themselves can be designed to develop specific sets of skills. These activities are designed to
develop:

- fundamental skills;
- exploration skills;

- directed experiment skills; and,
- independent investigation skills.

As a teacher, when you are planning science activities you can focus on any or all of these skills. There is no particular order to their introduction or particular age for which they are appropriate.

Fundamental skills

For children to be able to investigate effectively, they will need a number of basic or fundamental skills. These skills are not unique to science and can often be developed and practised in other contexts. For example, children need to manipulate materials and equipment (manipulative and motor skills), measure accurately using various instruments (measuring skills) and record and report in appropriate ways (language and communication skills, including IT skills). Initially, you will need to structure your teaching to ensure that the children have opportunities to use these skills in scientific contexts and develop facility at doing so independently.

Exploration activities

By organizing exploration activities, you will give children opportunities to observe scientific situations and events directly and to communicate their observations in some way. Young children, before they begin school, are already keen observers. They can also communicate what they have seen, heard or noticed in various ways. When they start school, they bring these skills with them, although at first they may be shallow and unfocused. As their teacher, you will have to provide opportunities to help focus and refine them. This happens through opportunities to:

- use physical aids for observations (like hand lenses, binocular microscopes, and good quality measuring instruments);
- use good quality source materials (like pictures, charts, computer software and television and videorecorded programmes);
- carry out focused observations (such as observing things from unusual angles or close up, for a particular length of time or for a particular specified purpose);
- record observations in a variety of ways (pictures, cartoon strips, tables, charts and graphs, writing, tape recording, photographs); and
- communicate observations to different audiences (to a partner, a group, the class, another class, at a parents' evening).

Remember that it is opportunity and variety which will develop these skills.

Directed experiments

Directed experiments are activities which are very much under your control as the teacher. You will have identified the focus of the investigation and structured the planning. The intention is to provide carefully managed opportunities for the children to find out more about some particular aspect of science. Directed experiments usually bring together a variety of skills, such as manipulating equipment, measuring effects, observing changes, recording results and communicating findings. They are also useful for introducing a new skill, perhaps by you demonstrating it first to the class or a group and then have them practise it for themselves. The important thing is that you will have a clear target and outcome in mind. You are controlling the scientific situation. Directed experiments are particularly useful for introducing the idea of fair testing and controlling variables, since you can prescribe the variables and the changes needed to give children the practise they need with appropriate support.

Independent investigations

As already mentioned above, children must be given opportunities to bring their skills and knowledge together in the context of open-ended investigations. As a teacher, you will find this very demanding. You will need to monitor the situation carefully, balancing their independence with the need to intervene in order to give support and avoid frustration. The latter is less likely to occur when the children have been thoroughly prepared through a range of activities beforehand.

Task 3.2 Practical activities in school	While you are on your visits to school, try to observe your class teacher (or another teacher) teaching a science lesson.

Classify the kind of activities the children are doing. Are they:
- developing fundamental skills?
- exploring?
- involved in directed experiments?
- carrying out independent investigations?

List the features of the activity that led you to this view.

COMMUNICATION AND THE ROLE OF DISCUSSION

Investigations and other forms of practical activity are essentially thinking activities. The children cannot do them effectively without thinking carefully about them. When children are involved in experimental and investigative science, opportunities for discussion are crucial for developing their ideas. You should make time for children to express and share ideas through small group and whole class discussions. These need to be as carefully planned and monitored as any other science activity would be, particularly with respect to the key discussion points, questions to ask and the focus for thinking. Children bring ideas about the world around them to their lessons. Discussion not only allows you to access their thinking, it enables the children's ideas to be translated into simple investigations. During discussions, other ideas emerge which may lend themselves to further investigation in the classroom, although it is equally likely that the ideas produced cannot be investigated. Setting a problem to solve might be a suitable alternative. The children then investigate systematically the idea that they have generated or the problem which has been presented to them. Discussions need to be as carefully planned and monitored as any other science activity. Communication in science is returned to in more detail in Chapter 7.

SOME HEALTH AND SAFETY ISSUES AND SCIENTIFIC INVESTIGATION

In a school, the Health and Safety Act makes safety the general responsibility of everyone. The local education authority or the school's governing body, will probably follow the *COSHH: Guidance for Schools* (HMSO, 1989) in drawing up a school policy statement for science. When you are in schools you should familiarize yourself with this policy document. Although they will be broadly similar, there will be variations from school to school and authority to authority on what you are and are not allowed to do.

However, when you are organizing science activities for your class, it is your responsibility as the teacher to ensure that all the resources and equipment you are using are safe and that there is nothing potentially hazardous about the practices and procedures you intend the children to carry out. Safety should be of paramount concern. In many schools, teachers carry out a *risk assessment*, a kind of safety audit of the science lesson they have planned. This will help you to think carefully about:

- the task/activity itself – what will the children be doing?
- the resources and equipment – what will the children be using?
- the interaction of the children – how will the children be working?
- your interaction with the class – what will you be doing?
- flashpoints in the lesson – how will you change tasks or end the lesson?
- anticipation – what else might happen?

The science co-ordinator, as part of his or her role, will carry out regular audits of equipment and resources to ensure they are safe. You should talk to him or her if you have any concerns or if there is anything you are not sure about. Also, report to the co-ordinator any faulty or damaged equipment for it to be dealt with in an appropriate way.

The ASE produce an excellent booklet on safety in primary school science, *Be Safe!* (ASE, 1990). You should try to obtain a copy before you begin school placements.

This has been adopted by many local education authorities to guide schools on their safety policy in science and risk assessment.

Be Safe! covers all of these matters and many more. Another source of help and advice is CLEAPSS – the Consortium of Local Education Authorities for the Provision of Science Services. Over 95 per cent of education authorities in England, Wales and Northern Ireland are members. CLEAPSS provide regular leaflets on primary science topics and themes, such as *Electricity* or *Pets in Schools*. They also run a telephone helpline for schools. You should ask your science co-ordinator for more details.

Task 3.3 Checking on safety   For each of the following situations, identify what you think is (1) unsafe (2) what your alternative might be.

(a)   You are doing some work on temperature and heat. You want the children to dissolve things in very hot water. You get the kettle from the staff room . . .

(b)   You want a heat source to melt chocolate. You have access to candles, a gas picnic stove, and an electric heating ring . . .

(c)   You want to grow a crystal garden. Some one tells you that copper sulphate and potassium permanganate work really well . . .

(d)   You are doing some work on teeth and dental hygiene. You would like the children to make impressions of their teeth by biting on plasticine . . .

(e)   One of the children has an uncle who is giving away a parrot and two terrapins. The child offers them to you for the classroom because you are doing some work on pets at the moment . . .

Construct some other situations of your own and decide how you would handle them.

PROCESSES AND PRODUCTS

The children you will be teaching must acquire a body of procedural knowledge which they can then practice and use in new, investigative contexts. However, skills cannot meaningfully be practised in isolation. Children need something to think about and work with, real contexts in which to apply their skills. In an ideal world, the children would generate these contexts for themselves, according to their particular interests. However, in the National Curriculum world, where time is limited, these contexts need to relate to the conceptual knowledge base we want children to acquire. Economy of effort, and often enhanced understanding, result from direct experience in this way. Through direct experiences, we develop children's understandings in science and introduce them to situations which highlight the target knowledge. These are the key concept areas which we want them to acquire, specified in the National Curriculum Order for Science as Sc2: *Life Processes and Living Things*, Sc3: *Materials and their Properties* and Sc4: *Physical Processes*. These areas of knowledge and understanding are the focus of the next three chapters.

SUGGESTED FURTHER READING

If you would like to explore further some of the issues touched upon in this chapter, the following should be of interest to you.

ASE (1990) *Be Safe! Some Aspects of Safety in School Science and Technology for Key Stages 1 and 2* (2nd edition), Hatfield: ASE
This is a 'must read' for any teacher of primary science. It covers a range of safety issues in aspects of biology, chemistry and physics, as well as considering problems in design and technology which will also be of use to you.

Gott, R. and Duggan, S. (1998) 'Understanding scientific evidence – why it matters and how it can be taught', in Ratcliffe, M. (ed.) *ASE Guide to Secondary Science Education*, Hatfield: ASE, pp. 92–99
Although the work has a secondary orientation, the points being made are equally valid for teaching primary science, and Gott and Duggan provide a very thorough and detailed discussion about the concept of evidence.

Wynn, C.M. and Wiggins, A.C. (1997) *The Five Biggest Ideas in Science*, New York: John Wiley & Sons, Inc
As mentioned in the previous chapter, Chapter 1 of this book provides an entertaining and easy-to-read overview of scientific method, while Chapter 7 (pp. 107–119) provides more detailed insights.

4 What Do We Mean by Life Processes and Living Things?

Life Processes and Living Things encompasses the whole of the biological world. It is all to do with being (and staying) alive. So what counts as being alive?

Task 4.1 Alive, not alive or never alive	How would you distinguish between the concepts: • alive; • not alive; • never alive? Think about, for example, a growing plant like an ash tree, a wooden ruler and a metal ruler. What is it that distinguishes them from each other in terms of 'life'?

We shall look at the features which are characteristic of all living things on our planet and these characteristics will be considered in particular by reference to humans and green plants as organisms. How living things pass on their characteristics from one generation to the next will be discussed, and how we sort and classify living things will be explained. Finally, we shall consider how different living things fit into and adapt to their environments.

FUNCTIONING ORGANISMS

If you are a Star Trek fan, you will be familiar with the small, hand-held life detectors used by the away teams. The crew use them to scan for signs of life. But what are the signs that indicate the presence of a living being? What is the life detector looking for?

Life Processes Characteristic To All Living Things

Organisms are usually classified as being alive because they can carry out a range of biological functions or processes normally associated with life. Many of these processes can be found occurring individually in some non-living things. It is their collective occurrence in an organism which allows it to be described as alive. There are usually seven processes which are described as characteristic of life on our planet.

- Maturation (Growth and change)
- Locomotion (Movement)
- Nutrition (Feeding)
- Respiration (Breathing)
- Excretion (Waste elimination)
- Irritability (Sensitivity to the environment)
- Reproduction (Producing offspring)

Maturation (growth and change)

All living things, whether plants or animals, have cycles of change to their lives. Their progress through these *life cycles* is usually described as growth. The stages which the living organism passes through completes the progress from the immature form to the mature form capable of producing offspring. Once maturity has been reached, there is usually a short period in which the organism's body is able to reproduce: the whole purpose of its existence. The rate at which different organisms go through their life cycles varies enormously, from days (mosquitoes) and weeks (sweet peas) to years (elephants) and centuries (the giant redwoods). During this period of growth from immaturity to maturity, the organism's body changes. New body structures are created and repairs are carried out. Eventually, when this is no longer possible, the organism dies. This usually occurs when the life cycle is complete.

Some non-living things appear to grow. For example, crystals increase in size under the right chemical conditions, but they cannot produce those conditions for themselves.

Locomotion (Movement)

All living things are able to move, although the degree of movement that is possible varies between organisms. This confuses children, who tend to associate movement only with animals. An animal's ability to move from place to place in order to obtain food or escape from danger is fairly easy to see. Plant movement is usually much more limited, occurring in response to stimuli like light or gravity. To children they often appear stationary. Certain plants, like the sensitive mimosa plant which can close its leaves when touched or the insectivorous plants like the Venus fly trap or the sundew, show much more obvious movement. Less obvious is the movement of daffodil flowers growing from bulbs in a pot on the window sill. Their bending towards the light is a much slower process and less convincing to younger children.

Some non-living things move. For example, water moves as it flows in a stream along a valley. The important thing is that the water does not generate its movement itself. It is being forced to move in response to the pull of gravity.

Nutrition (Feeding)

In order to carry out life processes, like growing and moving, all living things need energy. This is obtained from a regular supply of food. Green plants are able to make the food they need from the simple materials in the world around them − water from the soil and carbon dioxide from the air. This process in plants is called *photosynthesis*, and it can only work in the presence of a light source (the sun) which powers the system. A special light-trapping pigment − *chlorophyll* − is found inside the *chloroplasts* in plant leaves, and it is this pigment which gives the plant its green colour.

$$6H_2O \ + \ 6CO_2 \xrightarrow{} C_6H_{12}O_6 \ + \ 6O_2$$

| water | carbon dioxide | sunlight (light energy) | sugars | oxygen |

At the same time, plants are able to combine the sugars they have made with mineral salts extracted from the soil to make the proteins necessary for building and repairing cells.

Photosynthesis by the plants in the great rainforests of the world and by the green plankton in the oceans is an essential process for regulating the earth's atmosphere, as it increases the amount of oxygen while at the same time reducing the amount of carbon dioxide. Destruction of the rainforests or pollution of the oceans destroys this balance.

Animals, on the other hand, are unable to make their own food from these naturally occurring materials. However, they are able to move around in search of ready-made 'packages' of food in the forms of other animals and sometimes plants. Animals which eat only other animals are *carnivorous*. Lions and ladybirds, puffins and centipedes are all carnivores. Those animals which eat only plants are *herbivorous*. Guinea pigs, giraffes and millipedes are all herbivores. Those animals which can eat both are *omnivorous*. Humans and bears are examples of omnivores. Whatever the source of the food, in all cases it is broken down by the animal into the sugars that are needed for energy. Animals derive proteins from their food to build and repair body tissues. They also break down the fats and oils in foodstuffs, either for energy or to replace their own fatty tissues.

Some non-living things appear to 'feed'. For example, a motor car needs petrol as a fuel to do other things. However, the car cannot obtain or make that petrol for itself.

Respiration (Breathing)

The energy that an organism needs to carry out its life processes is only changed into a useable form when the sugars in the food the animal has eaten or which the plant has made are burned in the body, using *oxygen* from the air. This happens during the process of *respiration*. The term respiration is commonly used to describe the process of *breathing*, in which gases are exchanged. In animals, this involves the intake of oxygen from the surrounding environment and the release of carbon dioxide into the environment. In plants, during daylight when photosynthesis is occurring, carbon dioxide is taken in and oxygen is given out. During hours of darkness plants respire, giving out carbon dioxide and taking in oxygen.

However, respiration is more accurately described as the process by which complex organic compounds like sugars are broken down by plant or animal cells into simpler ones. During this process, energy is released. For most living things, respiration only occurs when oxygen is present. The oxygen from the air is combined with other substances, usually foodstuffs like sugars, and in the process heat is given off. We generally talk about this as combustion or 'burning', although it is more correctly called *oxidation*.

$$C_6H_{12}O_6 + 6O_2 \xrightarrow{\text{'burning'}} \text{Energy} + 6H_2O + 6CO_2$$

$$\underset{\text{(like glucose)}}{\underset{\text{sugars}}{}} \quad \underset{\text{oxygen}}{} \quad \underset{\text{Energy, ...)}}{\underset{\text{Chemical}}{\underset{\text{(Heat,}}{}}} \quad \underset{\text{water}}{} \quad \underset{\text{dioxide}}{\underset{\text{carbon}}{}}$$

When sugars are burned in this way, as well as the useful energy that is produced, there are also a number of waste products like water and carbon dioxide.

Some non-living things appear to respire. For example, a motor car engine needs oxygen to burn the petrol which enables the car to move.

Excretion (Waste elimination)

When animals feed and respire, the waste products that are produced by the chemical activity in the body are in the form of solid materials as well as water and gases. If these were allowed to build up in the body, they could be harmful. Carbon dioxide and some water can be breathed out. Water and dissolved salts can be sweated out when the animal perspires. The remaining water and the solid materials have to be eliminated by being pushed out of the body as urine and faeces. All of these ways of disposing of waste are described as excretion, although it is only the last which is commonly thought of in this way.

In plants, because energy is released from the burning of sugars which the plant has made, the waste products produced are mainly in the form of water and gas, neither of which is an obvious form of waste but is still excretion.

Some non-living things appear to excrete. For example, when fuel is burned in a motor car, waste gases, sooty smoke and water are produced which must be disposed of via the car exhaust pipe.

Irritability (Sensitivity to the environment)

All living things need to be sensitive to changes in their surroundings and must be able to respond in an appropriate way to ensure their own survival. Both plants and animals can respond to physical stimuli such as changes in temperature and light intensity and even to the force of gravity. In plants, the effect of such changes is to trigger events like leaf fall and dormancy. Animals store up food and hibernate. Living things also respond to chemical stimuli, for example, our eyes water in response to raw onions and dogs salivate when they smell food.

Some non-living things respond to stimuli. For example, an intruder alarm sensor detects movement in the area being scanned and triggers the alarm.

Reproduction (Producing offspring)

The whole purpose of existence for most living things is to perpetuate the species. All living things are capable of producing new, independent members of their species, although the way this process occurs varies enormously, not only between plants and animals but also within the plant and animal kingdoms.

Some non-living things might be thought of as being able to reproduce. For example, a spark from a burning log can start another fire.

Task 4.2 Life detection	Scientists made a simple version of a life detector for use by the Mars landing probe, but it was not very successful. The results were ambiguous. Think about the problems it might have to deal with.

How would it assess life that is not visible to the human eye?
How would it react to a powered alien vehicle?
How would it handle a non-carbon based life form?

As a life detector yourself, how would you respond to fire. Is it alive?

Humans as organisms

The study of humans as organisms involves an exploration of the various life processes exhibited by all living things as they apply specifically to humans.

Feeding and nutrition

Food is needed in order that the body can carry out its various life processes. If appropriate foods are not eaten, it is harder for the body to work efficiently. Once the food is taken into the mouth it follows a journey down the oesophagus (or gullet) and through the body's *digestive system* (Figure 4.1).

The process of breaking down food into smaller organic compounds which the body can absorb and use is called digestion. In humans, this process occurs internally in a specialized organ called the gut or *alimentary canal*. This is a tube which widens and narrows along its length and in which all the food eaten is processed. The canal begins

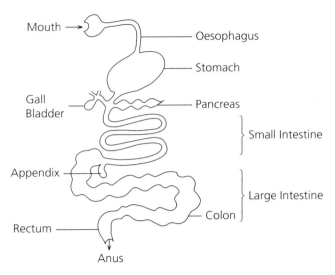

Figure 4.1 The human digestive system

at the mouth, where food is taken in (ingested) and ends at the anus where indigestible leftovers are passed out of the body. In between, the canal is divided into specialized areas which carry out particular functions. The actual breaking down of food (digestion) begins in the *stomach*, which has thick walls and and smooth muscles which contract in order to move the food around to aid the process. Glands secrete gastric juices (mucus, enzymes and an acid). With the help of powerful muscle action, a partially digested mass of food is then passed into the *small intestine*. Here further digestion occurs and absorption begins. More glands secrete *enzymes* and *bile*, so that fats, proteins and carbohydrates are broken down, stomach acids are neutralized, and nutrients can be absorbed. Next, in the *large intestine*, water residues are absorbed from the remaining materials and gut bacteria act to produce vitamins. At the end of the alimentary canal is the rectum, into which waste materials are stored as faeces, ready for elimination.

Teeth play an important role in the initial breakdown of food. Human teeth are described as heterodontic, that is the teeth are of a mixture of different types and sizes. A human with a full set of teeth will have 32, shared equally across the upper and lower jaw. On the top jaw, these are arranged as four incisors in the centre, two canines (one either side of the incisors), four premolars (two either side) and six molars (three at each side at the back of the jaw. The pattern is the same for the bottom jaw. In humans, each tooth is of essentially the same structure, although the shape varies according to function. The incisors are sharp, flattened teeth, edged like a chisel and used for biting or cutting food. Canines are conical teeth, sharp and pointed for puncturing and tearing meat. Premolars are cuboid, flat topped teeth used for grinding and chewing. The molars are similar, but usually broader, and used for grinding. The third molar on each side does not appear until early adulthood, hence its description as a wisdom tooth. In some people wisdom teeth do not appear.

All teeth have a hard coating of enamel covering the exposed tooth above the gum level. Enamel is smooth, white and very hard, and is made mainly of calcium phosphate and calcium carbonate. The enamel protects the inside of the tooth, which is mainly dentine, a material similar in composition to bone. However, dentine is different to bone in that it has tiny ducts through which blood capillaries and nerve fibres run. The dentine surrounds the pulp cavity, the heart of the tooth. The pulp cavity contains the blood supply and main nerves to the tooth. Once they are fully developed, our teeth stop growing and must be protected by careful dental hygiene from sugars and acids in particular.

The heart and blood circulation

The focus of the human body's *circulatory system* is the heart. It lies in the middle of the chest cavity, between the two lungs and is a hollow, muscular organ which acts as a pump to circulate blood around the body. It is divided into four chambers, two on each side. The upper chambers are the right and left *atria*. The lower ones are the right and left *ventricle*. In healthy people there is no connection between the two sides; each side works as an independent pump.

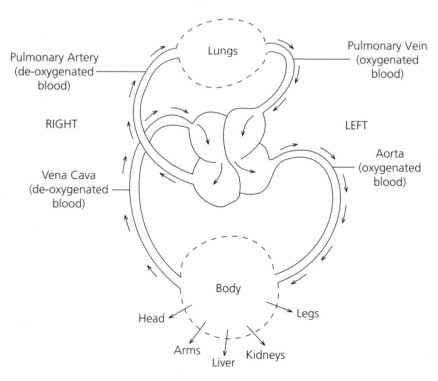

Figure 4.2 The human circulatory system

The flow of blood into and out of the heart follows a rough figure eight pattern (Figure 4.2). Begining with the left ventricle, the chamber contracts and oxygentated (oxygen-rich) blood is pushed with tremendous pressure into the *aorta*. From here, it passes along arteries to fine capillaries which supply blood to all parts of the body. The oxygen is removed from the blood by the body tissues and the de-oxygenated blood is returned to the heart by a network of veins. These eventually join up and lead into the right atrium. The deoxygenated blood passes through from the atrium to the right ventricle. A trapdoor-like valve prevents it from going the opposite way. The muscles of the right ventricle then contract and the blood is pushed into the pulmonery artery leading to the lungs. In the lungs, carbon dioxide is exchanged for oxygen and the oxygen rich blood is then returned to the left atrium. It is pushed through the trapdoor-like valve into the left ventricle where the journey begins again.

Blood circulating through the body provides a very sophisticated way to transport many substances. For example, the blood leaving the heart for the rest of the body carries oxygen while that returning carries waste carbon dioxide gas. Essential nutrients, such as sugars and fats, enter the blood from the intestinal walls and are carried to different parts of the body to be deposited. Waste products, like ammonia, are carried to the liver where they react to form urea which is then carried to the kidneys for excretion. Important hormones and other body regulators are secreted by endocrine glands and transported by the blood to their target cells.

Human blood consists of red and white blood cells, suspended in a watery medium called blood plasma. It also contains small, disc-shaped cells called platelets which are responsible for the blood clotting. The red blood cells are made in the bone marrow and contains the iron-rich protein molecule, *haemoglobin*, which gives blood its red colour. It is the haemoglobin which gives the oxygen molecules a piggyback ride from the lungs around the body. The white blood cells, or *leucocytes*, are larger and colourless blood cells. They are produced in the bone marrow and lymph nodes of the body and play an important role in the body's immune system.

Breathing, lungs and exercise

In humans, a pair of lungs is found in the thorax protected by the rib cage (Figure 4.3). Each lung consists of a thin, moist membrane which is much folded to increase the surface area through which gases (oxygen and carbon dioxide) can be exhanged. Air enters the body through the windpipe, or *trachea*, which branches into two *bronchi*, one for each lung. Further branching of the bronchi occurs, eventually forming a network of tiny *bronchioles* in the lungs. Each bronchiole ends in a tiny air sac, or *alveolus*, formed from a fold or crease in the lung membrane and fed by numerous tiny blood capillaries. It is here that gases are exchanged. The lungs have no muscles of their own. The respiratory movements of the muscular *diaphragm* ventilate the lungs, that is, cause them to inflate and deflate. When we inhale, the diaphragm flattens, making the lung cavity larger and thus reducing its pressure. This pulls air into the lungs. When the diaphragm relaxes, it becomes arch-shaped, making the thoracic cavity smaller, and pushing the air out of the alveoli. In other words, we exhale.

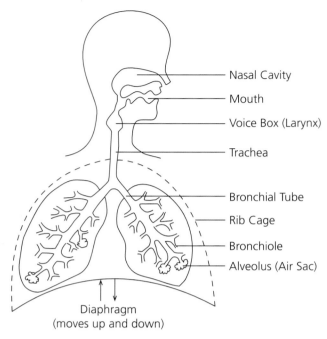

Nasal Cavity

Mouth

Voice Box (Larynx)

Trachea

Bronchial Tube

Rib Cage

Bronchiole

Alveolus (Air Sac)

Diaphragm
(moves up and down)

Figure 4.3   The human respiratory system

During exercise our bodies use more energy than when at rest. The energy is released by increasing the chemical and physical processes within the body, in other words the rate of metabolism. More oxygen is needed to fuel the various processes. We breathe faster to take in extra oxygen and get rid of waste carbon dioxide. The heart beats faster to pump blood more quickly around the body, carrying these necessary materials. This change can be measured by our increased pulse rate (the number of heartbeats per minute). If we clog up our arteries by eating the wrong foods, or if we coat the delicate membranes of the lungs with tar and other pollutants by smoking, the body's ability to function effectively in this way is greatly limited, sometimes with serious consequences.

Movement and the skeleton

Humans have an internal skeleton or *endoskeleton*. It is the whole structure which provides the framework of the body, as well as protecting the vital organs like the heart and lungs, and providing anchor points for muscles. The skeleton is built from hard connective tissue called *bone*, made from protein fibres and crystalline calcium phosphate salts embedded in bone cells. The human skeleton is made up of over 200 separate bones.

Bone is hard and inflexible, but it is given flexibility by a system of *joints* where one or more bones meet. Immovable joints occur where the flattened bones of the skull meet. Partly movable joints can be found between the vertebrae of the spine.

Freely movable joints (or *synovial* joints) are those which allow articulated movement of the limb bones. Hinge joints allow movement in one plane only, as with the knee and elbow joints. Ball and socket joints allow movement in more than one direction, as with the hip and shoulder joint. Ligaments link the bones in synovial joints. They are surrounded by a synovial membrane and bathed in a fluid to lubricate and protect the joints.

The movement or tension of the body skeleton is controlled by fibrous tissues called *muscles*. There are three types. Cardiac muscle is found only in the heart. Smooth or involuntary muscles are controlled by the autonomic nervous system and work automatically, producing for example movements in the intestines and respiratory tract. Striated or voluntary muscles are under our conscious control and produce movements of our limbs and joints. Striated muscles enable skeletal movement and consist of bundles of long fibres attached to the bone by *tendons*. One end of the muscle is fixed to a non-moving bone, while the other end is attached to a bone which can move. The striated fibres run long ways and contain proteins which can contract. Muscles operate in pairs. A *flexor* muscle contracts, becoming shorter and fatter and moving the bones closer together. An *extensor* muscle, on the opposite side of the joint, contracts in the opposing direction, pulling the bones away from one another. When one muscle of the pair is contracting the other is always relaxed, becoming long and thin.

The human life cycle

A life cycle is the total sequence of stages passed through by individuals, from the fusion of the *gametes* (male and female germ cells) in one generation to the same stage in the next. The visible signs of the human life cycle are the stages from birth through to maturity and the production of a new baby by the adults. Mature humans have specialized reproductive organs to produce the gametes (the sperm in the male and the eggs or ova in the female).

In females, the reproductive organs are the *ovaries* which are linked to the *uterus* (or womb) by the *fallopian tubes*. The uterus is connected to the outside by the *vagina*. Hormones control the release of *ova* (eggs) from the ovaries on a regular cyclical basis. Usually, one ripe egg is released from one of the ovaries about once per month, although occasionally more than one can be released. The egg awaits fertilization in the womb, which has a special lining of cells to nurture growth and development. If the egg is not fertilized, then it and the special womb lining are shed (*menstruation*) and the process begins again. The whole cycle takes about one month.

Fertilization occurs when a male germ cell, a *sperm*, fuses with the egg. Sperm are produced in the *testes*, the male reproductive organ. The testes are contained in a sac-like *scrotum* outside the body. Within the testes are tubules in which large quantities of sperm develop connected by two tubes, the *vas deferens*, to the outside through the *urethra*. The sperm are ejected down the urethra into the vagina and the sperm swim through the fluids towards the uterus and the egg. Thousands of sperm might be ejected but only one is needed for fertilization to occur.

In the womb, the fertilized egg now contains the full complement of genetic material needed for development (see the next section). The single cell goes through stages of development and cell division to produce the embryonic human. The mother's body, through the linking umbilical cord, nurtures and protects the embryo for nine months, providing all the nutrients and materials for growth. After this period, the baby is then ejected from the mother's body by strong muscular contractions of the uterus. However, the infant is still totally dependent on the parent for a number of years.

Green plants as organisms

We use plants for food, fuel, building materials and medicines. They remove waste carbon dioxide from the air and produce the oxygen which we breathe. They are essential for most animal life on earth and yet we seldom think of them as organisms which, just like us, go through similar life processes and have organs specialized for carrying out particular functions.

Leaves and photosynthesis

Unlike animals, green plants cannot collect and eat their food directly. They must make their food from simple substances, but to do this they need energy. The whole process is *photosynthesis*, from photo (meaning light) and synthesis (to make). To photosynthesize, they need carbon dioxide from the air, water from the soil and chlorophyll in their leaves to trap the energy.

$$\text{CARBON DIOXIDE + WATER} \xrightarrow[\text{CHLOROPHYLL}]{\text{SUNLIGHT}} \text{SUGAR + OXYGEN}$$

Most flowering plants are green because their cells contain this energy trapping pigment, chlorophyll. The upper surfaces of leaves have a layer of special cells, *pallisade* cells, which contain a lot of chlorophyll. These are usually protected by a waxy surface layer. The underside of the leaf contains more air spaces, and small air holes call *stomata* which are used for respiration. They can be opened or closed to control the amount of water lost from the leaf.

Roots and stems

As well as needing water and light for growth, plants need nutrients in the form of various chemicals. These are usually found in the soil and are taken up through the plant's root system. Nitrogen is needed for general growth, phosphorus for healthy roots and potassium for healthy leaves. Roots are usually covered with tiny hairs, increasing their surface area for uptake of materials, particularly water. The water passes up through the root system into the stem. The stem has tiny tubes called *xylem*, along which the fluid travels. Other tubes called *phloem*, lead from the leaves into the stem, and food passes down the phloem tubes to the rest of the plant.

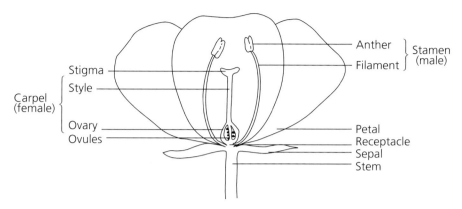

Figure 4.4 A flowering plant's reproductive system

Life cycles and reproduction

The flowering plant's reproductive system is the flower itself, which we tend to value for appearance and fragrance (Figure 4.4). Flowering plants have male and female germ cells (gametes) for reproduction, the pollen grains and the ovules respectively. The female reproductive organ of the flower is called the *carpel*, and comprises a stigma, a style and an ovary. The male reproductive part is the *stamen*, comprising the anther and filament. Inside each ovary, the ovules are made and inside each anther are the pollen grains. Most plants have both on one flower, although fertilization of the ovule may be required by pollen from a different plant of the same species (*cross-pollination*) rather than from the same plant (*self-pollination*).

Pollination is the transfer of pollen from the anthers of a flower to the stigma, so that fertilization can occur. This is done in several ways. The wind can blow pollen around. This is the way grasses and cereals are pollinated. Some flowers attract insects by having colourful petals or a scent or by producing nectar. Many common garden flowers are pollinated in this way. When the insect reaches down into the flower for nectar, the pollen sticks to the insect. When it visits another flower, it is brushed off onto the stigma. This is easy to see in plants like sweet peas and snapdragons. Once on the stigma, the genetic material of the pollen grains are transferred down the style to the ovule. When fertilization has occurred, the ovary ripens and *seeds* form.

The seed consists of an embryonic plant and tissue which supplies the nutrients needed for development. A protective seed coat, the *testa*, surrounds the whole. In true flowering plants, the ovule wall develops into a *fruit* which encloses the seed. Seeds provide protection and food for the embryonic plants, and can be dispersed by wind or by animals, particularly birds attracted to the fruit. Seeds are also an effective means by which the plant can survive winter until the conditions are appropriate for *germination*. This is the start of growth of the seed into the mature form. Various factors can trigger germination, for example, rising temperatures, exposure to light or rupturing of the seed coat by water. This process varies from species to species.

CONTINUITY AND CHANGE

Genetics and heredity

In the earlier sections of this chapter we considered reproduction as one of the characteristic functions of being alive. Living things reproduce to perpetuate their species although how they do so can vary. Individual members of a species can breed with one another, but reproduction between species cannot produce fertile offspring. This situation brings us to the process of inheritance. As materialistic human beings we can inherit property, money and other valuables from our ancestors. Biological beings also inherit the things which make them what they are, a tree or a grass, a mouse or a spider. Even within these large groups there is variety. Humans are male or female, tall or short, with black hair, brown eyes and so on. What makes this possible?

Cells: the building bricks of life

Although there are millions of different species of plants and animals on our planet, they all have one thing in common. Their bodies are all made from *cells*, the building bricks of life. Some living things are so small their whole body is just one cell. For example, the algae, *Chlorella*, that cause the green film on garden ponds or the protozoan, *Amoeba*, which lives in the pond, or the many bacteria which break down the dead materials in the pond are single-celled *organisms*. Other living things are larger and apparently more complex, like the goldfish swimming in the pond or the neighbour's cat trying to get to the goldfish. Small or large, simple or complex, all living things are made up of cells (Figure 4.5).

If we consider the two main kingdoms of living things, plants and animals, there are certain features common to all cells. The bulk of the cell is formed from a greyish, jelly-like material called *cytoplasm*. This cytoplasm is encased in a cell boundary. In animals, this boundary is a soft, elastic *cell membrane*. Think of it as a polythene bag filled with wallpaper paste. Materials can pass into and out of the cell through the cell

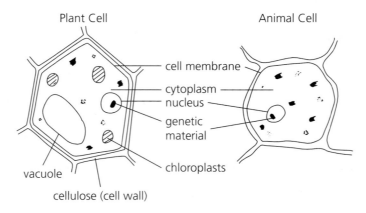

Figure 4.5 A typical plant and animal cell

membrane. In plants, the cell membrane is reinforced with a more rigid layer of *cellulose fibres* to form a *cell wall*. Imagine putting your paste-filled bag into a shoe box. The cell wall provides structural support for the plant cell. In addition, plant cells have tiny bodies called *chloroplasts* full of the green pigment *chlorophyll*. Cells also have bubbles or *vacuoles* in the cytoplasm. These are filled with fluids and gases and help to regulate the levels of sugars and salts in the cell. In animals, there are usually a few small vacuoles, but in plants there is usually one large one where it serves an additional role by expanding and contracting when the temparature falls or rises. This helps to prevent the plant cell from bursting in extreme conditions.

The most important feature of all cells is a tiny object called the *nucleus*. This is the control centre of the cell, determining all cell activity and containing the cell's genetic material, the *deoxyribonucleic acid* (DNA). The nucleus and its contents are crucial for the process of reproduction.

Reproducing without sex

Not all living things show the variety mentioned earlier. Some living things are identical copies of their parent. This is because of the way they reproduce. It is rather like being in a factory making plastic toy ducks for the bath. If the system is working perfectly, one duck is identical to the next. They all have a yellow body, a red bill, green feet and blue eyes. It is like this with some single-celled plants and animals. For example, amoeba produce offspring by a process called *fission*. They divide themselves into two identical pieces, although there is nothing simple about how they do this. It happens in several stages (Figure 4.6).

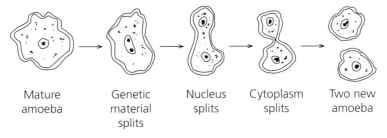

Mature	Genetic	Nucleus	Cytoplasm	Two new
amoeba	material	splits	splits	amoeba
	splits			

Figure 4.6   Asexual reproduction in a single-cell organism

If you were looking down a microscope, you would first see the strings of genetic material in the nucleus, the *chromosomes* with their DNA, become visible. Each of the two *chromatids* that make up each chromosome can be seen joined together by a *centromere*. Then the membrane of the nucleus disappears and a structure called a *spindle* appears, like two equilateral triangles joined together to form a diamond. At the equator of the spindle (where the triangles join) the centromeres cluster. Third, each centromere splits itself into two pieces, each of which has one chromatid. The chromatids move apart to opposite ends of the spindle. Finally, a nuclear membrane forms around each group of chromatids at the pole of the spindle, producing two new nuclei. This process is called *mitosis*.

The cell cytoplasm now divides to form a figure eight shape, taking a new nucleus into each part. The cytoplasm separates and two daughter cells have been produced, each with the identical genetic material of the parent which, of course, no longer exists. The offspring are *clones* of the original. So by this process, 1 gives 2 gives 4 gives 8 gives 16 gives 32 gives 64 gives 128 and so on. Before you know it, there are thousands or even millions of identical copies of the original parent. This is how bacteria multiply so efficiently and make us feel ill so quickly. It is also the kind of *cell replication* that occurs in the body tissues of more complex organisms as in the growth of our own skin cells.

But this means that cells replace like with like. The yellow plastic ducks are coming off the production line. How do we get variety in our plastic ducks? Sometimes, the red paint might run out and the ducks' bills might be yellow. Sometimes, the plastic-forming machine might become blocked and the tails develop a kink to them. Occasionally, the thermostat might break so the whole batch might overheat and melt, rendering them unusable. It is the same with asexual reproduction. Changes can occur to individuals because of *mutations* (a change in the cells' DNA) or effects of environmental changes. Sometimes catastrophes, like disease, can wipe out a whole species. But this cannot account for the tremendous variation we see not only between species but also between individuals within species. To explain this, we have to consider sexual reproduction.

Task 4.3 Dolly the Sheep

The offspring of this kind of cell division are *clones* of the original parent. A clone is an organism, a micro-organism or even a cell derived from one original parent by an asexual process. Dolly the sheep, produced by researchers at the Roslin Institute near Edinburgh in 1997, is an example of a cloned organism. A cell from the udder of a six-year-old ewe was implanted in an ovum (egg cell) which had had its genetic material removed. The egg developed into Dolly.

Explain why Dolly is female.

Why would Dolly's characteristics be exactly the same as those of the ewe which donated the udder cell?

Make a list of the possible advantages and disadvantages of cloning.

What do we need sex for?

Many organisms carry out a more complicated form of cell replication called *sexual reproduction*. This involves two parents, each contributing half of the necessary genetic material for the new offspring (Figure 4.7). Each parent has specialized organs which produce the *gametes* (the germ cells) by a process called *meiosis*. Meiosis involves similar stages to mitosis but each stage occurs twice. As a result, the gametes have only half the chromosomal material of the original cell. Those produced by the mother are female and are usually called ovules in plants or ova or eggs in animals. Those produced by the father are male and are usually called pollen in plants or sperm in animals.

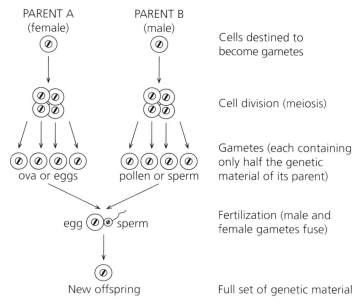

PARENT A (female)   PARENT B (male)

Cells destined to become gametes

Cell division (meiosis)

Gametes (each containing only half the genetic material of its parent)

ova or eggs   pollen or sperm

egg ⊘⊘ sperm

Fertilization (male and female gametes fuse)

New offspring   Full set of genetic material

Figure 4.7   Sexual reproduction in a multi-cellular organism

Because of meiosis, each gamete has only half of the required genetic material needed to produce a new organism and it is only when a male and a female gamete fuse that a complete new organism begins to develop. In plants this process is called *pollination*, in animals it is *fertilization*. By this process the parents survive to generate more than one offspring. The result is a new offspring which might resemble either, both or neither of its parents. But why is there such tremendous variation within species? To explain this we have to consider heredity.

Heredity

Going back to our ducks in the factory, imagine there is a control panel for making the ducks. It has eight buttons: a column of four for yellow bodies, red bills, green feet and blue eyes and a second column of four for white bodies, yellow bills, black feet and green eyes. By pushing one or other of each of the buttons on the control panels we could get sixteen possible ducks being produced. It all depends upon which buttons are pushed.

YELLOW	●	*Body*	●	WHITE
RED	●	*Bill*	●	YELLOW
GREEN	●	*Feet*	●	BLACK
BLUE	●	*Eyes*	●	GREEN

It is even more complicated with living things. When sexual reproduction takes place, characteristics of each parent are passed on to the offspring. Which characteristics are passed is quite random and we can be talking about hundreds or thousands of them. The characteristics are carried by the *chromosomes*, the strings of genetic material (DNA) in each cell nucleus. Each different species has its own specific number of chromosomes. For example, yeast cells have 16 chromosomes (8 pairs) while human cells have 46 chromosomes (23 pairs). Each chromosome is rather like two bead necklaces twisted around each other, the *double helix*. Each bead on the string has its own special position on the string and has its partner bead on the opposite string. In living cells, these pairs are the different characteristics or *genes*. So on your chromosomes you carry thousands of genes which determine everything about you that makes you you: your hair colour, height, size of feet, even the shape of your ears.

So, for our plastic ducks, there would be a pair of genes for body colour, two for the beak colour, two for the feet and two for the eyes. When sexual reproduction occurs and the chromosomes separate during meiosis, it is one half of the pair which is found in the germ cell (or gamete). The rules which tell us how these characteristics are passed on or *inherited* were first described by Gregor Mendel, an Austrian monk who experimented on plants in his monastery garden back in the nineteenth century. Mendel studied pea plants. He used plants with visible characteristics like flower colour (white or coloured), height (tall or dwarf), and texture of the pea seed coat (smooth or wrinkled). From his observations he noticed that depending on which parents he started with there were some regular patterns in the offspring. From these patterns, he identified what we now call Mendel's Laws of Inheritance. These tell us that:

1   Some basic characteristics (like height or colour) are determined by individual genetic factors which are passed on to offspring during sexual reproduction.
2   In normal cells, the factors for each characteristic exist in pairs.
3   When different factors are present in a pair, one factor can overrule (or dominate) the other. This is the *dominant* factor. The one overruled is the *recessive* factor.

What Mendel called factors we now call genes from the Greek meaning to give birth. We also know now that many characteristics are determined by more than one pair of genes. So, Mendel's pure-bred tall pea plants had a pair of genes for tallness (T and T), while the dwarf plants had a pair of genes for non-tallness or dwarfness (t and t). The pure-bred white flowered plants had a pair of genes for whiteness (W and W) while the coloured ones had a pair of genes for non-whiteness or colouredness (w and w). Impure plants, or *hybrids*, would have a mixture – Tt for height and Ww for flower colour. The appearance of the plant depends upon which gene is dominant. In the case of Mendel's peas, the hybrids looked tall with white flowers because T over-ruled t and W over-ruled w. This is shown diagrammatically in Figure 4.8.

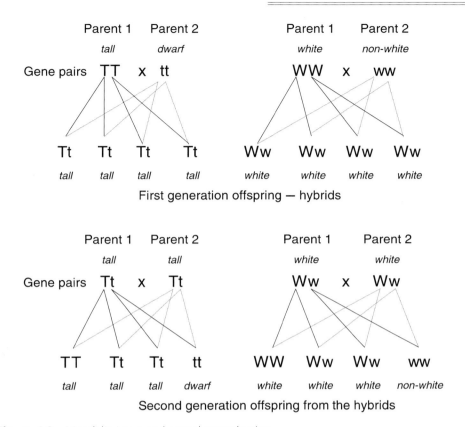

Figure 4.8 Mendel's Laws and sexual reproduction

Because there are hundreds of variable characteristics, this means there are millions of possible gene combinations for the offspring. This gives the great variation we observe in living things. Mendel's work with peas has been replicated with other plants and with animals. His laws have been found to hold true across the living world. Today, plant and animal breeders use Mendel's Laws when they try to breed new varieties of long-coated sheep or pest-resistant cereal crops, and horticulturalists have long used them to develop new varieties of carnations, roses and other flowering plants for events like the Chelsea Flower Show.

Task 4.4 Identical twins	In a recent magazine advertisement, there was a photograph of two couples, both of whom looked identical. Identical twin brothers had married identical twin sisters. Both women had become pregnant at the same time and given birth to sons on the same day.

Explain how, as well as being cousins the two babies can also, genetically, be considered brothers.

Evolution

The great variety of plants and animals on our planet is a result of a process of *evolution* in which new species have appeared and others have disappeared or become *extinct*. Until the nineteenth century, the general belief in Europe was that each species had been created about 4,500 years ago according to the account of Creation in the Christian Bible and that nothing had changed since then. This was known as *The Doctrine of Special Creation*. However, in the nineteenth century scientists were beginning to find evidence that the earth was considerably older than this and that plants and animals that are around today may be very different from some that existed a long time ago. Work of geologists like James Hutton and Charles Lyle helped to explain when and how the earth was formed and how the different layers of rocks, some with the fossils of animals not found today, came to be as they are. Probably the most famous name linked to evolution is that of Charles Darwin. Drawing on evidence he collected during his voyage around the world on *The Beagle*, Darwin created a theory of evolution. He published it in the book *The Origin of Species* in 1859.

In essence, Darwin's theory is based on three ideas:

- *A struggle for existence:* organisms produce far more offspring than can survive; they compete with one another for food and space as they struggle to survive.
- *The survival of the fittest:* generally, no two organisms are exactly alike; those better adapted to their environment or better equipped to survive are more likely to be successful in the competition for food and space; the fittest survive, breed and pass on their characteristics to their offspring.
- *Natural selection:* the better-adapted characteristics are likely to be favoured and selected for continued existence; they spread through the population and through the generations, becoming typical of the species; the better-adapted species are advantaged compared to other species when competing for food and space and ultimately new species appear while others die out; Darwin called this process natural selection.

Darwin's theory was strongly attacked at the time, by scientists as well as by clergy, but his theory is generally accepted today as a starting point for understanding the process of evolution. Evidence to support his ideas comes from many sources.

Geology: Modern technology has helped geologists to explore and explain how the layers of rocks forming the Earth's crust came to be the way they are. The fossils found in some of these layers provide extra evidence. How do fossils of sea creatures come to be found in layers of rock high up in mountain ranges, for example? Carbon dating techniques have also helped in this process by enabling us to locate with some accuracy when these layers were once at the bottom of lakes and seas and the fossil animals and plants were once alive. These dating techniques also enable us to identify when organisms that no longer exist, like trilobites, became extinct. We can build a time line to show the relationship between present-day species and their extinct ancestors.

Geography: The distribution of living things on the Earth's surface helps us to link the process of evolution to geological changes which have occurred over time. The movement of the Earth's surface resulted in the huge land masses being separated. Animals and plants which were once living side by side now have descendents on different continents separated by wide oceans. Their common ancestors form a strong link in evolutionary terms. For example, marsupials like kangaroos and wallabies are found only in Australia with the exception of the American opposum. We now believe that before the land mass separated, marsupials were quite widespread. When Australia split from South-east Asia, those marsupials in Australia were isolated geographically from the rapid development of mammalian species and so survived the competition for food and space. Those in the rest of the world were not so lucky and few marsupials survived.

Biology: If we look at the life cycles of many living things we find that although the mature form of many organisms may be very different, their early or embryonic stages are very similar. This is evidence of a common ancestor. So the aquatic larval stage of a frog (the tadpole), larval fish, and even the embryonic human all show signs of similar structures (like gills) and appendages (like tails). Similarly, in adult form, there are structural similarities between species. The pentadactyl (five digit) limb is found not only in humans, but also in a whale's flipper and in fused form in a bird's wing. Unless there is some relationship between these species, how can we explain the similar lines of development? Structural similarities due to common ancestors are called *homologies.*

Genetic engineering: As our knowledge and understanding of how characteristics are passed on from one generation to the next grows, so does the evidence to explain changes in populations and species. We can now deliberately engineer genetic changes in the laboratory which would have taken thousands of years in the natural world. Gene mapping of the DNA also helps us to match organisms, not just for immediate parentage but also for distant ancestry. For example, over 97 per cent of the DNA of a chimpanzee and a human is identical. We share a common ancestor in our evolutionary past.

The theory of evolution suggests that the more complex organisms have evolved from simpler ones. The latter have continued to exist when they have found a niche that the more complex ones could not occupy. So simple, single-celled plants and animals live side by side in the same pond with complex ones like pike, water lilies and frogs. We know that over millions of years there have been long spells of stability interrupted by changes on our planet, sometimes catastrophic, which have affected the life on the planet. This process is descibed as *punctuated equilibrium.* Organisms whose physical structures or biological responses enabled them to adapt more easily to such changes had an advantage over others. They were the fittest to survive. When such adaptations were due mainly to slight but significant alterations in the genetic material of the organisms, the characteristics could be passed on to offspring and new species could eventually evolve. With natural selection favouring the fittest, the original and intermediate species might even disappear altogether.

Ordinarily, extinction of a particular species can occur as a result of natural agencies, like disease, predation or even an environmental change. However, there are periods of mass extinction on Earth which are more difficult to explain. Perhaps the most famous one is that of about 65 million years ago which appeared to wipe out the dinosaurs. Evidence suggests that the atmosphere cooled rapidly, possibly as a result of volcanic activity or an asteroid hitting the planet. This probably resulted in acid rain and freezing temperatures. The dinosaurs were not the only living things to suffer. Many other species disappeared, including about three-quarters of the marine life and many terrestrial plants. This is one of those punctuations (or interruptions) in the equilibrium of life on Earth. However, what was a catastrophe for the dinosaurs and many other species became an opportunity for another group, the mammals. It is from this period, 65 million years ago, that our mammalian ancestors really emerged.

This view of evolution is divergent – spreading out from a single, common ancestral path. Not all evolution is like this. Occasionally, pathways converge. Two or more independent lines of evolutionary development bring about superficially similar results. This is usually as a result of different groups of organisms being subjected to the same natural selection pressures. They tend to evolve similar structural features to cope. For example, this is why whales and dolphins are often mistakenly thought of as fish. Their return to an aquatic life with the streamlined body shape and flipper-like limbs mirrors the development of fish like sharks and even some now extinct marine reptiles like the ichthyosaurs.

Over millions of years, species that were originally related could become so different that it is difficult to recognize the common ancestor. The intermediate groups are sometimes called the *missing links*, as with the links between humans and their ancestors. There is still a lot we do not know about evolution.

ECOSYSTEMS AND ENVIRONMENTS

Classification and the diversity of living things

Knowing that individual organisms carry out various life processes and pass on their characteristics to their offspring is still only part of the picture of the living world. If aliens visited our planet, how would they make sense of the vast diversity of life they would find? We need to sort and classify organisms into manageable groups which reflect the relationships between them according to particular features or characteristics.

Attempts to classify living things began as long ago as the time of the Ancient Greeks and different criteria have been used over time. For example, plants were once sorted into groups according to their use as food, medicines and perfumes. Later, they were sorted into groups according to shared visible features, like number of petals or shape of the leaves. These classification systems proved to be unreliable and resulted in plants like clover and wood sorrel, which both have three-leaf structures, being classified together when they are, in fact, biologically unrelated. They do not have the kinds of similarities we now use to group things together.

Modern scientific classification really stems from the work of a Swedish naturalist called Carl von Linné, or *Linnaeus*. He sorted plants into groups according to various similarities of structures, particularly in their reproductive structures. He identified each group of plants using two names, the *binomial* (two-name) system. The first part of the name identified the large group or *genus* to which the plant belonged. The second name indicated the subgroup within the genus, the specific or *species* name. His system of classification was later applied to animals as well as plants and is still used today.

The names used were Latin ones, to avoid variation in common names between districts and countries. For example, what is called a harebell in some parts of Scotland is not the same as what is called a harebell in the south of England. Thus the common daisy found on many lawns belongs to the same family as the mayweeds, the fleabanes and the ragworts, for example. To distinguish it from what we call the ox-eye daisy we use its scientific name. The common daisy is *Bellis perennis*, belonging to the genus *Bellis*, with a specific identity as being the perennial form, hence the species *perennis*. The ox-eye daisy, on the other hand, is *Leucanthemum vulgare*. It belongs to a totally different genus. Within the buttercup family (genus *Ranunculaceae*), we have a number of closely related members: the meadow buttercup (*Ranunculus acris*), the common water crowfoot (*Ranunculus aquatilis*) and the lesser celandine (*Ranunculus ficaria*). Similarly for animals, in the crow family (genus *Corvidae*) we have: rooks (*Corvus frugilegus*), ravens (*Corvus corax*) and jackdaws (*Corvus monedula*). Sometimes there are several different sub-groups of the species (or sub-species): the carrion crow (*Corvus corone corone*) and the hooded crow (*Corvus corone cornix*). To tell the difference between them, a third name has been added. Members of a species can interbreed with each other, but members of related species within a genus seldom do so. If they do, their offspring are usually sterile (as when a male donkey and a female horse produce a mule).

As a result of the work of Linnaeus and subsequent scientists, we now have a very comprehensive classification system for the vast number of living things on our planet. However, our ideas are constantly changing and developing as we gain new insights into what counts as alive. For example, although fungi were once classified as a major group in the plant kingdom, they are now thought by many scientists to be a kingdom in their own right, as are bacteria and viruses. There is currently a similar debate about the status of the Protozoa, a phylum in the animal kingdom. Some scientists argue it should be a separate kingdom.

When living things are classified in this way, a hierarchy emerges. That is, the higher the position of a group or category in the hierarchy, the fewer similarities exist between its member organisms. Figure 4.9 provides a summary of the classification of living things, although inevitably in the space available only those categories which might be encountered in primary science have been exemplified. At the top of the hierarchy are *kingdoms*. Two clear kingdoms exist in the living world, the plant kingdom and the animal kingdom. The plant kingdom is then subdivided into large groups called *divisions* and the animal kingdom into large groups called *phyla*. Each of these is then further subdivided into smaller and smaller groups, called *classes*, *orders*, *families*, *genuses*, and *species*. The lower down the hierarchy the plant is found, the greater are the similarities between the members of that group.

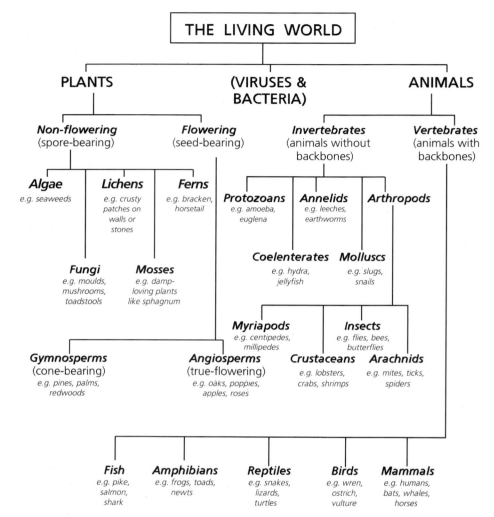

Figure 4.9 The classification of living things

Living things in their environment

All living things are connected to one another. We need to understand these connections and how the natural balance of living things in their physical environment can be maintained or, conversely, upset. Although living things affect the environment in which they live, they are also affected by it. Bees pollinating the fruit orchards of southern England may be killed by the insecticides sprayed onto crops to kill a harmful insect visitor. As a consequence, no fruit is produced. The balance is disturbed. Usually it can be restored naturally if the disruption is not too great, but human pollution of environments is slowly affecting this balance. In order to understand it we need to understand the various biological and physical components of the planet, that is the *biophysical environment*. The environment of any living thing comprises all the living organisms and non-living materials on which they depend. The science of *ecology* is the study of living things and how they are adapted to and exist within the different environments.

The basic unit of life in any environment is the individual *organism*. Most plants or animals can be recognized as individuals. Although they can often survive independently for a while, they seldom do so for long. Usually, they exist in larger groups or *populations*, living together and reproducing to continue the species. In any one place, or *habitat*, there will be several populations of different species, living together and satisfying their needs for food and space. In some habitats, there may be several populations of the same species as well as populations of different species of plants and animals. Sometimes the populations will be dense, as with grasses and groundbeetles. There will also be sparse populations, as with a single family of foxes or a lone pair of kestrels. All of these living things existing side by side are described as a *community* in which there is both co-operation and competition. These communities are dependent not only on each other but also on the non-living factors in their area, like the soil, the rainfall and the amount of light. The whole combination of the different plants and animals in their physical environment is called an *ecosystem*. There are many different ecosystems, such as a rocky shore, a pond, a wood and a water meadow. Each has its own unique balance.

Although ecosystems exist independently, and are organized and relatively self-sufficient, plants and animals from one can stray into another, as when seeds are blown by the wind or animals move in search of food. Large carnivores, such as foxes and hawks often roam across several ecosystems to feed. Smaller herbivores, like rabbits, may travel in search of plants. All living things are connected by their feeding relationships and ultimately all feeding relationships are dependent on the sun's light energy. We refer to this pattern or feeding relationships as the *energy flow* within the ecosystem.

The simplest feeding relationship is a *food chain*. This is the route by which energy is changed through a number of organisms (plants or animals) by one eating another from a different feeding level. At the beginning of a food chain is a primary producer, a green plant, which uses the sun's light energy to produce its sugars. The plant is consumed by the next organism in the chain, a herbivore. Herbivores are at the next level, they are primary consumers. These in turn are likely to be eaten by lower or top carnivores, the secondary and tertiary consumer levels. In reality, the situation is much more complex, with different plants being eaten by many different animals, and with animals that can feed at more than one level. The complex interconnection of chains in a community of living things is called a *food web*.

How many living things can occupy a particular habitat depends very much on the amount of food available to them. Animals which eat grass are abundant. Those that eat the grass-eaters have more competition and are therefore fewer in number. Moving up through the levels, each level can support a smaller number of organisms as the amount of available energy decreases. Eventually, there can only be one or two top carnivores. This relationship is sometimes called a *food pyramid*.

There is a great emphasis on environmental issues today and few people can have missed media reports on ecological disasters, depletion of the ozone layer or the effects of greenhouse gases. We are all encouraged to recycle waste materials, save energy, drive more economical cars and reduce exhaust emissions. Unfortunately, the emphasis is usually on the benefits to us as humans. But what of the benefits to the living things that were here before we were and to the effects on their environments?

Adaptation to the environment

Living things need to be adapted to the environment in which they live in order to survive. Adaptation describes when an organism – plant or animal – has evolved to function efficiently in its particular environmental niche. Adaptation can be *structural*, as with the thorns of a rose briar which enable it to use hedgerow plants to climb, or the tendrils of clematis which serve the same purpose. Similarly, the seeds of a dandelion allow easy dispersal by the wind, while those of goosegrass have tiny hooks to hitch a ride on any passing animal's fur.

Some adaptations are purely *functional*, enabling survival in different climatic conditions. Cacti in a hot, dry desert have barrel-like bodies to retain water, and tiny leaves (like spines) to minimize transpiration. Saxifrages high up on alpine mountainsides are low growing, with leaf clusters that hug the rock crevices. Some plants in very cold conditions even have a kind of antifreeze in their cells to stop the cells bursting as the temperature falls.

Some adaptations are to the organism's *mode of life*, for example for moving in different media (flying, swimming or burrowing) or for feeding on different food sources. For instance, moles are ideally adapted to their burrowing life style. Their powerful clawed feet enable them to dig their way through soil. Streamlined bodies, with short, dense fur and no external ear structures, enable them to move through the soil without being affected by the cold and wetness or sharp stones. Their digestive systems are adapted to their carnivorous diet, enabling them to take advantage of the worms and larvae found in the soil. They are able to function more effectively in this niche but bring them above ground and they are very vulnerable. Poor eyesight and legs adapted for digging not running through grass, make them easy prey for predators. In a similar way, plants exposed to strong winds and salt spray on the seashore have adapted to survive under those conditions by developing low growing structures and tough leaves which minimize dehydration and the effects of salt.

Not all adaptations are helpful to humans. For example, genetic mutations in some bacteria which cause disease have resulted in a resistance to antibiotics like penicillin.

WHAT DO PRIMARY CHILDREN ALREADY KNOW?

Young children already know quite a lot about life processes and living things before they start school. This does not mean that their knowledge is complete or even accurate, and they may have no deep understanding of the processes and ideas they can discuss with such confidence. Their ideas are based on limited experience of the environment in which they live and the children and adults with whom they interact. White (1988) suggests that such inaccuracies in children's ideas should be treated as 'informative rather than merely incorrect'. As their teacher, it will be one of your tasks to help them to clarify what they already know and use it as a relevant starting point for their new experiences of life processes and living things. However, children are often unwilling to change their ideas. Even when provided with evidence that what they believe is wrong, they can stubbornly hold on to something which seems to have worked for them for quite a while. According to Bradley (1996),

> This is because understanding is a process by which children test and modify their ideas. However, if their ideas are not in a form that is testable, no amount of evidence will help them to modify them.
>
> (p. 51)

So what kinds of ideas do children hold? If we begin with ideas about what is alive, people in the Zapotec civilization of sixteenth-century Mexico believed that something was alive if it had a vital force – 'breath' or 'wind'. Clouds moving across the sky, white water on the river and froth on a drink all had this vital force and were, therefore, alive. If you ask young children today what is alive, they are likely to tell you that people are, and possibly their pets. Things like plants and other animals are not seen as being alive. Nor do they see humans as animals. They place themselves in a separate group to plants and animals. Research with kindergarten children in Japan has shown that those who were given pet goldfish to raise at home had a greater understanding of animals and their life processes than the children who had no pets and only occasional contact with animals at school (Hatano and Inagaki, 1992).

It is hardly surprising that research tells us that children do not develop their ideas about these life processes all at once. Qualter (1996) provides a useful model to represent the development of children's understanding of the processes of life (Figure 4.10). It shows that young children first develop ideas relating to how things grow and move, and so topics in science could focus upon these life processes first, by looking at how the children, their pets and other animals like birds and minibeasts grow and

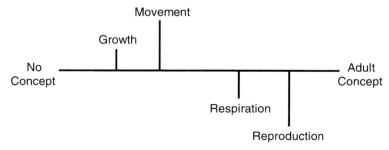

Figure 4.10 Qualter's model to represent the development of children's understanding of life processes

move around. Revisiting the experiences when the children are older could shift the focus to other life processes, particularly nutrition, respiration (or at this stage, breathing) and simple reproduction, with the various organs in the body being introduced for this purpose. The focus in the primary school should be on humans as organisms. A study of green plants at this stage can explore the parallel processes in plants.

To illustrate Qualter's developmental sequence at work, consider an idea commonly held by younger children in connection with nutrition.

> Lynsey, age six, held an extremely stable idea about the digestive system, which her teacher could not persuade her to change.
> 'First we chew the food up. Then there are two tubes, one for food and one for drink. Then some muscles mush it together. Then it comes out of one end.'
>
> (Bradley, 1996, p. 51)

Lynsey was clearly not ready for the more abstract ideas to do with feeding and digestion, although the basic ideas to do with food, muscles, change over time and so on are in place. When the children are older visual aids (such as pictures, charts or models) could help with the developing understanding although they made little impression on Lynsey.

Harlen (1992) provides many similar examples of children's ideas. For example, a developing chick inside an egg is thought by some primary age children to comprise a loose collection of body parts floating about until the time is right for them to join together and the bird to hatch from the egg.

Many young children fail to see green plants as living things at all or to recognize the life processes carried out by plants which parallel those in animals. For example, very young children know that animals move. Few, even at the end of KS2, recognize that plants also move. Animal movement is visually obvious but the movement of plants is much more restricted to slow responses to light and gravity, for example. Some children also hold the mistaken belief that plants get their food from the soil and that the food is in the same form as animal food. They see this as the purpose of the roots. This can be a difficult idea to change but opportunities to explore plants growing with and without soil can be a starting point.

Even at a young age, children show an ability to use a consistent and well-organized classification system (Sperber, 1994). This usually relates to simple, observable features, such as sorting by colour or number and later by shape. This can be the starting point for work on classification of living things, moving from the familiar and concrete to the less familiar and eventually abstract.

By the time they enter KS2 (around seven years) they also have reasonably well-developed ideas about some of the characteristics of seasonal change, and so can begin to explore these ideas in relation to physical states and properties of materials. However, they still maintain a belief in intentions, that is they attribute conscious choice to effects. For example, they believe trees lose their leaves in autumn because they want to or an animal grows thicker fur because it wants to. They do not yet appreciate the causal connection within these events.

WHAT DO THE CHILDREN NEED TO KNOW?

The experiences you organize for your class to introduce them to basic ideas associated with life processes and living things need to be related to the National Curriculum requirements for Sc2, summarized in Table 4.1. How do you begin to teach children about life processes and living things?

STARTING POINTS FOR THE CLASSROOM

Underpinning the National Curriculum Order for Science and the Circular 4/98 guidance, there are a small number of fundamental concepts which you will want your children in the primary school to acquire. These are:

- some things are alive, some were once alive but are no longer, and some things were never alive;
- there are a number of life processes characteristic to all living things;
- humans are living things which exhibit these characteristic processes;
- green plants are living things which exhibit these characteristic processes;
- living things – plants and animals – can be classified into groups according to certain characteristic features;
- plants and animals can be found in a range of different habitats;
- plants and animals are adapted to the environments in which they live; and
- plants and animals depend upon one another and upon the non-living environment in which they live.

The children themselves and their families, their local environment and the plants and animals in the locality can be the starting point for many of the experiences you plan for them. Some ideas for starting points are listed below.

Life processes and being alive

Initially, with children, studying humans as organisms and green plants as organisms can be little more than a labelling task to develop their awareness of the names of different parts of the plant or human body and then tying in the different parts to the various activities carried out. Once these are established, more complicated links need to be identified, for example, noses are used for breathing as well as smelling, muscles in our legs get tired after we run around, and to stay healthy we need regular food and rest. Throughout these experiences, an understanding of similarities and differences can be developed. The similarities with other animals can be pointed out, for example, that just like pets, we need food and water and our bodies grow and change with time. At this stage it is the simple patterns in the human body's behaviour which can be identified through topics like *Ourselves, Growth and Change, Seasonal Changes* or *The Senses*. These are then elaborated upon in more detail at Key Stage 2. With older

Table 4.1   Overview of Sc2 of the National Curriculum Order for Science for Key Stages 1 and 2

◆   *Life Processes and Living Things*   ◆

Life Processes

KS1: 1a – *differences between living, once living and non-living things;*
KS1: 1b – *animals, including humans, move, feed, grow, use their senses and reproduce;*
KS1: 1c – *relate life processes to animals and plants found in the local environment;*
KS2: 1a – *nutrition, movement, growth and reproduction common to animals, including humans;*
KS2: 1b – *nutrition and reproduction common to plants;*
KS2: 1c – *make links between life processes in familiar plants and animals and the environments in which they are found.*

Humans and other animals
KS1: 2a – *recognise external parts of the body;*
KS1: 2b – *need for food and water to stay alive;*
KS1: 2c – *exercise and the right food help to keep humans healthy;*
KS1: 2d – *role of drugs as medicines;*
KS1: 2e – *how to treat animals with care;*
KS1: 2f – *ability to produce offspring which grow into adults;*
KS1: 2g – *senses and the ability to sense the world;*
KS2: 2a – *function of teeth and dental care;*
KS2: 2b – *food for activity, growth and health;*
KS2: 2c – *model heart and its pump action;*
KS2: 2d – *pulse rate and effect of exercise and rest;*
KS2: 2e – *muscles, skeleton and movement;*
KS2: 2f – *main stages of human life cycle;*
KS2: 2g – *harmful effects of tobacco, alcohol and other drugs;*
KS2: 2h – *importance of exercise for good health.*

Green Plants
KS1: 3a – *plants need for light and water for growth;*
KS1: 3b – *recognize and name parts of a flowering plant*
KS1: 3c – *seeds grow into flowering plants;*
KS2: 3a – *effects of light, water and temperature on plant growth;*
KS2: 3b – *role of the leaf in producing new material growth;*
KS2: 3c – *role of the root to anchor plants and in transportation of water and minerals around the plant;*
KS2: 3d – *the parts of a flower and the life cycle of flowering plants, including pollination, seed formation, seed dispersal and germination.*

Variation and classification
KS1: 4a – *similarities and differences between themselves and other pupils;*
KS1: 4b – *grouping living things according to observable similarities and differences;*
KS2: 4a – *make and use keys;*
KS2: 4b – *identifying and assigning locally occurring plants and animals to groups.*
KS2: 4c – *variety of plants and animals makes it important to identify and assign them to groups.*

Living things in their environment
KS1: 5a – *variety of plants and animals in the local environment;*
KS1: 5b – *identify similarities and differences between local environments;*
KS1: 5c – *care for the environment;*
KS2: 5a – *living things and environments need protection;*
KS2: 5b – *different habitats have different plants and animals living there;*
KS2: 5c – *plants and animals are suited to their different habitats;*
KS2: 5d – *food chains show feeding relationships in a habitat.*
KS2: 5e – *food chains usually start with green plants.*
KS2: 5f – *different habitats have both helpful and harmful micro-organisms.*

children, the focus shifts to a more careful analysis of some of the particular processes, all at an introductory level.

There is a range of topics which lend themselves well to exploring processes and characteristics of life.

Area	Topic
Food and diet	Harvest festival, Foods we eat, Healthy eating
Growth and development	Growing things, Baby animals, Seeds, Spring life
Health education	Myself, My body, Good health, Teeth,
Change	The seasons/Spring, Summer, Autumn, Winter

Starting from stories is a popular approach with younger children. For example, traditional tales like *Jack and the Beanstalk* can start a topic on growing things. Roald Dahl's story *The Very Hungry Caterpillar* can be used to introduce life cycles. For older primary school children, this usually means considering key incidents in the life cycle, like birth, infancy, young childhood, adolescence and adulthood. Pictures of themselves and members of their families at each of these stages helps to construct the pattern. For younger children there are some excellent large-piece wooden jigsaws, available through commercial suppliers, to show life cycles in flowering plants and animals. However, ultimately the aim should be to involve children in observing and investigating the processes of life with the real thing. A parent with a new baby can be a starting point for the human life cycle. Seeing the baby fed, bathed and changed introduces various life processes. Photographs of children as babies and parents and grandparents when younger can help to introduce the sequence and time scale, expecially with older children.

Skeletons and models of different organs and parts of the human body help to show internal as well as external features, and there are also some excellent computer packages available for this.

Animals in the classroom can help children to observe life cycles, although local and national regulations must be followed carefully. Certain animals are not allowed in schools because of health risks. However, local vets and pet shop owners will often bring approved animals into school and give talks on the animals and their welfare. Spider jars, ant farms, wormeries and snail houses can all be established temporarily to show children a complete life cylce. Instructions on how to set up and manage these can be found in many commercial science schemes.

Although the emphasis is on the various processes of life, there is an additional dimension to this work. Children learn about the care of and respect for all living things, including themselves. Attitudes and values develop early in life and once established are difficult to change. Observing, investigating and caring for living things helps to set children off in the right direction.

Classifying living things

With primary age children, the starting point for sorting living things into groups should be those features of plants and animals that are easy to see. You can build on work in other areas of the curriculum, for example mathematics, where the children sort shapes according to the number of faces or edges, or their colour or thickness. In other aspects of science the children will probably have sorted objects according to what materials they are made from (wood, metal, plastic, . . .) or the properties of the material (insulator, magnetic, elastic, . . .).

You could begin to focus on living things by asking them to record ten things they notice about the goldfish or the geranium. Where possible, real organisms should be used, as with samples collected on a minibeast hunt or when pond dipping. Plants should be observed *in situ*, unless they are plants you are bringing from your own garden. Again, care for and responsibility towards all living things must be emphasized. By observing living things and noticing their observable features with younger children, you are laying down the ground rules for careful and accurate observation as well as providing the starting points for using classification keys at KS2.

Sorting keys, used to classify living things, can take several different forms. The common ones for older primary children are branching keys (sometimes called YES–NO keys) and GOTO keys. The former start with a question, like

Does your animal have wings?

If the answer is Yes, the children move down one branch, if No, they move down the other. There is a further question at each branch end which gives them a YES–NO choice, until they reach the correct answer (the name of the plant or animal).

GOTO keys work in a similar way, but each question is numbered. Question 1 would say,

Does your animal have wings?   If yes, GOTO question 2.
If no, GOTO question 6.

The children go to the relevant question and continue answering yes or no until they reach the name of the plant or animal they are looking at. At this stage the children use observable features to take decisions about which line or branch they move along or which step they go to next.

Groups of objects can easily be sorted in this way and with younger children it is sometimes useful to start with familiar objects like fruit and vegetables, leaves of different shapes, or blocks of different colours and shapes, until they get used to the process.

The important thing to remember about keys is that they should be relevant to the topic you are studying (Pets, Minibeasts, Farm Animals, Birds, The School Field, The Local Wood, . . .) and also to your locality. Published guidebooks to wildlife often have classification keys in them but they can be very confusing as they cover so many living things. You should design your own key for a limited number of plants or animals which are common to your locality, perhaps no more than four or six to begin with.

There are limits to the range of living things that can be brought into the classroom. A visit to a local farm, zoo, garden centre or park can help to expand children's experience of the variety of life. In addition, television programmes and video record-ings can be used, as can books and computer packages. Games like Animal Snap, Plant Snap, Animal–Vegetable–Mineral or Who Am I? can all help to extend their vocabulary and knowledge of living things.

Genetics and heredity

This is an area of study which is really only suited to older KS2 pupils. Even at this level, it is better confined to the study of cells. This can be approached through a topic like *Ourselves*, *New Life* or *Changes*. If the school has access to microscopes, single-celled organisms are easy to collect from local ponds. If you are lucky enough to capture an amoeba, it may even be possible to see fission occurring. It is also easy to see the cellular structure of thin slivers of onion skins. Health and safety rules forbid the use of blood or cheek scrapings to show cells, but pre-prepared slides of these can be easily obtained. Model cells can be made from polythene bags filled with water. A table tennis ball inside the bag on which a patch of genetic material has been drawn with a black pen represents the nucleus. This is a sterotype of an animal cell. If it is then squeezed into an empty plastic sweet jar, the jar is like the cellulose that forms a rigid cell wall. Green counters, glued to the inside of the jar, serve as the chloroplasts. However, it is difficult to seal the bags to prevent leakage so this is best demonstrated over a dish.

Grains of rice on a chessboard demonstrate nicely the way asexual reproduction increases the numbers of the organism (or cells) rapidly. Place one grain on the first square, two on the second, four on the third, eight on the fourth and so on. Unman-ageable numbers are reached before the children are far along the board. For sexual reproduction, it is better to leave the focus on the basic processes and life cycles, rather than get into the much more complicated area of inherited characteristics.

Evolution

Because children's own concepts of time are often uncertain, evolution can be a difficult idea to introduce. However, few primary children have no interest in topics like Dinosaurs or Fossils, and recent films like *Jurrasic Park* have helped fuel this interest. These are excellent ways to explore some of the simpler ideas of evolution. Depending upon the location of the school, a visit to a pebble beach or a safe, disused quarry can be a good way to encourage children to observe, ask questions and generate ideas. They can also use a range of research skills to find further information, as when using the library or the computer.

Ecosystems and environments

By studying different habitats children are given opportunities to explore and invest-igate scientifically. Studying a single habitat the children employ a range of skills, from close and detailed observation, sorting and classifying living things, comparing and contrasting organisms for adaptation to niches, recording and reporting observations in appropriate ways, and designing investigations to test ideas. Studies can range in scale from looking at the life in a spadeful of soil or a bucketful of leaf litter, to a study of a complete ecosystem like a rocky shore or a wood. Children can also focus on one individual, like an earthworm or a full community. They can represent food chains and food webs for their ecosystems as well as considering human influences on the habitats they are exploring.

SUGGESTIONS FOR FURTHER READING

If you would like to explore further some of the issues touched upon in this chapter, the following books should be of interest to you.

Driver, R., Leach, J., Scott, P. and Wood-Robinson, C. (1995) 'Young people's understanding of science concepts' in Murphy, P., Selinger, M., Bourne, J. and Briggs, M. (eds) *Subject Learning in the Primary Curriculum: Issues in English, science and mathematics*, London: Routledge, Chapter 14, pp. 158–183
A number of cross-age studies of children's ideas in science have been carried out over the last ten years or so. For example, the CLIS team (Children's Learning in Science Research Group) at Leeds University researched the ideas held by children between the ages of 5 and 16 years in areas like ecology, the structure of matter and the physical properties of air. A comprehensive overview is provided by some of the team in Chapter 14 of their book.

Farrow, S. (1999) *The Really Useful Science Book*, 2nd edition, London: Falmer Press
The basic ideas of science are introduced at a level suitable for primary teachers to help them to meet the requirements of the National Curriculum Order for Science. Section Two: *'Life processes and living things'* (pages 9–78) covers all the key ideas, from the characterisitics of living things (2.1) through to energy transfer in an ecosystem (2.6). It provides the necessary detail to those ideas explored briefly in this chapter.

Wenham, M. (1995) *Understanding Primary Science: Ideas, Concepts and Explanations*, London: Paul Chapman Publishing
This book could be a useful alternative to Steve Farrow's. In Chapters 2–5, he looks at life and living processes, humans as organisms, plants and variety, adaptation and interdependence.

5 What Do We Mean by Materials and their Properties?

Life processes and living things encompass the biological world, but we also live in a physical world in which both natural and synthetic materials play an important part. In this chapter, we shall look at the types and properties of materials to be found in our scientific and technological environment. We shall also consider the nature of these materials, the atoms and molecules which form the 100 or so elements from which everything is made and the various ways in which these atoms and molecules can combine and behave.

Task 5.1   Materials – what are they?

1   When you think of the word 'material' what immediately springs to mind? Try to construct two definitions of a 'material', one which a non-scientist might use to mean material, and one which a materials scientist might use.

2   When you are on a school experience placement, ask three or four primary children what the word 'material' means to them.

3   Compare your definitions and the children's responses. What do they tell you about the language of science and children's ideas?

4   What can you learn from this as a prospective primary teacher?

MATERIALS

There are several major ideas to explore here, each of which will be discussed in turn.

- What exactly are materials?
- What are the particles from which all materials are made?
- How do materials react?
- How do materials change?

What are materials?

The development of humans as problem solving, technological beings is tied in many ways to how humans have come to terms with the material world. The historical ages – the stone age, the bronze age, the iron age – all reflect the degree to which people learned about the properties and uses of those materials that gave the age its name. Materials like stone (as in flint and clay for *ceramics*) and *metals* (like iron, bronze and tin) were central to the everyday tasks of capturing, killing, cooking, storing and transporting food. *Composite* materials like bone and wood were readily available and were used in a variety of ways, as were *fibrous* materials like hides and hair. In modern times, we could just as easily recognize the steel age or the plastics age. These materials have not only been used and shaped by us; their properties and uses have shaped the technological evolution of mankind.

Classifying materials

The term *materials* has become a part of our everyday language to refer to the 'fabrics' or substances from which things in our physical environment are made. Thus we talk about wood or metal, plastics or ceramics, yarns or cloth. For the materials scientist, materials are classified into groups according to their composition:

> *metals:* such as copper, tin, aluminium, lead and platinum;
> *alloys:* such as steel (carbon and iron), bronze (copper and tin) and brass (copper and zinc);
> *ceramics and glass:* such as earthenware pots, bone china, bricks, tiles and glassware;
> *polymers:* natural fibrous materials such as hair, skin or rubber, and synthetic fibrous materials such as plastics;
> *composites:* combinations of materials such as chipboard, fibreglass or reinforced concrete.

An alternative way to classify materials reflects the ways in which they can be of use to us. Categories can reflect whether or not they float, are waterproof, conduct electricity, are attracted to a magnet or are flexible or elastic.

However, the term *material* also has a very specific scientific use. It refers to the form of *matter* from which substances are made. Usually this matter is in a *solid* form, but it can also be in the form of a *liquid* or even a *gas*. These are known as the *states of matter*.

Matter and mass

Matter is the material from which all things in our universe are made, living as well as non-living. It is any substance that occupies space and has mass. The word 'mass' actually comes from the Greek, *maza*, meaning lump. Think of a common lumpy object, like your bath sponge. Wherever the sponge is in the universe it still has the same amount of matter and occupies space. It might be squashed into a small space, as when you squeeze it, or spread out over a larger space, as when you stretch it, but the amount of matter it is made from − its mass − is still the same. Mass is a measure of the amount of matter in an object and we usually measure it in grams (g) or kilograms (kg).

The mass of an object is commonly determined using weighing machines, like kitchen or bathroom scales. These machines measure the pull of gravity on the object. This is the gravitational attraction between the object and the Earth. (We shall return to this in the next chapter.) When the mass is acted on by the force of gravity, it is pulled towards the planet's surface by that force and so it is described as having *weight*. Weight is the force due to gravity. On Earth, an object with a mass of 6 kg has a weight of 6 kg force. (Actually, the weight varies slightly over the Earth's surface because of variation in the Earth's shape and composition but the mass never changes.) The special unit we use to describe a kilogram of force is the newton (N), named after the scientist Sir Isaac Newton, who studied gravity in detail. 1 kgf = 10N, so the object with a mass of 6 kg will have a weight of 60N.

Adrift in space, far from the Earth, other planets and the Sun, there appears to be no gravity. Drifting objects in space would have zero weight, that is, they would be *weightless*. However, they still have the same amount of matter in them so their mass is still the same as on Earth.

On some other planet or moon, the mass of the object would be the same, but the weight could be different because the pull of gravity on the planet may be different from that of Earth. For example, on the Moon, gravity is one-sixth of that on Earth and so the 6 kg object would weigh one-sixth of what it did on Earth, 1 kg force or 10N.

Atoms and molecules

One of the most successful of scientific theories is based on a very simple idea which is actually very old. The Ancient Greek philosopher Democritus, who lived over 2,400 years ago, suggested that the materials are all made from *tiny particles* but the particles vary in different materials, hence they are different. That is what makes a material like gold different from iron. Alchemists over the ages have wasted a lot of time trying to change iron into gold.

Atoms and atomic numbers

Today, we call these tiny particles *atoms* (from the Greek meaning unsplittable) and atoms group together to form the *elements* from which all matter is formed. We now know that an atom is the smallest particle that makes up the element while still keeping the chemical properties of the element. Elements are substances which cannot be split into simpler substances. They can be thought of as the pure substance like oxygen, helium, lead or zinc.

Atoms, in turn, all have the same basic design. They consist of even smaller particles which include positively charged protons (p) and neutral neutrons (n) which clump together to form a tiny nucleus. Around the nucleus negatively charged electrons (e) move, rather like planets orbiting the Sun. In a balanced atom there are always the same number of protons and electrons, so the atom has no net electrical charge. Often, two or more atoms combine to form a molecule of the element. This is what happens with gases like oxygen. Two atoms of oxygen (O + O) combine to give a molecule of the gas oxygen (O_2).

The number of protons in the nucleus of an atom is called the *atomic number*. All atoms of the same element have the same number of protons and so the same atomic number. The atomic numbers of some common elements are:

hydrogen (H) = 1   carbon (C) = 6   oxygen (O) = 8
sodium (Na) = 11   calcium (Ca) = 20   iron (Fe) = 26

Iron, for instance, has 26 protons in its nucleus.

How many protons and electrons are present in an atom, and how the electrons behave under different conditions, allows scientists to sort them into groups and also to classify them as metals and non-metals. This classification system is called the *periodic table* and was begun by Mendeleyev.

Dalton's ideas

Altogether, there are about one hundred natural elements and a few artificial ones. Everything on our planet is made from these basic units. Some two thousand years after Democritus the famous chemist, John Dalton, developed his ideas about how the tiny particles combine to give the wide variety of substances in the world around us. In the early nineteenth century, Dalton began to explain the regular composition of different substances. Because atoms exist, they have mass (*atomic mass*), occupy space, and are affected by gravity, albeit on a very tiny scale. Dalton put forward a theory that the particles (atoms) of the basic materials (elements) have different *specific weights*, with hydrogen being the lightest. He began to use chemical symbols to stand for elements, an idea which we have refined and still use today (for instance, we use H to stand for hydrogen and O for oxygen). Dalton also suggested that combinations of these particles (atoms) give tightly bound chemical *compounds*. So when hydrogen and oxygen combine in the right amounts, two atoms of hydrogen (2H) with one atom of oxygen (O), we get the compound water, H_2O. Similarly, one atom of carbon (C) combines with two atoms of oxygen (2O), to give carbon dioxide (CO_2). For example, when you strike a match you start a reaction between various atoms in the match and the oxygen atoms in the air. They combine to form new materials which include ash, which you can see, and carbon dioxide gas, which you cannot see. In addition, some energy changes occur, with heat and light being released. This, of course, is the reason for striking the match in the first place.

It took Dalton's ideas to help us to understand how different elements and compounds react with one another.

| Task 5.2 Atoms, elements and compounds | The basic units of matter are elements. Every substance on earth is made from these basic units.
Iron is a basic element. It cannot be broken down into simpler units. |

Explain why wood is not an element.

Think of an analogy that would help you explain this to a primary child who classifies wood as a pure substance along with iron and gold?

Chemical changes to materials

Chemical reactions can be fast, like a firework exploding, or slow, like the growth of a child. The changes that result are the outward signs that some kind of interaction is taking place. The components involved in the reaction are joining together chemically in very specific proportions and in the process heat is usually absorbed or released.

There are many different kinds of chemical reactions. How atoms react with one another depends upon the electrons they have around them and how easy it is for an atom to lose or pick up electrons from other atoms. There are some common reactions with which you will be very familiar.

Burning

Probably one of the most familiar chemical reactions is *burning*. We burn bread for our breakfast and call it toast. We burn petrol in the car engine to make the car move. Slow burning is something which is going on inside our bodies all the time. What is common to all of these examples is the presence of oxygen as part of the change process. The molecules of oxygen exist in the air.

In our bodies, when we breathe in air, the oxygen molecules are absorbed into our blood stream. In our red blood cells, the haemoglobin molecules which contain a lot of iron act as a carrier for the oxygen and transport it around the body. In tissues like muscles, the oxygen molecules are exchanged for carbon dioxide molecules by the haemoglobin. The latter are carried back to the lungs and we then breathe them out. In the meantime, the oxygen that was left behind reacts (chemically combines) with food molecules and they 'burn' to release the energy needed for movement and the other life processes. In the process, some heat energy is released, which keeps us warm, and some of the carbon from the fats and sugars combine with the oxygen to form the carbon dioxide. This is really no different to when we burn toast or ignite fuel in a car engine, except that these reactions tend to happen more quickly than those in our bodies.

Another example of a chemical reaction involving burning is *rusting*. When we think of burning we tend to think of heat and dryness but rusting can take place when it is damp and cold. When a car door is scratched, atoms of iron are exposed to the air, resulting in oxygen molecules from the air slowly reacting with the iron. Iron oxide is produced (two atoms of iron, 2Fe, with three atoms of oxygen, 3O, to give one molecule of iron oxide, Fe_2O_3). We call this rust. This is why we try to keep air away from iron surfaces with paint, grease, or by galvanizing the body with a thin layer of zinc.

Photosynthesis

We have already considered how plants, in the presence of sunlight, take in carbon dioxide from the air and combine it with particles of water to make the complicated carbohydrates like sugars and cellulose. We have a chemical reaction between two compounds, water (H_2O molecules) and carbon dioxide (CO_2 molecules) to form a molecule of the carbohydrate.

Brewing

Many people make their own beer or wine at home. Even in the big breweries, the process is the same, bringing about a chemical change. The yeast cells used by brewers grow and multiply by reacting with the sugar. One of the chemicals they make during the reaction is alcohol. This process is called *fermentation*.

With chemical reactions it is often difficult to reverse the process and obtain the original substances. For this reason, many chemical reactions are described as *irreversible reactions*.

Task 5.3 Other chemical reactions	Some simple chemical reactions can be useful tests. Find out more about the following chemical reactions which are used as indicator tests:

- iodine as a test for starch;
- litmus as a test for acidity;
- cobalt chloride as a test for moisture.

How do disclosing tablets work as a test for plaque on teeth?

Find out about the chemical reactions which are taking place when you hard boil an egg.

Physical changes to materials

Not all particles join together and combine as easily as those described above. Sometimes, no chemical reaction occurs at all; the changes are purely physical. They can be quite sudden, like what happens to a car when the driver collides with a wall. They can be slow, as with the geological erosion of the landscape by a river. Physical changes are often easier to spot than chemical ones. Physical reactions change the shape or form of the original substance, although the matter from which it is made remains unaltered. As a consequence the properties of the material, for instance its strength, can sometimes be changed.

Changing shape and properties

A lump of clay is soft, moist and malleable. It can be rolled into a ball. It can be elongated into a sausage shape. It can even be moulded into a bowl shape. It is still a lump of clay. The matter from which it is made has not been altered. Even if the clay bowl is left to dry, it is still made from the same particles. It is possible to break the dry bowl into small fragments, replace the missing water and reconstitute the clay. Up to this point the process is reversible. However, if the clay bowl is put into a kiln and heated, its properties will be changed. It is still a bowl but now it is hard, fragile and (if it has been glazed) also waterproof. The changes are now irreversible.

Similarly, try to stand an A4 size sheet of paper on its long edge and balance a mass of 100g on the top edge. Impossible! But change the shape of the paper. Make it into a tube or zig-zag shape. Now it can carry the load.

Mixtures

Sometimes we can take substances and combine them so that the changes are purely physical, rather than chemical. Many common materials around us are simply *mixtures* of different elements or compounds. The different elements or compounds still exist but they are now sharing the same space. The components of a mixture can be present in differing proportions. So orange juice can be very concentrated (a lot of juice and a little water) or very dilute (a lot of water and a little juice).

Air is a mixture of substances. It comprises several different gases, notably nitrogen, oxygen, carbon dioxide. There are also tiny particles of solids, like dust and even lead near busy roads. Rocks are mixtures of lots of different minerals. Petroleum is a mixture of several different hydrocarbons. The different components of mixtures can always be separated from one another by physical means, although this may not be as easy as it sounds.

The component particles of a mixture can be quite tiny, as with molecules of gases, or quite large, as with stones in a soil sample. They can be soluble in water, as is sugar, or insoluble, as in sand. The properties of the different components give us a way of sorting and separating them.

Task 5.4 Sorting and separating mixtures

Listed below are some common methods used to sort and separate mixtures. For each, explain how the process works and then give an example of where we might use it in everyday life.

- filtering
- decanting
- centrifuging
- evaporating
- distilling

What is chromatography? Find out how the procedure works and suggest how it might be useful to the police for solving crimes.

Often two or more solids are mixed together. Sometimes this happens naturally, as with pebbles and sand. These can usually be separated by sieving. A gardener would use a riddle to separate pebbles and other lumps from the soil. Sometimes, the two solids can be separated by adding water and dissolving one of the solids, as with a mixture of sand and sugar. If the sand is removed, and the sugar solution is left to evaporate, crystals of the sugar should re-appear. Often, when two solids are mixed together, it is as a step in a process which involves a chemical reaction as well. For example, a builder would mix sand and cement before adding water. A chemical reaction then occurs. Similarly a cook would mix the dry ingredients to make a cake before adding egg and milk and then baking the cake.

Solids and liquids are often mixed together to produce *solutions*, *suspensions* or *gels*. With a solution, when the two substances are mixed together the solid seems to disappear. The *solute* (the solid) has dissolved in the *solvent* (the liquid) but it is still there. Salt mixed with water gives a solution which looks much like the original water. When tasted, it is obvious that the salt is still there. The process can be reversed by leaving the solution in a warm place for the water to evaporate. The salt crystals will be reconstituted. In a suspension, the solid particles are still there, suspended in the liquid. Straining or sieving will remove the solids. This is easy to see when you use a coffee filter. With a gel, the solid particles trap the liquid particles so that the liquid can no longer flow. This is what happens with jelly, when we added the crystals or cubes to hot water. The liquid is spread throughout the solid and locked in place. (Gels are a kind of *colloid*, more often seen as emulsions when two liquids are mixed, and as foams (a liquid and a gas).)

When two liquids are mixed they do not usually form layers. This happens when orange juice and water are mixed and is described as *miscible*, which simply means mixable. Sometimes, however, the liquids are *immiscible*, they will not mix. This happens when oil and water are added together. Two distinct layers are formed. If we break the oil down into very tiny particles it becomes partly miscible as an *emulsion*. This is, of course what happens when a cook makes mayonnaise. Mayonnaise is an emulsion and so is handcream.

It is also possible to have mixtures of liquids and gases. The result is either *fizz* or *foam*. For example, mix carbon dioxide gas into a solution of water, lemon and sugar and you have fizzy lemonade. To begin with the gas is in solution. Sometimes a mass of small bubbles of gas form on the surface of a liquid producing a froth or foam, as with beer. Occasionally, we deliberately introduce a gas (air) into the liquid and then heat it to trap the shape of trapped air. This is how we produce meringue.

With physical reactions it is often possible to reverse the process and return to the original substances. Most physical reactions are *reversible reactions*. It is also important to realize that often changes can involve both physical and chemical reactions simultaneously.

PARTICLE THEORY AND THE CONSERVATION OF MASS

That all substances are made from tiny particles called atoms has already been explained. One thing which all these tiny particles seem to have in common is that they are very active. To understand how this happens, we have to think about the *kinetic theory of particles*. Kinetic means 'on the move'.

The kinetic theory of matter

The kinetic theory of matter explains how all substances are made from tiny particles and these particles are constantly on the move. They are *vibrating*. Sometimes they do not move or vibrate very much. This is when something is in a solid state. The particles tend to vibrate about fixed positions, which is just as well, otherwise tables, chairs, books, clothes would all just disappear in front of us!

On the other hand, this is just what many liquids do. Water particles vibrate more freely and slowly drift away from one another and mix with other particles in the air. Higher temperatures gives them more kinetic energy (movement), so they vibrate more and move faster. They escape into the air as a vapour, that is, they evaporate. A wet towel on a hot radiator will lose its water as vapour much faster than the same towel left on a cold radiator. The water has changed from its liquid form into its gaseous form.

In gases, like the mixture of gases we call air, the particles are more active than in solids and liquids. They move very quickly and, as connecting bonds break, they spread out into the surrounding space. If an ice cube is heated, this is what happens. The particles in the solid water (ice) are vibrating slowly. The heat gives them energy to move more quickly and so bonds holding the particles together begin to loosen. The particles vibrate more vigorously and the solid water (ice) changes to a liquid. If we continue to heat the liquid, the rate of vibration increases and the loose bonds break apart. The liquid changes to a gas (vapour) and the gas particles shoot off into the surrounding air. This change from liquid to gas is *evaporation* and can occur at any temperature. Occasionally, there is a very rapid change from a liquid to a gas at a fixed temperature (depending on the pressure) and we call this *boiling*. The temperature at which this happens is the *boiling point*. For water, the boiling point (sea level) is about 100°C, depending on the air pressure.

So, the kinetic theory of particles gives us four very simple ideas.

1   All matter is made from tiny particles, so small we cannot see them except with special equipment, and then only in the case of the largest particles.
2   These particles are constantly moving, some slowly and some quickly.
3   The particles will move faster if the temperature is higher.
4   More massive particles are more difficult to move and therefore move more slowly than less massive particles at the same temperature.

Solids, liquids and gases

Each pure substance has its unique *freezing* and *boiling* point which gives us the three states of matter: solids, liquids and gases.

In solid form, the particles vibrate around fixed positions. The bonds holding them together are strong. The substance keeps a fixed shape and a fixed volume. The particles are:

- closely packed together;
- arranged in a neat, regular pattern;
- vibrating on the spot;
- held strongly in place by bonds to neighbouring particles.

As a result, solids have a fixed shape. They can be dense which means they can be very heavy for their size and may not be easily compressed. They can also be very strong.

In liquid form, the particles have some freedom of movement and so they have a fixed volume but a variable shape. There are still loose bonds holding them together but they can move much more easily around each other. The substance can move to take up the shape of the container. The particles are:

- closely packed together;
- arranged in a loose, irregular pattern;
- vibrating more freely and slide over each other;
- held weakly in place by bonds to neighbouring particles.

As a result of this, liquids have a variable shape, depending upon the container they are in. They are relatively dense which means they can be heavy for their size and not easily compressed. They are not very strong.

In gaseous form, particles can move independently within the space available. They have both a variable shape and volume. The particles are:

- not packed together at all so they spread out;
- not arranged at all, so they can move randomly;
- vibrating freely of their own accord;
- not bonded to neighbouring particles at all.

As a result, gases have no fixed shape. They are light and easily compressed and are very weak. They mix or spread very quickly with other substances.

Task 5.5 Solids, liquids and gases	Use your understanding of solids, liquids and gases to explain why:

- we can smell a curry cooking even before we enter a room;
- when we drop a glass of water, there always seems to be more liquid than when it was in the glass;
- a bucketful of snow does not produce a bucketful of water when it melts.

Most substances can exist in all three states. The form they take depends upon the temperature. For example, at less than 0°C, water is a solid (ice). Between 0°C and 100°C it is a liquid (which we tend to call water because that is its common state for normal temperature ranges). Above 100°C, it is a gas (vapour). There are different ways to change a substance from one state to another but the most common is by heating or cooling it. See Figure 5.1.

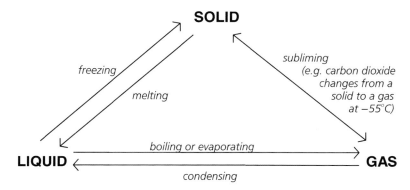

Figure 5.1 The different ways that a substance can change state

The conservation of mass

Even though matter may be changed by mixing, by chemical reactions or by changing its state, the matter still exists. It still has mass and occupies space. No new matter has been created nor has any been lost or destroyed. The total mass has been conserved.

WHAT DO PRIMARY CHILDREN ALREADY KNOW?

Primary age children have already had quite a lot of experience of the material world before they start school. Through their toys, their clothes and their home environment they will have encountered a variety of materials and be familiar with some of their properties. However, these ideas will be relatively random and disorganized.

To begin with, children use everyday labels for things. To them, materials will be the fabrics used to make curtains and clothes. The concept of 'a material' will be new to them. They will also have a non-scientific concept of 'properties' related to how things are used. So a fork made from metal or plastic will be described according to its purpose (for eating) rather than its scientific properties (metal, flexible, light weight and so on). They may have the idea that candles are made from plastics, and gas is air. These are quite rational ideas to them. Different sub-groups within a category of material (such as sub-dividing metals into iron, copper, zinc, and so on) may be quite a sophisticated level of classification for some children.

Even towards the end of KS2, some primary children may still find the concept of reversibility difficult. They tend to see changes as a chain of events in one direction. They may have difficulty with concepts requiring thinking in two directions, like changes of state from solids to liquids to gases and back to liquids and solids.

Older KS2 pupils are more confident with the concept of 'liquid' than with 'solid'. They confuse melting and dissolving, often using the former for the latter. When water boils, they argue that the boiling process is causing the air to leave the water. They do not see the water changing state to the gaseous form. For them, 'gas' is not a substance at all, since they do not see a gas as having mass or weight.

WHAT DO THE CHILDREN NEED TO KNOW?

The experiences you organize for your class to introduce them to the basic ideas associated with materials and their properties need to be related to the National Curriculum requirements for Sc3, summarized in Table 5.1. Circular 4/98 identifies how you might use your knowledge and understanding of materials and their structure to support the teaching of the KS1 and KS2 Programmes of Study. How do we begin to teach children about materials and their properties?

STARTING POINTS FOR THE CLASSROOM

Underpinning the National Curriculum Order for Science and the Circular 4/98 guidance, there are a small number of fundamental concepts which you will want your children in the primary school to acquire. These can become your targets (or objectives) for lesson planning. They are:

- Materials in our environment show great variety and can be grouped in different ways according to their properties.
- Different materials have different properties, which enable them to be used for different purposes.
- Some materials occur naturally and some have been made by people.
- In general, a substance can be classified as a solid, a liquid or a gas.
- There are differences in the ways substances behave when they are in different states or forms.
- Substances can be mixed together to form mixtures.
- Mixtures can be separated into pure substances.
- Pure substances may react together to form new substances with different properties to those of the constituent substances.
- Some substances will mix together well; some will dissolve; some will absorb liquids and others will resist them.
- Some substances change when they are heated.
- Sometimes these changes can be reversed, and sometimes they cannot.

Table 5.1 Overview of Sc3 of the National Curriculum Order for Science for
Key Stages 1 and 2

◆ *Materials and their Properties* ◆

Grouping and Classifying Materials

KS1: 1a – *use senses to explore and recognize similarities and differences;*
KS1: 1b – *sort objects into groups on the basis of simple material properties;*
KS1: 1c – *recognize and name common types of materials and recognize that some are found naturally;*
KS1: 1d – *find out about the uses of a variety of materials and how they are chosen for specific uses on the basis of their simple properties;*
KS2: 1a – *compare everyday materials on the basis of their properties and relate these properties to their everyday use;*
KS2: 1b – *know that some materials are better thermal insulators than others;*
KS2: 1c – *know that some materials are better electrical conductors than others;*
KS2: 1d – *describe and group rocks and soils on the basis of their characteristics;*
KS2: 1e – *recognize the differences between solids, liquids and gases.*

Changing Materials ──────────

KS1: 2a – *find out how the shapes of objects made from some materials can be changed;*
KS1: 2b – *explore and describe some ways some everyday materials change when heated or cooled;*
KS2: 2a – *describe the changes that occur when materials are mixed;*
KS2: 2b – *describe the changes that occur when materials are heated or cooled;*
KS2: 2c – *that temperature is a measure of how hot or cold things are;*
KS2: 2d – *that some changes are reversible, including dissolving, melting, boiling, condensing, freezing and evaporating, dissolving, melting and boiling;*
KS2: 2e – *know about the water cycle and the role of evaporation and condensation;*
KS2: 2f – *know that non-reversible changes result in the formation of new materials;*
KS2: 2g – *burning materials results in irreversible changes.*

Separating Mixtures of Materials

KS2: 3a – *how to separate solid particles of different sizes by sieving;*
KS2: 3b – *know that some solids dissolve in water to give solutions and some do not;*
KS2: 3c – *how to separate insoluble solids from liquids by filtering them;*
KS2: 3d – *how to recover dissolved solids by evaporating the liquid from the solution;*
KS2: 3e – *use knowledge of solids, liquids and gases to decide how mixtures might be separated.*

- The processes of melting, freezing, evaporating and condensing do not change what a substance is made from.
- All changes in materials are caused by interaction with other materials or by energy changes.

As with living things, the experiences offered to children to introduce them to materials and their properties should be made explicitly relevant to them by basing them on those materials familiar to them within their immediate environment. Their everyday uses, their physical properties and their composition can be exemplified by introducing work on such materials.

Many materials can be distinguished from others simply by their appearance or behaviour. Often, all that is needed is the direct application of the senses. For instance:

Sight: shape, colour transparency, whether the material is obviously a mixture or appears uniform.
Touch: weight of the material, texture, state (solid, liquid or gas), temperature.
Smell: odourless, sharp, sweet, sickly, smelling of something in particular.
Hearing: the sound the material makes when it is dropped or struck (thud, crack, click, swish, etc.).
Taste: not generally used, since many household materials are unpleasant or harmful.

Note   Caution is needed when testing materials using the senses. Adequate safety precautions must be taken. Dangerous fumes can be produced (for example, if plastics are heated or certain kitchen materials mixed) and some common materials are poisonous, caustic or otherwise hazardous. This is a good opportunity to introduce health and safety issues to the children.

Some properties may require the construction of a fair test, involving some measurement and recording and interpretation of results. For example, children can carry out fair tests to investigate the effect of load, pressure or impact, the effect of warming or cooling the material or the effect of water on the material. This is a good way to introduce the children to data handling and the use of information technology in science (see Chapter 7 for more on this).

Some tests will produce temporary changes in the materials, as when squashing a sponge, melting chocolate or dissolving salt in water. On releasing the sponge, cooling the chocolate and evaporating the water, the materials return to their original state (although not necessarily their original shape). Other tests may produce more or less permanent changes, as when twisting a piece of wire, baking dough, or mixing vinegar and baking powder. Children should experience a range of everyday permanent and temporary changes in materials. Often such changes take place unnoticed in household tasks like baking and cooking. Sometimes the changes will be noticed, as with melting snow. The infant who brings a snowball in from play time to save until later notices that it has been replaced by a soggy pocket and a puddle.

Some other changes that can lead to productive exploration and investigation include:

- *Life cycles:* animals (frogs, butterflies and moths, spiders, pets or chicks), plants (examples of flowering plant life cycles).
- *Plants:* growth rates and conditions for growth, changes in seeds (size, shape, germination rate), seasonal changes and their effects on life.
- *Ourselves:* changes as we grow older (birth through to old age), changes during exercise (pulse rate, heart beat, breathing rate), changes to fit our environment (clothes, food, home).
- *The environment:* seasonal change, weather and climate, tree diaries through the year, plants and animals seen at different times of the year, rocks and soils.
- *Materials:* weathering effects (wind, rain, ice), rusting (compare iron with other materials), dyes and dying (using natural and cold-water dyes), fading (card shapes on sugar paper).
- *Water:* changes in the state of water, changing the shape of water (using bottles of different shapes to freeze fixed volumes of water), the water cycle and evaporation and condensation, solutions and solubility (using common kitchen powders and crystals), cleaning water (filtration and the water works).

The ways in which changes affect the materials can be explored, leading to work on solids, liquids and gases and making and separating mixtures. Various sorting and classifying activities can be used to introduce the concepts of mixtures and pure substances. Children can be given various mixtures of solids and asked to invent a way to separate the materials. For example, peas and marbles (by hand), peas and sand (by sieving), sand and iron filings (using a magnet), sand and water (by filtering through cloth), sugar from sand (by dissolving the sugar and sieving) and sugar from a sugar solution (by evaporation). In order to select the appropriate way to separate the materials, the children need to know and understand something about the properties of the materials.

The enormous range of materials available, and their wide variety of properties and uses, can make the study of materials a large and sometimes confusing topic. You will need to begin your planning with a very clear purpose and use it to control the direction the work takes. Infant exploration of materials could begin with a simple exploration of properties using the senses, as listed above. The touch table and the feely box or bag can be used to raise awareness of texture, increase tactile discrimination and develop powers of description. Common items made from different materials and found in the classroom can be selected, sorted and classified into groups. The origin of many materials is a mystery to KS1 pupils. The grounds can be laid for classifying materials as either natural or manufactured by making some materials like paper and clay pots. A visit to manufacturers (a bakery, pottery, brickworks, or similar places) can help to develop the realization that cups and saucers, knives and forks and the bread we eat are all produced from other materials.

Opportunities for the scientific investigation of materials can arise from something as simple as a *Keep Our School Tidy* campaign. A study of the litter found in and around the school lends itself to investigating properties of the various materials used to make drink cans, crisp packets and so on. KS1 pupils can also begin to investigate some of the properties of solutions and mixtures: dissolving sugar in water or jelly crystals. One disappears and looks just like water but now tastes different. The other disappears but colours the water and sets solid. Would it make a difference if the water used was cold instead of hot or if we used more or less water?

While such opportunities will normally be arranged by you as the teacher, there are also accidents which can be used to good effect – as with the child who left the snowball in his coat pocket for later. Where did the snow go? After determining the cause of the inevitable change, an investigation into whether it would have made any difference if the snowball had been bigger might follow. Does a bucketful of snow make a bucketful of water?

At KS2, pupils should continue to observe and investigate the properties of materials, making finer discriminations between them. Materials and their properties is an important area for activities in design and technology, and many of the science investigations can be used as precursors to designing and making activities during D&T lessons.

SUGGESTIONS FOR FURTHER READING

If you would like to explore further some of the issues touched upon in this chapter, the following books should be of interest to you.

Farrow, S. (1999) *The Really Useful Science Book*, 2nd edition, London: Falmer Press
  The basic ideas to do with materials and their properties are introduced at a level suitable for primary teachers to help them to meet the requirements of the National Curriculum Order for Science. Section Three (pp. 79–123) covers this area, supplementing the ideas introduced briefly in this chapter.

Wenham, M. (1995) *Understanding Primary Science: Ideas, Concepts and Explanations*, London: Paul Chapman Publishing
  In Chapters 6 to 11, Wenham covers States of Matter and Physical Change, Mechanical Properties of Materials and Objects, Explaining Physical Changes, Chemical Changes, Obtaining and Making Materials, and Earth Science.

6   What Do We Mean by Physical Processes?

We live in a biophysical world. In other words, the world comprises an interaction between physical events and biological entities. To understand our world fully it is not sufficient to look only at living things. It is also necessary to understand the physical processes which are at work.

Physical processes involve forces and energy. This chapter will examine and attempt to explain these two concepts. Each has a number of different facets, so each of these will be explored separately and the significant characteristics of each will be explored. We will begin by looking at forces.

FORCES AND MOTION

This list contains a number of aspects of forces to be considered but what exactly are they and what can they do?

Forces – what are they and what can they do?

Put very simply, forces are pushes, pulls and twists. Not a second of our lives goes by without us being affected by the action of forces in some way. From when we get out of bed in the morning to going to bed at night, we are subject to forces. Even while we are in bed, sleeping, forces hold us in place and hold the sheets and covers on top of us.

We use forces to make things happen: pushing our feet into our slippers; pulling on a dressing gown; turning on a tap. We also use forces to prevent things from happening: gravity holds a paperweight in place which stops papers blowing away; the grip of clothes pegs holds things safely on the line; the grip of elastic stops our underwear from falling down. Even when we are relaxing on a beach, forces are at work. Gravity pulls us down on to the sand, friction holds our bathing costume in place, upthrust makes the ice cubes float in the cool drink and pushes, pulls and twists are all at work when we remove the top from the tube of sun-screen, squeeze it on our skin and rub it in.

We teach children about forces because they are everywhere. Often they are unnoticed and taken for granted. The concept of *force* is essential to our understanding of the physical and technological world. Machines would not exist (think of the forces at work in a bicycle) and even if they did, people would not be able to operate them (think of the forces at work when riding a bicycle).

| **Task 6.1 Pushes, pulls and twists in life** | Work your way through a typical day, from waking up in the morning to going to bed at night. List the forces |

which affect you in one way or another. Is there any part of your day where you are not subject to forces? Classify the forces you have listed into pushes, pulls or twists.

Think of these common children's toys. What forces are at work when the children play with them?
- a doll's pram
- a two-wheel scooter
- building blocks for construction activities
- a ball
- a skipping rope

As a primary teacher, how could you use toys as a starting point for some work on forces with a KS1 or KS2 class?

Measuring forces

What name do you associate with forces (or more specifically, one particular force, gravity)? Hopefully, you thought of Sir Isaac Newton. He was a famous natural philosopher and mathematician who lived in the seventeenth and eighteenth centuries (1642–1727). Among other things, Newton studied the force of gravity, something we shall return to later. Because of this work, his name is used as the unit of force: force is measured in *newtons*. A force of one newton (1N) is quite a small force. It is the pull needed to lift a small container of cake decorations with a mass of about 100g. It might take only about one thousandth of a newton (0.001N) to lift a small feather. On the other hand, a large rocket could generate a thrust (push) of over ten million newtons (10,000,000N).

Measuring the forces we experience around us is easy: we use *force meters*. Force meters come in all shapes and sizes, the most familiar being bathroom and kitchen scales. In the classroom, you will also have spring balances. Those bought as force meters will be marked in newtons. Older ones might use a gf or kgf scale. For the purposes of

---

Task 6.2 Feeling forces

Weight is a measure of the force of gravity on an object. Mass is the amount of matter in the object. We use Earth's gravity as our standard, so on the Earth's surface a 100g mass experiences a force of about 100gf or 1N. We measure mass in grams (g) and kilograms (kg). We measure its weight in grams force (gf) or kilograms force (kgf) or newtons (N). One newton (1N) is about 100gf. So,

0.01N is like lifting a marble of mass 1g
0.1N is like lifting a ball-point pen of mass 10g
1N is like lifting a small bar of chocolate of mass 100g
10N is lifting a bag of sugar of mass 1kg

Try lifting each of these items and see what the forces feel like. How might you use this idea with children? Find objects which have a mass of 50g, 500g and 2kg. Feel the forces involved in lifting them and convert their masses to a weight in newtons.

---

science, they should be converted to newtons by sticking a strip of masking tape or paper over the old scale and marking on a new one. For instance, you can change the 100g and 200g points on the existing scale to 1N, 2N, and so on or you can re-calibrate it by hanging 100g masses on it and marking where the pointer comes to rest.

There are *push*, *pull* and *twist* meters. Pull meters usually have a spring inside which is stretched or extended by external forces like a spring balance. The stronger the spring, the more force is needed to extend it. Push meters usually have a spring inside which is squashed or compressed by an external force. The stronger the spring, the harder it is to compress it, that is, more force is needed. Some exercise equipment (like hand grips) work on this basis. Car mechanics use twist or torque meters for checking the amount of twisting or turning force needed to tighten nuts and bolts such as those on a car wheel.

The laws of motion

So what exactly do forces do to things? If all the forces on an object are balanced, nothing happens and it stays where it is. If not, the object will *move*. If a skateboard is standing in the middle of the floor, a push will move it to one side if there is nothing to balance that push. Once you start pushing the skateboard, if you keep pushing, it will move faster and faster, that is, it will *accelerate*. However, if you stop pushing on the skateboard, it slows and stops (Figure 6.1). Why? Although your push was large enough to make the skateboard move, as soon as you stop, the effects of other forces make themselves more apparent. In particular, there will be the force of *friction* between the wheels and the axle and between the wheels and the surface on which they are rolling, so the skateboard loses speed, that is, it *decelerates*.

Isaac Newton summarized the ways objects, like the skateboard, behave in his *Laws of Motion*.

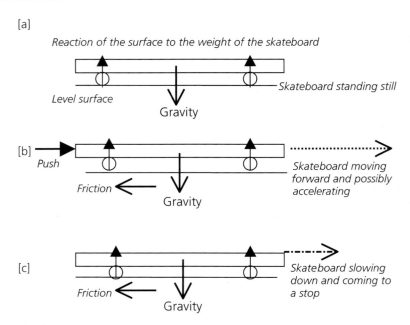

Figure 6.1   Forces acting on the skateboard

Law 1a: *Even when a massive object is free to move, it can be difficult to start it moving*
Have you seen the party trick where a smooth table cloth is pulled from underneath the cups, saucers and plates, and nothing is damaged? The crockery has enough mass to resist motion when the cloth is tugged from underneath. An alternative version of this is to place a coin (like a 50p piece) on a small square of card (about 10 cm by 10 cm) which is itself lying on a cup. Quickly pull the card sideways and the coin falls into the cup. The reluctance of an object to begin moving is called its *inertia*. Big coins have more inertia than small ones, so the trick works better with a 50p than a 1p coin.

Law 1b: *Once the object is moving it can be difficult to stop it or make it change its direction of motion*
Have you ever been on roller skates or ice skates? Once you are moving, it is difficult to avoid someone who skates in front of you – stopping or even changing direction can be quite a problem. Think of a large vehicle like a lorry parked on a level road. Even if the handbrake is released, it would be very difficult for someone to push it and make it move (Law 1a). However, once it is moving, it would be just as difficult to stop or deflect it. The more inertia it has, the harder it is.

Law 2a: *If you push an object, it accelerates (providing there is no other force to balance the push); the bigger the push, the greater the acceleration*
Think of the roller skates again. If someone gives you a push you start moving. If they keep pushing, you often move faster. The more they push, the faster you go. Friction

tends to mask some of these effects, because it opposes the motion. Thus, on a lawn or a carpet the acceleration would be less than on a smooth floor.

Law 2b: *When you push less massive objects steadily, they will accelerate more than massive objects (provided there is no other force to balance the push)*
If you push a small child on a bicycle, he will accelerate more than a large child on the same bicycle with the same push.

Law 3: *Every action has an equal and opposite reaction. Push an object and it pushes back*
Imagine two children on roller skates and facing one another. Jill pushes Jack. Jack, as you would expect, rolls backwards. But Jill rolls backwards, too, just as though Jack had pushed her. The action (Jill's push on Jack) produced an equal and opposite reaction. In the same way, a gun recoils (reaction) when it is fired (action). If Jill crashes into a wall on her roller skates, it is no different to the wall crashing into her: the effect is the same. If the wall did not push back it would give way and behave as if it was not there. Perhaps backing the car into a lamp-post is a better example – this is where we wish the post had not pushed back, because of the physical changes which result on the car bumper. Everything pushes back to some degree.

At the heart of Newton's Laws of Motion is the idea of balanced and unbalanced forces. When an object like an ice skater or a lorry is stationary or is moving at a steady speed, all the forces acting on the object are in balance. Consequently, if nothing changes, the skater or lorry will continue to be stationary or to move at a steady speed forever. However, if the forces are out of balance, changes in motion can occur.

Gravity – a weighty business

Isaac Newton realized that gravity was just like other forces as far as its effects were concerned. Most people will have heard the story of Newton and the apple,

> *Sir Isaac Newton tells us why*
> *An apple falls down from the sky ...*

The story is probably apocryphal, but he would certainly have known that once the apple left the branch, it would accelerate until it hit the ground. When on the ground, the apple is still subject to Earth's gravity. Only the solidity of the earth's crust prevents it from continuing on its journey to the centre of the planet. If a 600g apple is placed on a set of kitchen scales, gravity pulls it towards the centre of the earth, and hence makes the pointer on the scales move to read about 6N (or 600gf), the force of gravity on the apple.

The Moon is smaller than the Earth and so its gravitational pull is less, only about one-sixth of that of Earth. So although the mass of the apple is still the same, 600g, the force of gravity on it (its weight) would be only one-sixth of what it is on the Earth, that is 1.0N (or 100gf).

Friction, drag and resistance

Sometimes, we only notice a force when it is too large or too small. *Friction* is a force like this. If we try to push a heavy wardrobe away from the wall, we wish there was less friction. On the other hand, if we are running for a bus when there is ice on the ground, we wish there was more friction. When friction is an asset, helping us to do something, we tend to take it for granted, as when shoe soles grip the floor or nails and screws stay in place in furniture. As with most forces, friction can be both a boon and a bane. Whatever the case, *friction is a force which opposes* (or resists) *motion* (or movement).

Everyday experience tells us that friction between solid surfaces depends upon the materials involved. Rough surfaces, like sandpaper, can produce more friction than smooth, glassy ones like ice. As such, it usually acts between surfaces – the soles of your shoes and the floor covering, the tyres of a bicycle and the road surface, your hand and the glass you are holding. It is the result of the way in which the two surfaces catch on each other – how easy or difficult it is for one surface to move over or slide across the other. The harder it is, the more friction there is; the easier it is, the less friction. We can make friction greater by making the surface rougher (for example, change smooth shoe soles for rough, textured ones, or walk on a carpet rather than on smooth tiles). Alternatively, we can make it less by making the surface smoother (for example, by rubbing soap onto your finger to remove a ring which will not come off, or oil the cogs and gears in a car engine to reduce the wear). A dry hand can pick up a dry glass with no problems. With hand cream on your hands the glass slips through your fingers because you have reduced the grip. Sometimes, we roughen things deliberately to increase the grip. Spikes on running shoes are an extreme example of this.

Task 6.3 Fact and friction	The three things that matter when thinking about friction are:

The three things that matter when thinking about friction are:
- the texture (roughness) of the surface;
- the weight of the object on the surface; and,
- the area in contact with the surface.

How would you investigate the claims that:
- Maker X's training shoes have more grip than Maker Y's?
- The new floor covering gives more grip than the older one?
- Rubbing butter on a ring will remove it more easily than soap?

So far, we have only considered friction between solid surfaces. Does friction occur in liquids and gases? Water runs through our hands easily so it seems that there is very little friction, but if you run through water you can feel the *drag*. Increase the size of an object in contact with the water (as in the case of a large person in the swimming baths) and the drag increases. This type of friction depends on the liquid. Change the water for a thicker, more *viscous* liquid (like treacle) and the friction is greater. Try it with three tall bottles, one full of water, one of treacle and one of cooking oil. Drop identical plastic beads in each. What do you think will happen? Time how long they take to reach the bottom of the bottles.

Imagine holding a group of objects on a flat, wooden board, one large, one small, one very heavy and one quite light. If we could remove the effects of all forces other than gravity, what would happen when we tip the board? All the objects would fall from the board at the same time and be pulled towards the Earth by gravity. Each atom and molecule would accelerate at the same rate, regardless of mass or weight. Therefore, all four objects would reach the ground at the same time. This does not happen in real life because other forces are involved. Air resistance, in particular, slows down falling objects. Objects with large surfaces will be slowed down more than those with small surfaces. Try this with two identical sheets of paper. Crumple one into a ball. Drop them both from the same height and observe which hits the ground first.

Air is less viscous than liquids but it still opposes motion and resists movement through it. The resistance of air is generally so small that we seldom notice it. Cycling, however, can make it more noticeable. Waving sheets of cardboard makes it noticeable, too. The constant friction of the air on the hull of an aeroplane like Concord raises the outer hull temperature so that it would be hot to the touch. On the other hand, sky divers, parachutists and hang-gliders use air friction to control their descent. When a sky diver has arms and legs outstretched, he or she falls more slowly. Curling up into a ball makes the descent quicker. Nature uses the same principle to disperse seeds. Some seeds have wings for gliding (maple or sycamore, for example) or canopies for floating in air (like dandelion seeds).

In economic terms, unwanted friction can be a costly business and industry spends a lot of money trying to reduce it. Axles, for instance, contain steel ball bearings which roll rather than rub as the wheels turn. Lubricants, like oils, are used to separate parts so they do not rub together. Car, boat and aeroplane bodies are streamlined to reduce resistance in air and water, just as are birds and fish.

On the other hand, there are times when we want more friction, not less. Birds like swans and ducks can be seen braking to increase friction – that is, they push their large webbed feet out in front of them, increasing resistance so they slow down. Vehicles like cars going for land speed records or space shuttles coming in to land have parachutes to do much the same thing. Carpet tape fixes a rug in place, ridges on bottle tops and jars increase grip, shoes have textured soles, and tyres have tread on them. These all depend on naturally high friction surfaces or on forces which press the surfaces close enough together to increase the friction. The weight of the car is great enough to press the tyre tread to the road surface but nevertheless, all that friction can be lost in heavy rain so that the car 'aquaplanes' or slides on the water.

Speeding along

We can capture some of the things we know about forces and motion in some simple formulae. These are:

$$\text{Distance (D)} = \text{Speed (S)} \times \text{Time (T)}$$

$$\text{Speed (S)} = \frac{\text{Distance (D)}}{\text{Time (T)}}$$

$$\text{Time (T)} = \frac{\text{Distance (D)}}{\text{Speed (S)}}$$

- So, a car travelling 10 miles at 30 miles per hour (mph) will take:
  D = 10 miles; Speed = 30 mph; Time = ?
  10 mls = 30 mph × T hrs
  T = 10/30 hour = 1/3 hour = 20 minutes

- A cyclist travelling 4 km at 10 km per hr will take:
  D = 4 kilometres; Speed = 10 kmph; Time = ?
  4 km = 10 km per hr × T hrs
  T = 4/10 hrs = 4/10 of 60 mins = 24 minutes

- A train travelling 100 miles in 50 minutes would be travelling at:
  D = 100 miles; Speed = ?; Time = 50 minutes (or 50/60 hours)
  100 mls = S × 50/60 hrs
  S = (100 × 60)/50 mph = 6000/50 mph = 120 mph

- An aeroplane travelling at 500 km per hr for 2.7 hours will travel:
  Distance = ?; Speed = 500 km per hr; Time = 2.7 hours
  D = 500 × 2.7 km = 1350 km

However, remember that this is just arithmetic: the science is in the words.

Task 6.4   DST   Try these for yourself.
  1   How far will a bus travel at a speed of 40 mph for 2.5 hours?
2   At what speed must someone run to cover 7 km in 1hr 45 min?
3   How long will it take a train to travel a distance of 180 miles at 75 mph?

Invent some questions of your own to practise using the relationship between distance, speed and time.

[You should have the following answers: (1) 100 miles; (2) 4 km per hr; (3) 2 hrs 24 mins.]

In everyday language we tend to use the term *velocity* in much the same way as we use *speed*. In science, these two words have different meanings so must be used with care. Speed describes only how fast something is moving (for example, 20 metres per second or 60 miles per hour). But velocity is more than that. It is both how fast something is moving and the direction it takes (20 m per sec NW or 60 mph S). With young children, the word you would tend to use would be *speed*.

Things do not spend all their time moving along at a steady speed. They have to speed up (*accelerate*) or slow down (*decelerate*). Imagine driving a car. To make the car move you have to press the accelerator. In other words, the engine provides a continuous push to make the car move from stationary to the target speed. The car has to overcome the resistance of the road surface and the air resistance (friction), to build up to some steady speed or to accelerate. Some cars do this better than other. A small engined car will generally accelerate more slowly than a powerful sports car, if both cars have the same mass. We sometimes see advertisements which say things like, *0 to 60 miles per hour (mph) in just 12 seconds* or *0 – 60 mph in 7 seconds*. Which do you think has the greater acceleration? Which could be a sports car? Acceleration is the rate at which speed increases. For example, a car which accelerates from 30 mph to 40 mph in 2 seconds speeds up at the rate of 10 mph in 2 seconds, that is, it has an acceleration of 5 mph per second.

When we are travelling at a steady speed and see a red traffic light, we need to decelerate. This is the opposite of acceleration. By pressing the brake pedal, you increase the friction between the spinning brake disks and the fixed brake pads. This slows the wheels. Brake hard enough and you will come to a stop. Deceleration is the rate at which speed decreases. For example, a car which decelerates from 70 mph to 30 mph in 5 seconds slows down at the rate of 40 mph in 5 seconds, that is 8 mph per second.

MAGNETISM

Words associated with magnetism and its effects have slipped into common use in a surprising number of ways. We talk about someone having a magnetic personality or magnetic attraction between people. Usually, such phrases are meant to indicate something positive. But a magnet can repel as well as attract. A magnetic personality could also be a disadvantage.

Many actions in everyday life involve mechanical forces, the pushes, pulls and twists described in the earlier section. We see objects move up to one another, push, make things move, or pull. Mechanical forces in action are often obvious. It is also helpful to think of magnetism as the source of forces like these. A magnet, however, can be less obvious in its action than the mechanical forces described above and is more selective about what it acts upon. Place a small magnet near an iron nail and we see nothing reaching out from the magnet to the nail, yet the nail is pulled towards the magnet. Replace the iron nail with a copper one and nothing seems to happen. What, then, is magnetism?

Magnets and what they do

The unusual ability of some materials to pull others towards them was noticed in rocks from the mountains near the city of Magnesia in northern Greece – hence the name *magnet*. When suspended in a paper cradle held by an untwisted thread or floated on a small piece of wood in a bowl of water, a finger-shaped piece of this rock always turned to point in the same direction. As such, they were described as lodestones or *leading stones* – stones which lead (or point) the way. They became a useful aid for seafarers. Today the magnetized needle of a plotting compass serves the same purpose.

These natural magnets were also found to have another unusual property. They were found to attract small pieces of iron, such as pins, and other *ferrous* (iron-based) materials. Since they had such remarkable properties, it is not surprising that people began to ascribe other powers to them. Magnetic stones were thought to cure aches and pains, correct speech impediments and even, if placed under the pillow, improve sex lives. It was also believed that magnets became weaker at night and lost their magnetic abilities if rubbed with garlic. Such beliefs were, of course, found to be unjustified but you might have children investigate the effects of garlic on the strength of a magnet.

Modern magnets are made from *steel* (largely an alloy of iron and a little carbon). They tend to be stronger magnets than lodestones and keep their magnetism reasonably well if not dropped too often or heated (two ways to weaken magnets). They can be quite heavy and cumbersome, and generally are available as bars, rods and horseshoe shapes. More recently, *ceramic magnets* have been developed, made largely from a mixture of clay, iron and carbon. These can be moulded into any shape and are relatively cheap to make although they can be fragile.

Magnetic poles and lines of force

Like a lodestone, a steel bar magnet floated on a piece of wood in a dish of water will turn so that one end will point towards the north and the other towards the south. The end that points north has been named the *North Pole* of the magnet and is often painted red or has a letter N or a dot stamped on it. The other end is named the *South Pole* and is sometimes painted blue.

The pushing and pulling force of a magnet can be shown in many ways. Many ferrous materials (but not stainless steel) are strongly attracted to a magnet. An interesting way to show this is to tie a short (15cm) piece of thread to an iron paper clip. Hold the free end of the thread firmly on the table with one hand. Bring a bar magnet near to the paper clip so that the latter is free to move towards the magnet. Slowly, raise the magnet into the air so that the paper clip follows the magnet but does not touch it. Hold the paper clip vertically using the magnet. Why does gravity not pull the paper clip down?

Nothing is visible in the gap between the paper clip and the magnet. It is as though there are invisible fingers stretching out from the magnet to pick up and hold the paper clip. What can these invisible fingers penetrate? With care, sheets of different materials can be slipped between the clip and the magnet. Will the magnetic pull penetrate a sheet of paper or card or plastic or aluminium foil or wood?

The field of influence around a magnet (where these invisible fingers can reach) is not normally visible, but it can be made so using iron filings. Use an A4 size sheet of paper or a transparent acetate sheet. Sprinkle fine iron filings onto the sheet like icing sugar to form a very thin, even coating. Slowly, lower the sheet over a bar magnet on a flat surface and tap it gently. The iron filings will respond to the magnet's influence and produce what are known as *lines of force* around the magnet. Iron filings can be difficult to remove if they are allowed to stick directly to a magnet so it is useful to wrap the magnet in plastic film before using the filings.

> **Note:**   Iron filings are safe to use when handled carefully. However, like any tiny, hard particles, they can get into eyes if blown about, so care is needed. Some LEAs do not permit their free use in the primary school. Some commercial suppliers sell flat plastic boxes with iron filings sealed between the sheets of plastic as an alternative.

Try placing the paper clip (still attached to its thread) near to one pole. The lines of force should be seen reaching out towards the paper clip to pull it to the magnet. The same pulling power can be shown clearly with two bar magnets, provided that *unlike poles* (that is, a north and a south pole) are used. Try putting two *like poles* together to see what happens to the lines of force (a north with a north or a south with a south pole). Repulsion occurs. The invisible force seems to be pushing the two magnets away from one another and the patterns in the iron filings will show this.

William Gilbert and the Earth's magnetism

In the time of Queen Elizabeth I, navigation of the oceans for both political and commercial reasons was of great importance. Sailors used lodestones to 'point the way' but no one had explained why they worked like that. The queen's physician, William Gilbert (1544–1603), tried to find out. In 1600, he found that if he made a model world with a magnet inside it, lodestones suspended near the model's surface would turn and point to the magnet, just as on the real Earth. Gilbert concluded that the Earth behaved as though it had a magnet in it. Since the north pole of a lodestone (or bar magnet or compass needle) is attracted towards the Arctic, it is as though there is a south pole of a magnet under this region. If you were to follow a compass into the Arctic Circle, it would not lead you to the *true* or *geographical North Pole* (the axis on which the earth turns) but to the *magnetic North Pole* which is some distance away in Greenland and changes its position slightly every year. The converse is true for the Antarctic. Geophysicists have now explained more completely the magnetic effects of the Earth's ferrous core and shown that Gilbert's ideas, 400 years ago, were in essence correct, although of course there is not a bar magnet inside the Earth.

Magnetic induction

Sometimes, you can take a screwdriver from a drawer and find two or three iron tacks attached to it. In the same way, scissors sometimes attract dressmaking pins to them.

Objects like pins, scissors and screwdrivers can become slightly magnetized when left in the Earth's magentic field. Such magnetic effects are, however, weak. It is possible to magnetize a steel object using a process known as *magnetic induction*. The easiest way is to use something like a steel knitting or darning needle. First, check it is not already magnetized by testing it with some iron filings. Then use a bar magnet and stroke the darning needle. Rub the north pole of the magnet along the length of the needle, always starting at the same end and finishing at the other end and using large loops to move back to the starting point. Do this at least twenty times and then test the needle on the iron filings again. Before being magnetized, the needle behaved as though it was full of tiny magnets, each pointing randomly in different directions, and cancelling one another out. What you have done is re-oriented some of the particles in the darning needle. When the bar magnet stroked the needle, it turned some of these so that they were pointing (or aligning themselves) in the same direction., with north poles at one end and south poles at the other. In some kinds of iron (called soft iron) the particles rearrange themselves again very quickly so the magnetic effect you have *induced* does not last for very long. In steel, the particles stay re-arranged for much longer and we have a more or less permanent magnet.

Electromagentic induction

It can be difficult to produce strong magnets but this can be done using electricity. When Michael Faraday (1791–1867) was carrying out his investigations into electricity, he found that an electric current in a coil of wire made the coil behave like a magnet. We call this effect *electromagnetism*. It can be shown easily using a battery, a bulb in a bulb holder, some wires and a plotting compass. Make a circuit using the battery, bulb and wires. Twist one of the wires around your finger to form a coil with five or six large loops in it. Slowly, put the plotting compass inside the loops of the coil and watch what happens to the needle as you do so. Move the compass in and out of the coil and watch the needle. You should see it move in response to the magentic effects of the current. If you wrap the coil around a soft iron nail the effect is stronger and the nail may pick up steel pins.

Electromagnetism is an important property and it is central to the action of an electric motor, a buzzer, a doorbell or an electic crane in a scrap yard. The advantage of an electromagnet is that it can be switched on and off. In an electric door bell, this is exactly what we do. We shall explore more fully what is happening in the section on electricity.

ENERGY

In the previous section we looked at forces, the pushes, pulls and twists which cause an object to move or to change the way it is moving. When we think of forces, we can usually visualize a force acting on something and the consequential effect. Some people confuse forces with *energy*. As a concept, energy can be as elusive as a wet bar of soap. You think you have grasped it and it slips away. We describe children as being full of energy, some drinks as boosting our energy, and the need to save energy around the home. Whoever we are talking to understands what we are talking about, but if you ask them to explain what energy is, we run into difficulties because energy is not something concrete. Children are no more full of energy than they are full of pinkness or bendiness. Energy cannot be saved in a piggy bank like money. We cannot see the energy in the drink that is going to give us the needed boost. So what exactly is it?

Mechanical energy – something waiting to change

One productive way to think about energy is to think about how things are arranged. If something is arranged in a way that can change by itself or can do so with a little help to get it going, then there is energy 'available'. We could say something is 'waiting' to change. When it does change it may do something useful in the process. For example, think about a wind-up toy mouse. After being wound up, the spring is ready to change back to its loose, unwound state. Put it on the floor and it unwinds, moving the mouse across the floor in the process. We can say that there is energy available in the wound-up arrangement of springs in such toys and the energy can be used to turn the toy's wheels. This action can easily be demonstrated using a strip of stiff paper. Cut the paper to about the size of a 30cm ruler. Hold one end of the strip firmly between finger and thumb and wrap the rest of the strip around them to make a coil. Still keeping hold of the inner end, release the outer end. The coil unwinds, turning as it does so. The coiled-up paper was waiting to change. When it did, it turned rapidly. It is this turning motion that is put to use in turning the toy's cogs and wheels.

Another familiar child's toy looks like a bug sitting on a long, loose spring fixed to a base plate. When the spring is compressed and then released, the bug leaps 20 or 30 cm into the air. This time it was the length of the spring that was changed. It had energy available in the compressed arrangement that could be used to do something useful when it was released. In this case, the available energy threw the bug into the air.

Springs can be stretched as well as compressed. In the stretched arrangement, there is also energy available to do something useful. Perhaps a stretched spring could pull something when the spring is released. A catapult works the same way. Stretch the elastic band, release it and the elastic contracts and hurls a stone. A rubber band behaves like an extended spring.

A scientist would define energy as *the capacity to do work*. All this means is that energy is available in some 'pent-up state' and when we allow it to change it can do something useful for us. It is not only toys and entertaining novelties that demonstrate this. In the world around us, energy changes are occurring all the time. Sometimes these are the result of natural processes, sometimes they are produced by human technology and engineering. Energy can be difficult to explain to young children but the 'something waiting to change idea' is a good starting point. Care must be taken, however, since inanimate objects cannot be said to 'wait' like people. Here, the word is used metaphorically.

Gravitational energy

An object on a table, like a book, appears to be in a state which cannot change, but push it over the edge and it falls to the floor. Its height has changed. Tie a piece of thread to a child's toy car. Place a lump of plasticene to the end of the thread and hang the thread over the table's edge. As the plasticene falls (changes height) it pulls the toy car across the table. Because it is gravity which changes the height of the book or the plasticene, the energy available is called *gravitational* energy. Gravitational energy is involved when a river flows from the hills to the sea and turns turbines in a hydro-electric power station or the wheel on a water mill. It is also what turns the mechanism in a pendulum clock as the heavy weights slowly fall. We pull the weights to the top of the case and as they are slowly pulled back down by gravity, the clock ticks away the seconds.

Chemical energy

You will be aware that not all energy changes fit into the pattern outlined above. Mechanical changes such as changes in shape, height and position are not the only sources of energy but they are amongst the easiest to see. But what is waiting to change in a toy car powered by batteries? The battery looks the same when it is new and after use. What has changed? What changes are the chemicals inside the battery. When they change, one effect is to make an electric current flow through the circuit in the toy car's motor. Sometimes, if an old battery is left unattended, the chemicals cause the casing to decay and the changes are more obvious and unwelcome. In some batteries the changes are permanent. The chemicals cannot be turned back to their original state and re-used. However, in rechargeable batteries the change is reversible. The chemicals formed when using the battery can be separated and re-arranged again so that the battery can be re-used.

Energy and living things

What happens inside a battery is, in some ways, very similar to what happens inside the bodies of living things. When we eat, the food changes inside us, providing energy as well as nutrients. One of the things it does is keep us warm. To release heat, the body allows the food to burn very, very slowly, that is, combine with oxygen and break down. The same food could have been burnt in an oven to the same end, giving off a lot of heat very quickly. There is energy waiting to change in the mix of chemicals which form foods, like peanuts, sugars and bread. When we allow these chemicals to change and combine with oxygen from the air (through breathing), we experience this energy as heat loss. A peanut, for instance, can be ignited by a match and will burn unaided, showing it to be a source of energy.

Energy and fuels

We sometimes describe food as the body's fuel. The word *fuel* is often used to describe a substance that can be burned and, in the process, produces lots of heat as a source of energy to do something else. There are a number of natural fuels in our environment such as the *fossil fuels*, like coal, natural gas and oil. They are the remains of ancient plants and animals, changed by heat and pressure over millions of years into the forms we see today. Some fuels are by-products of processing fossil fuels. For example, petrol is a fraction of oil. All these fossil fuels have one thing in common; once they have been used they cannot be renewed. As we consume them, the stocks get less. For this reason, we should husband the Earth's fossil fuels and look for alternatives. An ideal fuel would be one that does not harm the environment, is cheap and is *renewable*. Managed forests are a possible source of a renewable fuel. Scientists, technologists and engineers have been looking for others, exploring the potential of the sun, tides, wind power and water flow as renewable energy sources.

The development of photoelectronic cells means that we can convert sunlight directly into electrical energy. *Solar energy* is used on a small scale in watches, calculators and light meters. On a larger scale, there are sheets of solar cells on the 'wings' of satellites. The cells provide the electric current to operate some of the devices on board the satellite. Another use of solar energy is to heat water directly as it trickles through blackened pipes on roof panels. The heated water is then used as part of the domestic hot water system. Solar energy is also used in solar furnaces. The heat turns water to steam which turns an electric generator. In the Majove Desert in California, one of these solar furnaces produces enough electrical energy for 5000 homes. Nearly 2000 moveable mirrors, each about the size of the floor of a double garage, are controlled by computer and track the sun's position in the sky so that the maximum heat is reflected onto a boiler at all times.

We already have successful *hydroelectric* power stations and *wind* farms. Here, turbines are turned by flowing water and wind respectively, driving electric generators. Turbines in the barriers on *tidal* estuaries, like that on the river Rance in France, are producing electricity as the tides flow in and out. Even the Earth itself provides *geothermal heat*. Subterranean hot rocks heat water that can be piped to the surface for use in hot water supplies and steam-driven generators. In countries like Iceland, where there is a lot of geothermal activity, towns can be heated in this way.

Nuclear reactors are devices that release energy from the nuclei of atoms under controlled conditions. Particles are separated or split from the nuclei of radioactive elements like uranium 235 in a reactor's fuel rods, a process called *nuclear fission*. When this happens, heat is released and this is used to change water into high-pressure steam which turns turbines.

You may have heard of *fast breeder reactors*. Think about this.

- Most nuclear power plants use uranium 235 as their fuel, but the supply of U–235 is limited.
- Most of the natural uranium we mine contains less than one per cent of U–235. The rest is U–238, which is not usable as a fuel.
- When U–235 is fissioned (split) in a nuclear reactor, it gives off particles.
- If U–235 is surrounded by U–238, the particles convert the latter into an artificial radioactive element called plutonium, which can be used as a nuclear fuel.

But: Plutonium is highly toxic and can be used in fission bombs. We appear to get something for nothing. Is it worth it?

Conservation of energy

I have been writing about something waiting to change and when it does change, it may do something useful for us. Energy has different forms. For instance, there is mechanical, chemical, heat, light, sound, electrical or nuclear energy. We can often change energy from one form to another. For example, strike a match and chemical energy is changed to heat and light energy. Plants are very efficient at converting the sun's light energy into chemical energy. Riding a bicycle involves changing chemical energy (in muscles) into mechanical and heat energy. Electrical energy is changed to sound energy in loudspeakers. Energy can neither be created nor destroyed but it can be changed from one form to another.

ELECTRICITY

The story of our knowledge of electricity begins a long time ago and with the material amber, perhaps more familiar in jewellery. Over 2,500 years ago, the Greek philosopher Thales described how a piece of rubbed amber would attract small pieces of chaff. If you rub a plastic comb on a piece of soft cloth, it will attract small pieces of tissue paper in exactly the same way. Thales probably never imagined he was writing about something we would come to depend on in almost every part of our lives. At the heart of what Thales saw is the *electron* – a word we have taken from the Greek word for amber.

Flowing electrons

As we have already seen, all materials contain atoms which comprise negatively charged electrons orbiting a nucleus with neutral neutrons and positively charged protons. Some materials, like copper and nickel, are described as *good conductors* of electricity. This is because some electrons can be dislodged from their atoms in these materials and made to drift through the material fairly easily with the help of a battery. In many materials, like wood or plastics, making electrons drift like this is usually very difficult. We call these materials *poor* or *bad conductors* of electricity.

The *flow* of these electrons constitutes an *electric current*. The electrons are so small that we cannot see them. Even an electrical spark is simply the glowing trail of air along the path the electrons have taken. It can help to use an analogy to describe electrical current. The most common one is water flow. Electrical current in a wire behaves something like the flow of water in a pipe. Loosely speaking, the battery is like the pump which keeps the water flowing. Just as we can change the rate at which the pump pushes the water, we can use batteries of different 'strengths'. In the water circuit, we can make the flowing water do something useful for us, such as aerate an aquarium or turn a water wheel. In the same way, we can make the flowing electrons do something useful, such as to make a buzzer sound or heat a wire to make it glow in an electrical heater. Just as in the water circuit and the electrical circuit, the circuits need to be complete otherwise they will not function as intended. However, like all analogies, the water circuit analogy has its limits. For instance, a broken pipe lets water run out but a snapped wire does not let the electricity run out. A very simple water circuit which you can set up at home is shown in Figure 6.2.

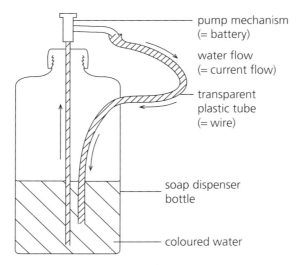

Figure 6.2 A simple water circuit

The soap dispenser pump on the bottle takes the part of the battery. The plastic tubing through which the water can flow is like the wire. If you use a little soap solution or food colouring in the water, it is much easier to see the movement of the water. Pump the dispenser and the water flows. Pump harder and the flow is faster.

So what exactly is waiting to change in the electrical circuit and what can we make it do that is useful?

Batteries and chemical charge

Earlier we were thinking about batteries in the context of chemical change. Chemical changes in a battery produce direct current – that is, the electrons tend to flow in one direction around the circuit. There are many different kinds of battery, sometimes called cells. They generally have the same basic structures: two *electrodes* made from two different materials in contact with an *electrolyte*. An electrolyte is a liquid or paste which reacts chemically with the electrodes. Figure 6.3 shows you a cross-section of a common torch battery.

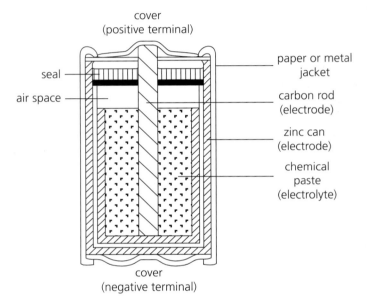

Figure 6.3   Cross-section of a typical torch battery

The cylindrical container is made of zinc and acts as one of the electrodes. The other electrode is a carbon rod which runs down the centre of the battery. The container is filled with a paste containing ammonium chloride. When connected in a circuit, the chemicals react and electrons flow from the zinc to the carbon rod. If an atom passes one of its electrons on to a neighbour, that electron needs to be replaced (so that the atom remains electrically neutral). Like a game of 'pass-the-parcel', electrons are passed on from one atom to another around the circuit. Once the circuit is broken and there is nowhere for these electrons to go, the chemical reaction stops. Current is not used up or consumed and is the same in all parts of the circuit.

Solar cells are the cleanest form of battery. No chemical changes are involved and they are very reliable. Sunlight causes one of the electrodes in the solar cell to release electrons to flow through the circuit (a watch or calculator, for example) and then back to the other electrode. The stronger the sunlight, the greater the voltage produced.

Resisting the flow

A battery that is near the end of its life can be connected to a bulb in a circuit and the bulb will glow weakly. This weakly glowing bulb may be examined with a magnifying glass to see the hot coil of thin wire. The electrons in the circuit are able to flow through the thick copper or nickel wires in the circuit without difficulty. It is rather like shoppers moving along a broad arcade. They move smoothly and keep their distance from one another. But if the arcade suddenly narrows, there is a bottleneck and the people have to squeeze together to flow through. All the pushing and shoving makes the shoppers hot and bothered. With the electrons, something similar happens. When they reach the thin coil of wire in the light bulb they squeeze through but the thin wire *resists* the flow. The electrons jostle the atoms of the wire which vibrate and the wire looks and feels hot. This is what happens in the coils of an electric heater, toaster and in some electric ovens. *Resistance* is a measure of how difficult it is for electrons to flow in the material. Some materials resist the flow of electrons more than others. Tungsten has a greater resistance to electron flow than copper of the same dimensions.

A bulb connected to a new battery will glow brightly. If we add a second bulb, so the two bulbs form a line, one after the other *in series*, the bulbs are less bright. This is because there are now two thin coils resisting the flow of electrons so only half as many electrons flow through them in each second as compared to when there was only one bulb in the circuit. There is less jostling and thus less heat and glow. On the other hand, if the bulbs are connected in *parallel* to one another, the bulbs should be just as bright as one bulb on its own. Whichever route the electrons take, only one bulb filament opposes them. The battery now delivers twice as much electrical current to share equally between the bulbs. Series and parallel circuits are shown in Figure 6.4.

Most metals are good at conducting electricity but other materials are often poor conductors. The carbon in a soft pencil lead (for example a 3B drawing pencil) is one of the better of these poor conductors and can be used to show the effect of resistance quite easily. Figure 6.5 shows you how to do this.

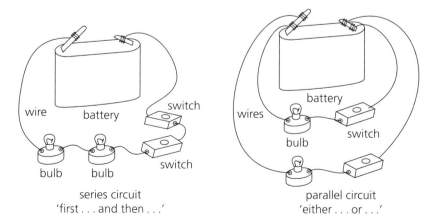

Figure 6.4 Series and parallel circuits

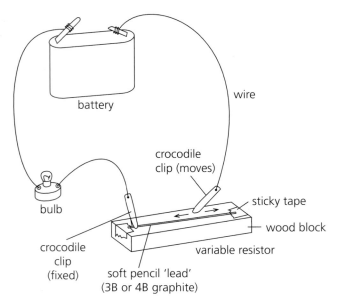

Figure 6.5 Including a variable resistor in a circuit

Pencil 'lead' is no longer made from lead, which is poisonous, but from graphite, a form of carbon. Although carbon does allow electrons to flow it is not a very good conductor. The longer the piece of carbon that the electrons have to flow through, the harder it is and the dimmer the light bulb. If a length of soft pencil 'lead' is included in a circuit, with one end of the wire free to slide along its length, you will see the variation in the brightness of the bulb as the the electrons have a shorter or longer distance to travel in the carbon.

Task 6.6 Uses of resistance	Variable resistors are used in all sorts of electrical equipment around the home, from dimmer switches to adjust lighting to sliding volume controls on television and hi-fi sytems to control

knobs on ovens to change the temperature.

Explore your own home and identify as many items as you can which use variable resistance. Explain what is being varied in each case and try to find out how they operate.

Circuit training

When we describe how electrical components are fitted together we call the arrangement a *circuit*. (A useful analogy is with the circuit that a runner would follow around a track: it is a closed loop.) A simple electric circuit might have a battery, a bulb in a bulbholder and two wires. Other components may be added to it – bulbs, wires and batteries, buzzers and variable resistors. We may also add instruments for measuring voltage and current. The components can be arranged in series or in parallel. To make circuit diagrams easier to read, the components are drawn using standard symbols. Some common ones are shown in Figure 6.6 and Figure 6.7 shows an example of a circuit diagram.

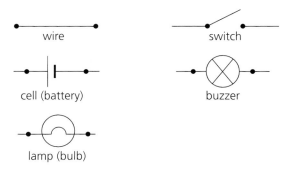

Figure 6.6 Symbols for a circuit diagram

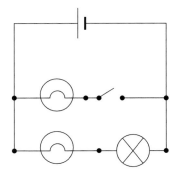

Figure 6.7 An example of a circuit diagram

Task 6.7 Circuit diagrams	Try designing some simple circuit drawings with bulbs in them. Predict what will happen to the brightness of the bulb(s) when you change the arrangements.

Bringing it all together

There are some very simple ideas to do with electrical circuits:

- the 'strength' or *voltage* of the battery;
- the flow of the electrons or electrical *current*;
- how much *resistance* to electricity the materials have; and,
- the rate at which energy is transferred in a device or its *power*.

The 'strength' of a battery is more properly called its *electric potential*. It is measured in *volts* after the scientist Alessandro Volta (1745–1827) who experimented with batteries. One volt (1V) is the measure of the energy needed to carry a current of one amp between two points in a conducting material. The voltage of a single battery (or cell) is about 1.5V when new. We sometimes use more than one battery at once, as in a torch (2 × 1.5V). Cycle lamps often use 4.5V batteries, which are really three 1.5V cells wrapped in one package. These batteries will not give an electric shock but the voltage of the mains supply is 240V and is very dangerous. Not only will it give a shock, but it may kill. That in the overhead cables between electricity pylons may be several hundred thousand volts and is very dangerous.

To count the number of electrons flowing past any particular point in a circuit in each second is impossible. There could be millions of them. To make life easier, we measure the flow of electrons in *amps*. The unit is named after Andre Ampere (1775–1836), a French scientist who investigated the magnetic effects of an electric current. A current of one amp (1A) amounts to 6,000,000,000 (six thousand million) electrons passing a point in a wire every second.

Resistance (or how much something resists the flow of electrons) is measured in *ohms*, again named after a famous scientist, Georg Ohm (1787–1854). For some common materials (like copper wire or pencil 'lead') under certain conditions (such as when the material remains cool), doubling the voltage doubles the current. For instance, if a 1.5V battery makes 0.5A flow in the circuit; then two 1.5V batteries in series (that is, 3V) will make about 1A flow; and, three 1.5V batteries (4.5V) will make about 1.5A flow. This pattern is captured in the formula:

$$\textbf{V}\text{oltage equals } \textbf{R}\text{esistance multiplied by } \textbf{C}\text{urrent}$$
$$\textbf{V} \quad = \quad \textbf{R} \quad \times \quad \textbf{C}$$

Try fitting some numbers into the rule to work out the effects of changing the voltage (1.5V, 3V, 4.5V, 6V, etc.), when the resistance to the flow of current is 2 ohms.

Finally, we need to consider the *power* of devices such as bulbs, heaters and motors that might be in a circuit. Power is the rate at which electrical energy is fed into or taken from an electrical device or system. It is measured in watts, named after James Watt, the Scottish engineer. One watt (1W) is equivalent to one joule of energy each second. The wattage of a household light bulb is often about 60W. This means it takes 60 joules per second to operate normally. An electrical kettle might take 750 watts (750W) or 0.75 kilowatt (0.75KW). An electric heater can take 1000 watts (a Kilowatt, 1KW) or more, usually about 1KW for each bar. Again, there is a simple pattern which shows the relationship between the power consumed and what is going on in the circuit: the PVC rule.

$$\textbf{P}\text{ower equals } \textbf{V}\text{oltage multiplied by } \textbf{C}\text{urrent}$$
$$\textbf{P} \quad = \quad \textbf{V} \quad \times \quad \textbf{C}$$

So,   60W light bulb = 240V (mains electricity) × 0.25A (current)
       40W light bulb = 240V (mains electricity) × 0.1667A (current)
        3KW⋆ cooker = 240V (mains electricity) × 12.5A (current)
       (⋆ 3000W)

Why do you think having the right fuse (for example, 13A for a kettle but 3A for a lamp) is important?

The power consumption of an electrical device is usually printed on a label attached to it. Have a look at some household electrical equipment and see what the power consumption of each is.

LIGHT

Most of us take light for granted and yet we are very dependent upon it. Think about how people react during a power cut, or an eclipse or even on a dark night. In fact, most life on our planet depends upon light. So what is light? In this section, we will consider the nature of light. We are familiar with its usefulness, whether it is sunlight making plants grow for us to eat and powering solar cells for watches and calculators, or artificial light providing illumination in homes and street lights. So what exactly is it?

A keyboard of light

Think of standing on the seashore, watching the waves run up the beach. Sometimes, a lot of wave peaks come in close together in quick succession. Sometimes, they are more spaced out. Sometimes the waves are high, sometimes quite low. We can think of light as being a kind of wave. It can differ in wavelength and intensity. When the light wave has lots of peaks close together, we see it as blue–violet light. When the wave peaks are farther apart, we see it as red–orange light. Between the two are all the colours of the rainbow, that is, the light *spectrum*. You probably learned a rhyme when you were young to remember the colours of the rainbow: **R**ichard (red) **O**f (orange) **Y**ork (yellow) **G**ave (green) **B**attle (blue) **I**n (indigo) **V**ain (violet). In reality, listing seven colours is just a matter of convention as one colour shades into the next. There are as many colours as you want; the important thing is that there is a spread of light with different wavelengths.

But this visible spectrum of colours is only a very small part of an invisible, bigger spread. It is rather like a keyboard on the piano where we can hear only three or four keys either side of middle C. Other keys exist on the keyboard and we cannot hear the notes they make, but we may sense them in other ways. At a higher frequency than violet, where the wave peaks are closer together, there is ultraviolet light (which we cannot see but some animals can), X–rays and gamma rays. These waves are very energetic, so much so that they are able to penetrate and kill living cells. Waves with peaks farther apart than red light are infra-red and radio waves. These are much less energetic. This enormous keyboard, of which we can see only a few keys, is known as the *electromagnetic spectrum* (the em-spectrum) and is shown in Figure 6.8.

A rainbow is a spectrum from that part of the em-spectrum visible to human eyes. When a mixture of all these colours enters our eyes at once, the impression we get is one of white light. Pass a ray of white light through a crystal on a chandelier or droplets from a hosepipe or a clear plastic ruler and you may split it again into its

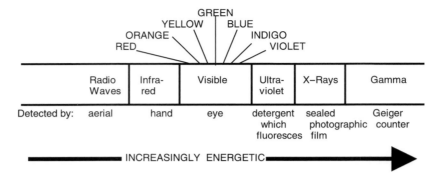

Figure 6.8 The electromagnetic spectrum

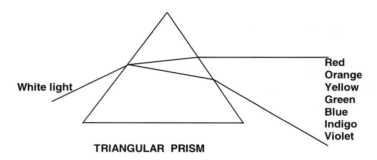

Figure 6.9 Splitting white light

constituent colours (Figure 6.9). This is what may happen with raindrops in the sky on a showery day to produce a rainbow.

Colour and light

In science, red, green and blue are called the *primary* colours of light. (Note that in art, red, yellow and blue are commonly called the primary colours.) When these colours overlap, we see the *secondary* colours: yellow (red + green), magenta (red + blue) and cyan (green + blue).

Sir Isaac Newton invented a colour disc that, when spun quickly like a top, presents all the colours to the eye which recombines them into white light. This disc is easy to make from a circle of card about the size of a saucer. Divide the card into seven segments (like pie slices) and colour each segment lightly in one of the colours of the rainbow. Spin the card on a pencil point and view it to see the colours combine. Crayon or paint pigments are seldom pure, so the effect is greyish rather than white. A disc with two primary colours can be used to produce a secondary colour.

Black objects absorb light of all colours and reflect none, hence they look black. White objects reflect all colours, so look white. Green objects tend to absorb all

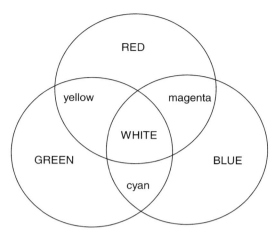

Figure 6.10   The primary and secondary colours of light

colours except green which they reflect and so look green. We see red curtains because the other colours are being absorbed but the red light is being reflected. The colour of objects depends upon which wavelengths of the light they absorb and which they reflect.

Light sources and light travel

Think of the things that produce light. The Sun, at the centre of our solar system, and other suns (stars) in other systems are all sources of light. A candle flame or a torch also produce light. But light can also be bounced off things, or *reflected*. Light from the Sun is reflected by the Moon. People tend to say that the Moon is 'shining' but this is definitely an incorrect description of what is happening. Similarly, a mirror, aluminium cooking foil, smooth water on a lake, silver spoons all reflect light. Even coloured paper reflects light although not as completely as white paper or as faithfully as a mirror.

Rays of light travel in straight lines. Even a young child knows this subconsciously when he or she draws a picture of the sun and puts lines radiating from it. The beam from a torch, car headlights or the warning light from a lighthouse on a foggy night all provide evidence that light travels in straight lines. Even better is evidence provided by a laser. Surveyors use lasers to find a straight line between two points. Army personnel sometimes use laser-sighted guns which send beams of light to targets. The red spot shows where the bullet will land. You can show light travels in straight lines quite easily. Use a short piece of garden hose, about half a metre in length. Pull the hose taut and you should be able to see through it. The light from the other end of the hose can enter the hosepipe and travel straight along it into your eye. Allow the hose to sag slightly and the light can no longer travel in a straight line, so you cannot see out of the other end. Light cannot travel around curves or corners of its own accord. This is known as the *rectilinear propagation of light*. It just means that light travels in straight lines.

Light travelling in straight lines causes some interesting effects in our world, such as *inverted* (upside–down) images in cameras and in the eye (see Figure 6.11). In the pinhole camera, light from a window passes through the pinhole in the box. Because light travels in straight lines, the rays of light from the top of the window travel straight into the pinhole and on until they hit the bottom of the screen at the back of the box. Light from the bottom of the window ends up on the screen at the top of the box. The rays of light from other parts of the window and from objects on the window sill end up between these two extremes. As a consequence, the image formed on the screen in the box is inverted. Pinhole cameras are easy to make from shoeboxes and greaseproof paper. Make the hole bigger with your thumb and the picture is brighter but blurred. A lens in front of the hole will now focus the picture and we have a lens camera. Replace the screen in the box with photographic film and we have the camera.

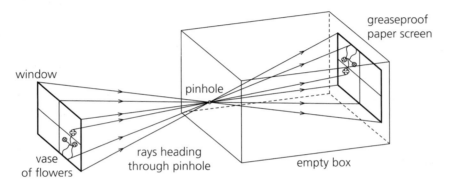

Figure 6.11   A pinhole camera

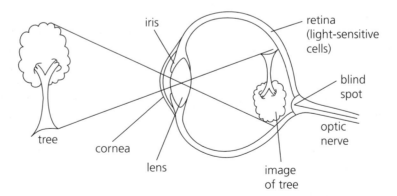

Figure 6.12   Cross-section of a human eye

Much the same thing happens in the eye, as shown in Figure 6.12. The *iris* (the coloured part of the eye) behaves like a lens shutter, opening and closing the *pupil* (the black part of the eye which is really a hole) to change the amount of light entering the eye. On bright, sunny days the pupils will be very small to keep out bright light.

At night, in the dark, the pupils will be very large to allow as much light as possible to enter the eye. If someone shines a torch in your eyes, you will be dazzled for a few seconds until the pupils adjust by closing down to cut out some of the bright light. The light enters the eye and falls on the *retina* (which acts as a light sensitive screen) producing an inverted image. The cells that form the retina pass the information to the *optic nerve* which carries it to the *brain*. The brain, of course, deals with the information so that we 'see' the image the correct way around. The eye also has a lens to keep the image in focus. This is just behind the pupil and is soft and adjustable so that it can change shape to keep the image in focus.

Another effect of light travelling in straight lines is the production of shadows. Because light cannot bend around objects, it is stopped by opaque objects that block its path. Light cannot reach behind the object so there is a shadow there. Shadows are formed when any solid object is placed in the path of a light source, large or small. Obstacles can be huge, as when the Moon lies directly between the Sun and the Earth to produce an *eclipse* of the Sun. Directly under the shadow no Sun will be seen and there will be total darkness. Just outside the total shadow, light from the edges of the Sun reaches the Earth and so there is a partial shadow – a kind of twilight. This is where there is a partial eclipse. When the source of light appears to be small, the edges of the shadow tend to be sharp and clear. However, when the source of light appears to be large, the shadow's edges become blurred because of these partial shadows.

Reflection of light

We see things because light is either given off by the object or the object is reflecting light from another source into our eyes. Some materials are good reflectors of light, others are not. White paper reflects light well. Black paper absorbs most of the light. It appears black due to the absence of reflected light.

Even amongst good reflectors, there are differences. Smooth surfaces like glass, metal foil, stainless steel and gloss paint all reflect light in a regular, even way. These smooth surfaces behave like mirrors, with the rays of light bouncing off them like balls bouncing on a smooth path. Rough or uneven surfaces, on the other hand, bounce light rays in all directions. This is like balls bouncing on an uneven cobbled path. This is shown in Figure 6.13.

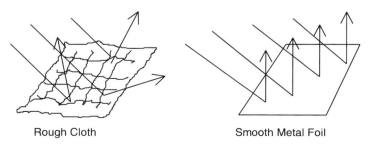

Rough Cloth   Smooth Metal Foil

Figure 6.13 Reflection of light from rough and smooth surfaces

The regular way that light reflects from a mirrored surface is described in another law of science: *the angle of incidence (the angle at which the ray approaches the mirror) equals the angle of reflection (the angle at which it leaves the mirror)*. The image in the mirror is also turned around or *laterally inverted* (Figure 6.14).

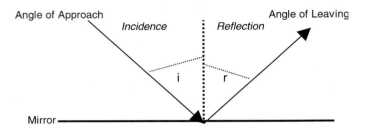

Figure 6.14   Light approaching and leaving a mirrored surface

Not all mirrors are flat. They can be hollow (*concave*) or bulging (*convex*). As with the flat (or *plane*) mirror, the angle of incidence and the angle of reflection are the same. However, because the surface of the mirror is curved, the rays of light tend to give a strange image. Try looking at yourself in the surfaces of a shiny table spoon. Your image can look fat or thin or upside-down. In an amusement park, the hall of mirrors uses curved mirrors.

The speed of light

Light is the fastest thing we know. In just one second, light can travel 300,000 kilometres (over 186,000 miles). In the blink of an eye light would have circled our world eight times, or be two-thirds of the way to the moon. During a thunder storm, we see the flash of lightning before we hear the thunder because light travels so much faster than sound. Similarly, at a sports event it is possible to see the smoke from the starter pistol before we hear the noise.

Astronomers talk of distances in terms of light-years, that is, the distance travelled by light in one year. A light-year is a useful unit for an astronomer because it lets them avoid huge numbers when they are talking about distances to planets and stars. For example, Proxima Centauri (the star nearest to our solar system) is 4.3 light-years away. Since a light-year is roughly 9.5 billion kilometres (or about 6 billion miles), this puts Proxima Centauri almost 41 billion kilometres away, a number so huge it is difficult to comprehend.

SOUND

Sound as a means of communication or of entertainment is something we probably take for granted. What is sound and how can we say that it is a form of energy?

Something waiting to change

Think of the different ways to make a sound. You could clap your hands or stamp your feet, or you might use an object like a piece of wood vibrating against a surface. Sometimes sounds can be musical. A stretched rubber band or a ruler over the edge of the table can be vibrated to produce vaguely musical sounds. In the case of the rubber band and ruler you can actually see something happening. They *vibrate* backwards and forwards and push at the air on either side of them. A tuning fork does the same thing. Hit it on a book and you will hear the musical note it produces and you may see the tines vibrate. You can demonstrate the vibration by dipping the tines into a glass of water. (At home, you can try this with a pair of tweezers.)

Sound is produced by vibrating things although we may not always be able to see the vibrations clearly. Loudspeakers in televisions, radios and hi-fi systems produce sound. The cardboard cone at the front of the speaker vibrates in response to the changing electrical current. You can demonstrate this by disconnecting a speaker from an old radio. Remove the cloth cover if it has one. Connect one of the wires from the speaker to a contact on a 4.5V battery. Scratch the other speaker wire onto the other contact. The cone in the speaker will vibrate and make a scratching noise as you move the wire across the contact.

Sound recording converts sounds into a permanent form that can be stored and reproduced later. The first sound recorder was made by Thomas Edison (1847–1931), and comprised a wide horn receiver into which he spoke. At the narrow end of the horn was a disc which was made to vibrate by speaking loudly into the horn. Attached to the disc was a short needle that pressed against a rotating drum covered with wax. As the cylinder rotated, the needle created a wavy groove in the wax that mirrored the vibrations produced by the sound. By replacing the needle in the groove and rotating the drum, the disc could be made to vibrate and produce sounds through the horn. This kind of sound recording was popular for many years until magnetic-tape recording was developed. Instead of grooves in wax or plastic, a plastic strip is coated with tiny particles of magnetizable materials (such as iron oxide). Electrical current from a microphone passes to the recording heads. These are small electromagnets that line up the ferrous particles according to changes in the current. They produce magnetized stripes on the tape, rather like a bar code. Compact disks (CDs) represent the most recent technological development in sound recording. Here, instead of a needle and wax, a laser leaves a trace on a sheet of thin metal foil.

If sound is the result of something vibrating, how does it reach us? As the rubber band, ruler, loudspeaker cone and your voice box vibrate, they repeatedly push at the air around them. This produces *compression waves*. These are pulses of air which travel in all directions from the source of the sound, rather like the ripples that spread out from where a stone is thrown into a pond. A good way to visualize this is to use a slinky spring. Fix one end of the spring to a chair leg and stretch the spring. Hit one end of the spring in a line along its length and watch the wave travel down the spring to the chair leg and then bounce back again. (This is like the sound vibrations returning as an echo. Note that just behind the compression is a place where the spring is stretched more than is normal. Each compression is accompanied by this *rarefaction*.)

These vibrations are a form of mechanical energy. As they hit something, they make it vibrate and energy is transferred. In the process, we can make it do something useful. Air vibrations produced by a whistle can make electric key rings bleep so you can locate your keys. They can make lamps switch on or alarm clocks switch off. And, of course, they provide us with a means of communication.

Ears – our hearing aids

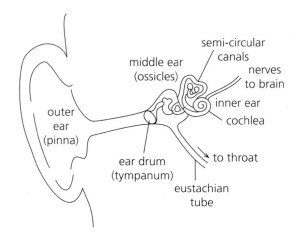

Figure 6.15 Cross-section of a human ear

We sense the vibrations in the air with our ears (see Figure 6.15) although some animals, like worms, sense vibration with their bodies. When a sound pulse reaches the *outer ear*, the latter behaves rather like a funnel and channels the pulse down the tube to the *ear drum*, a taut disc of skin stretched across the funnel. This makes the ear drum vibrate and the vibrations are passed to the *middle ear*. Here, they shake a tiny set of bones, the malleus, incus and stapes (sometimes called the hammer, anvil and stirrup bones because of their appearance and action). Under the stirrup bone is another membrane separating the middle ear from the *inner ear*. This comprises the *cochlea* which sorts out the sound into its different pitches and also, incidentally, acts as the body's balancing organ. The sorted sounds make hairs in the cochlea vibrate and nerves attached to them send electrical currents to the brain for interpretation.

Some animals have much better hearing than we have. Their ears have adapted to pick up air vibrations very easily. Having upright ears that move helps; think of a horse and the way its ears prick up and move to locate noises. Having extra large ears also helps, as with a bat whose ears seem out of proportion for its size and work as sound catchers. Make a large cone of cardboard and place it over an ear. You should be able to pick up sounds more readily than before; this is how the old-fashioned ear trumpet worked.

Pitch and loudness

Not all sounds are the same. Just as with the waves on the beach or the light waves we discussed earlier, sound waves come in all shapes and sizes. Short, fat, slack rubber bands produce a different sound to long, thin, taut ones. A ruler with only 5cm sticking over the edge of the table and twanged produces a much higher note than one with 15cm sticking over the edge. Similar effects can be heard with many other things that vibrate: tuning forks, guitar strings, xylophone bars and air in organ pipes.

Task 6.8 Musical interlude	Make a list of as many different musical instruments as you can think of. Beside each one, identify what it is that vibrates to produce the sound. Sort them into groups accordingly.

Think of some home-made musical instruments that children might make. How is the sound produced in each of them?

In organ pipes, it is the columns of air that vibrate. Changing the length of the column changes the *pitch* of the sound. All else being equal, the longer the column of air (or rubber band or ruler) the lower the pitch. The pitch describes the frequency of the sound produced, that is the number of vibrations per second. Shorter, lighter materials generally vibrate more quickly, that is, at a higher frequency. Longer, thicker or heavier materials vibrate more slowly, producing lower notes.

The range of frequencies that people can hear is relatively limited when compared with some other animals, like dogs or bats. We tend not to hear very low notes, less than about 20 vibrations per second. Nor can we hear very high notes, above about 20,000 vibrations per second. A dog whistle, at over 20,000 vibrations per second, is generally inaudible to us, but the response of the family pet indicates that it can hear it. Similarly, bats use high frequency sounds for echolocation. (You may find that 'vibrations per second' is referred to by the short-hand unit *hertz*. For teaching purposes in the primary school, the longer version is more meaningful.)

We can keep the pitch or frequency of the sound the same but alter its loudness. Large vibrations will produce louder sounds than small vibrations. The word *amplitude* is used to describe the maximum displacement of a vibration from its resting position and this is an indicator of loudness.

Noise versus sound

Unwanted sounds are usually called noise, sound in the wrong place or at the wrong time. How do we distinguish between welcome and unwelcome sounds? One kind of unwelcome sound is that which is found to be excessively loud. Loudness of sounds is measured on the *decibel scale*. For example, a rough guide to loudness might be:

Silence .... 0 db
Breathing .... 10 db
Whispering .... 20 db
Bird song .... 30 db
Background music .... 40 db
Quiet talk .... 50 db
Loud talk .... 60 db
Party noise .... 70 db
Football crowd .... 80 db
Pneumatic drill at work .... 90 db
Underground train going past ....100 db
Thunder overhead ....110 db
Jet aeroplane taking off ....120 db

Health workers tell us that exposure to sounds in the range of 100db to 130db for longer than 15 minutes can cause headaches, nausea and hearing damage so workers in noisy factories and on industrial sites often wear ear protectors. Sounds over 200db can lead to death because of the physical damage produced by such large vibrations.

Sound travelling

So far, we have only considered sound travelling in air. Sound can also pass through liquids and solids. Such materials affect the speed that sound can travel. Films show the cowboys of the American West putting their ears to the metal railway tracks to check if the train is coming just as the Native Americans would press their ears to the ground to listen for galloping horses. Beethoven lost his hearing in later life and it is reported that he gripped in his teeth a piece of wood nailed to his piano. The sound vibrations passed from the piano through the wood to the bones in his head, by-passing the outer ear.

Sound also travels efficiently through water. Explosions under water can deafen swimmers. In films, we see submarine crews whispering so the sound detectors of the enemy cannot pick them up. I have a coffee mug which plays a tune that can be heard even when it is submersed in washing-up water. Other materials can absorb sound. In concert halls, the fabrics of the seats and curtains absorb it and affect the quality of the music. We encounter a similar effect if we wear a coat hood or a hat that pulls down over the ears. Sound waves are absorbed by the fabrics so covering the ears means that we cannot hear so well. This could be dangerous when trying to cross a busy road.

That sound needs some material to travel in is demonstrated by placing an alarm clock in a jar and removing the air. Initially, the alarm can be heard, but as the air is removed and a vacuum is created, there are no air particles to vibrate and pass on the sound, so we cannot hear the alarm. It is the same in the vacuum of space. When we see spaceships exploding on films, the blast is often accompanied by a loud noise. In reality, there would be none.

EARTH AND BEYOND

To those living in the ancient world, the planet Earth was flat and at the centre of the universe. They believed that the Sun, Moon and other heavenly bodies revolved around the Earth because that is what observation told them. In the Middle Ages, Nicolaus Copernicus (1473–1543) took a different view. For him, it was the Earth that revolved around the Sun. We now know, not just from earth-bound observations but from direct observation from space, that our *planet*, Earth, is a fairly ordinary planet travelling through space in an orbit around a fairly ordinary *star*, the Sun. It is not unique as there are eight other planets travelling around the Sun, too.

You may have learned a rhyme to remember the names of the planet: **M**an (Mercury) **V**ery (Venus) **E**asily (Earth) **M**akes (Mars) **J**ugs (Jupiter) **S**erve (Saturn) **U**seful (Uranus) **N**ecessary (Neptune) **P**urposes (Pluto). The rhyme not only tells us the names of the planets. It also tells us their order, Mercury being the planet closest to the Sun. If you were to make a scale model of the solar system, with the Sun 3 metres across (300cm, that is about the size of one wall of a room) then the planets would have the following diameters:

Planet	Average Distance from the Sun		Size
Mercury	35 million miles =	12cm	1.0cm
Venus	67 million miles =	23cm	2.5cm
Earth	93 million miles =	32cm	3.0cm
Mars	142 million miles =	49cm	1.5cm
Jupiter	485 million miles =	167cm	30.0cm
Saturn	875 million miles =	300cm	26.0cm
Uranus	1750 million miles =	600cm	10.0cm
Neptune	2615 million miles =	900cm	10.0cm
Pluto	3700 million miles =	1270cm	1.0cm

Earth – a closer look

The planet earth was probably formed about 4.5 thousand million years ago (4,500,000,000 years). It is sometimes called the blue planet, because from space it looks blue. It may be the only planet in our solar system with free liquid water on its surface because its surface temperature makes that possible. Over two-thirds of Earth's surface is covered with water and the whole is enveloped in an oxygen-rich atmosphere. If we were closer to the Sun, the water would all evaporate. If we were further away, the water would be permanently frozen. The iron core of Earth produces a powerful magnetic field which stretches out into space. Earth also has its own satellite, the Moon, which is quite large compared with the size of Earth. Earth is roughly spherical and has a circumference of approximately 24,000 miles. As far as we know at the moment, it is the only planet which supports life in our solar system.

Like all planets, Earth is not a source of light. From space it appears to shine because of the reflected light of our nearest star, the Sun. Imagine spinning a ball fixed to a string around your head. The ball represents Earth and you are the Sun. The string represents the Sun's powerful gravity which keeps Earth in place. If you release the string, the ball's momentum will carry it off at a tangent, as shown in Figure 6.16. This is what Earth is doing. Its orbit is the result of a compromise to GO and FALL at the same time. Earth makes one complete cycle of the sun in about 365.25 days, although we call a year 365 days. Every fourth year we have to add an extra day (the leap year of 366 days) to catch up with the left over quarter days.

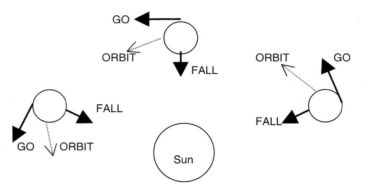

Figure 6.16   How the Earth orbits the Sun – the planet tries to move forward (GO) but at the same time is pulled towards the Sun (FALL)

But what is a day? From a space ship looking back at Earth, the cause of day and night is easy to see. As already mentioned, Earth has no light of its own. It can only reflect light that falls on it and the major light source in our part of space is the Sun. Because Earth is spherical, the hemisphere facing the sun is illuminated and the hemisphere facing away from the Sun is in darkness. (Remember, light travels in straight lines, so it cannot curve round earth to light up the half farthest from the sun.) However, Earth also rotates on its own north–south axis, as shown in Figure 6.17, so half of the world is in sunlight, where it is day, but the part facing the Sun constantly changes.

Earth rotates on its axis once in 24 hours. This means that for any place on Earth, the time taken to rotate from early morning through day and night back to early morning

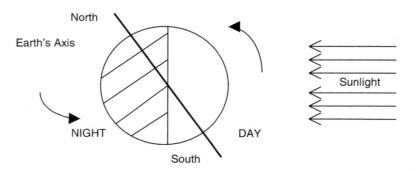

Figure 6.17   Rotation of the Earth to produce day and night

is twenty-four hours. At midday in winter, the Sun will appear directly overhead. British Summer Time is about an hour ahead of true time. Even in winter this is an approximation, because Britain is a wide enough island for midday to occur at different times according to longitude. If viewed from above the north pole, Earth rotates anticlockwise. This means that Sun appears to rise in the east (Earth is turning towards the east) and set in the west (Earth is turning away from the Sun in the east). If you were standing on the equator, the ground beneath your feet would be moving at a speed of about 1,000 miles per hour because Earth's circumference is about 24,000 miles. But of course, you would not notice it because you and everything around you, including the atmosphere, is moving at the same speed. You can easily demonstrate day and night using a geographical globe and a torch. Set the globe spinning anticlockwise and see the countries move through day and night. Place a piece of plasticene on the equator on the globe and you can see how the piece on the equator has to travel farther in the same time so the speed must be much greater at this point than at the poles.

Another thing you will notice is that the axis of the globe is tilted, to reflect the fact that Earth's axis is tilted by 23.5°. This tilt causes the *seasons* and the associated variations in light and temperature at different times of the year. This is shown in Figure 6.18. The equator, an imaginary line around the middle of Earth at right angles to its axis and like a belt, divides the planet into the northern and southern hemispheres. As Earth travels around the Sun, one hemisphere is tilted towards Sun (summer) and the other away from it (winter). Summer receives more heat per square mile and so days are warmer. The reverse is true in winter. The transitions into and out of summer (spring and autumn respectively) are, therefore, periods midway between these as far as the amount of heat received from the sun is concerned.

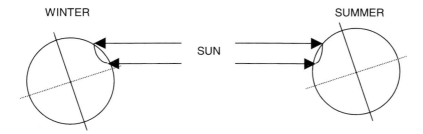

Figure 6.18   The seasons in the northern hemisphere

The Moon is only about one-quarter of the size of Earth. It does not spin on its own axis so it keeps the same face towards the Sun at all times. Although astronomers have known for centuries what the surface facing Earth looked like, it was not until the early 1960s that the first pictures of the far side of the Moon were available. The Moon revolves around Earth in roughly 28 earth days or a month. Like Earth, it produces no light itself but reflects the Sun's light, and hence appears to 'shine'. From earth we see different proportions of the illuminated side of the Moon during its lunar cycle as shown in Figure 6.19.

The Moon is a dry, airless place. For people to survive there without support from Earth they would need to build a self-contained space station in which they could

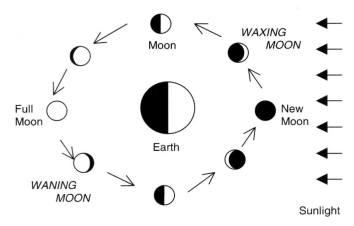

Figure 6.19   Phases of the moon

produce food and water and also maintain an oxygen-rich atmosphere. Because it is smaller than Earth, it has a gravitational pull that amounts to only about one-sixth of Earth's gravity. This would make the lifting of the materials for building a space station much easier than on Earth.

It is the Sun's light that has enabled life to develop on Earth. It is also responsible for day and night, the seasons, and shadows and eclipses. Most life on our planet is dependent upon the Sun for light and heat energy. However, the Sun will not last forever as it is now. As its helium and hydrogen gases run out, life as we know it will disappear on Earth, although not for millions of years.

The other planets

We now know quite a lot about some of the other planets from the information sent back by long distance probes as well as by direct observation through telescopes.

Mercury

This is the closet planet to the Sun and it is only slightly larger than the Moon. Because it is close to the Sun, it travels around it in only 88 days. Because it spins very slowly on its own axis, the days and nights are very long. Consequently, the temperatures on the planet's surface are extreme. On the side facing the sun, it reaches 400°C while on the night side it falls to −180°C.

Venus

The next planet out from the sun is Venus, a very romantic name for a very unromantic planet. It is almost the same size as Earth but if we were to travel there we would be suffocated by the corrosive atmosphere, crushed under its enormous pressure and roasted by the high surface temperature (over 450°C). Even the rocks would glow in the dark. Venus rotates on its axis in the opposite direction to the Earth so the sun appears to rise in the west and set in the east. However, its cloud blanket is so dense that we would probably never see the Sun rise or set.

Earth

Earth has already been described. It lies at a distance of about 93 million miles from the sun. The balance of light and heat from the Sun and of gases and water on the surface provide the necessary components to create and sustain life. This balance is precarious and the planet's dominant species – humans – can easily upset it.

Mars

Called the Red Planet because of the rusty red dust which blows around in strong winds and covers the surface, Mars is only about half the size of Earth. It is a planet covered with mountains, canyons and flat plains, some of which are far larger than anything found on our planet. For example, Olympus, a volcanic mountain, is three times higher than Everest. Because Mars is a long way from the influence of the Sun, it is a cold planet with surface temperatures seldom rising above freezing. Any water on Mars is under the surface or possibly at the poles as frost caps. It has two small moons, Phobos and Deimos.

Jupiter

The giant of our solar system is Jupiter. It is so huge that all the other planets, their moons and all the asteroids and other space debris in our solar system could fit inside it with room to spare. Its diameter is eleven times greater than Earth's but it is not a rocky planet. It is made almost entirely of gases like methane, ammonia, hydrogen and helium. They are under such great pressure that, below the atmosphere, they have changed state and become liquid. It is possible that at the heart of the planet the hydrogen may even have become solid. Jupiter also produces a powerful magnetic field, 20,000 times greater than Earth's magnetic field. Fierce storms rage across the planet's surface producing strange effects like the Great Red Spot. Jupiter also spins very quickly on its axis, so that days and nights are short, about 10 hours in total. It has seven moons. Ganymede, the largest, is bigger than planets like Pluto and Mercury. The other moons include ice-covered Europa, volcanic Io and crater-peppered Callisto.

Saturn

Saturn is another giant planet, about nine times the diameter of the Earth. Like Jupiter, it is composed of gases with a solid core. However, it is very unlike Jupiter in that its density is so low that it would float on water if you could find a large enough dish for it. It has several moons, the largest of which is Titan, but its most spectacular feature is the band of icy fragments that girdles its equator and stretches out into space. Until the late eighteenth century, people thought that Saturn was the outermost planet of our solar system.

Uranus

Four times the size of the Earth and twice as far away from the Sun as Saturn, Uranus is another giant planet. It is mostly composed of frozen materials and is unusual in that it lies on its side. Uranus takes 84 Earth years to orbit the Sun, and it appears to be a featureless planet with no weather activity. Like Saturn, ice fragments girdle Uranus, although the rays they produce are narrow and faint. It has 15 moons.

Neptune

Astronomers calculated Neptune's position before they actually saw it. This is another icy giant, about the same size as Uranus. However, unlike Uranus it has tremendous storms and winds, which stir up the nitrogen and methane atmosphere and create spots like the Great Dark Spot. The gases are frozen at the south pole, forming a pale pink ice cap. Neptune is also circled by small moons and dusty rings. The largest of the moons is Triton and it is thought to be the coldest place in the solar system, with temperatures below −230°C.

Pluto

Pluto is the smallest planet in our solar system and also the most distant for most of the time. It is only two-thirds of the size of Earth's Moon and it takes 248 earth years to orbit the sun once, following an elliptical path which brings it inside Neptune's orbit occasionally.

Deep space

Once we move out of our solar system, we really are into unknown territory. We know that our star, the Sun, is just one of billions of stars in our galaxy, the Milky Way. This is a flattened, spiral shaped disc, rather like a Catherine Wheel firework. On a clear night, away from the light pollution of towns and cities, it is sometimes possible to see the Milky Way. We are looking across the disc, so it appear as a stripe of dense stars across the night sky.

Because the Earth orbits the Sun, we are constantly changing position relative to the other stars in the galaxy. Consequently, we see different arrangements of stars at different times of the year. We call these clusters of stars *constellations*. In ancient times, the constellations were given names of gods, monsters and mythical animals, probably to help people remember them. The 12 figures of the zodiac, mythical animals like

Pegasus (the winged horse), or heroes like Orion with his belt and sword, or the twins Castor and Pollux, can all be found in the night sky. In reality, the clusters of stars do not mean that the stars are actually close together. The star patterns are nothing more than accidents of perspective. What we tend to forget is that these other stars, like our own sun, are in motion. So the patterns change very slowly over time. However, because the distances are so vast, the motion is imperceptible except over very long time scales.

Our galaxy is only one of millions, perhaps billions, of galaxies which make up our *universe*. Astronomers believe the universe was first formed billions of years ago and is still expanding.

WHAT DO PRIMARY CHILDREN ALREADY KNOW?

As with other areas of science, children come to their science activities with a number of ideas relating to physical processes. Their ideas vary in accuracy and appropriateness. Initially, 'magic' may be how a number of phenomena are explained. By Key Stage 2, there are some common misconceptions that you may have to deal with. For example, with *Forces*, young children may believe that the higher an object, the more it weighs. They justify this by reference to the greater impact it makes when dropped. With magnetism, until they can distinguish different types of metals, they are likely to identify things made from any metal as being attracted to a magnet. Osborne and Freyaberg (1985) found that 9-year-olds use a 'pulling' or 'sucking' model to explain magnetism – the magnet sucks the object to it.

The media have promoted the idea of *Energy* as a physical entity. Advertisements on television show boxes of electricity being sold over the counter in a shop, and tell of the stored energy in drinks, sweets and batteries and glowing children. Indeed, teachers themselves often talk about 'stored' energy. Very young children can have the idea that electricity, like water, is 'stored' behind walls. Press the switch and, like turning on the tap, electricity pours out. If the switch is left in the on position and nothing is plugged in, electricity will slowly run out and disappear. Another idea is that the electricity flows from a battery to a bulb and is used up lighting the bulb so there is no need for a return wire to complete the circuit.

There has been a lot of research into children's understanding of how we see. Primary age children often hold a model in which light 'rays' travel from the eyes to the object. Similarly, they are confused over sources and reflectors of light, particularly in connection with the Moon which is seen as a light source in its own right. Even something like shadows can create problems. Place an object in the shadow of another, larger object and some children believe that the former will have a shadow twice as dark as the latter.

With the topic *Earth and Beyond*, young children may initially believe in a flat Earth, rather like a floating dustbin lid. This is slowly modified with time and the Earth assumes a flattened ball shape with people living at first only on the upper flat part. Later, people live on both sides although sometimes on their heads on the lower surface. As the model of a spherical earth develops, children's lack of understanding of gravity may still lead them to draw people in the opposite hemisphere standing on their heads. Night and day and the Earth's rotation can also be a problem. Initially, the Sun is seen as moving, not the Earth. The space between Earth and 'sky' is sometimes seen as a void, with objects like the Sun, clouds and stars hanging from the underside of the sky. Clouds may also be used by children to explain the phases of the Moon and eclipses.

WHAT DO THE CHILDREN NEED TO KNOW?

The experiences you organize for your class to introduce them to the basic ideas associated with the physical processes need to be related to the National Curriculum requirements for Sc4, summarized in Table 6.1. So, how do you begin to teach children about the physical processes?

STARTING POINTS FOR THE CLASSROOM

Underpinning the National Curriculum Order for Science and the Circular 4/98 guidance are a few fundamental concepts that you will want your children to acquire and understand. These can become your targets (or objectives) in lesson plans and assessment. These are:

Forces and motions

- Forces may be pushes or pulls which act on things in particular directions and can be measured.
- When objects are stretched or compressed, they also exert forces on whatever is stretching or compressing them.
- Forces may change the shape of something, make things move or change the way they are moving.
- When something is not moving the forces acting on it are balanced; unbalanced forces make things speed up, slow down or change direction.
- Gravity is a force which pulls things towards the Earth and it is this which gives objects weight.
- Friction is a force which resists movement and it affects the size of the force needed to move things.
- Magnets attract or repel other magnets, depending upon which poles are brought together.
- Magnets exert noticeable forces on some other materials and can be used to make something move.
- When they are able to move freely, magnets align themselves roughly north–south.

Table 6.1 Overview of Sc4 of the National Curriculum Order for Science for Key Stages 1 and 2

♦ *Physical Processes* ♦

Electricity

KS1: 1a – *know about everyday appliances that use electricity;*
KS1: 1b – *know about simple series circuits;*
KS1: 1c – *how a switch can be used to break a circuit;*
KS2: 1a – *how to construct circuits to make electrical devices work;*
KS2: 1b – *how to change the number or type of components in a series circuit to make a bulb brighter or dimmer;*
KS2: 1c – *how to represent series circuits by drawings and conventional symbols and use these to construct circuits.*

Forces and Motion

KS1: 2a – *find out about and describe the movement of familiar things;*
KS1: 2b – *know that pushes and pulls; are examples of forces;*
KS1: 2c – *recognise that when things speed up, slow down or change direction there is a cause;*
KS2: 2a – *about forces of attraction and repulsion between magnets and magnetic materials;*
KS2: 2b – *that objects are pull downwards because of gravitational attraction between them and the Earth;*
KS2: 2c – *know about friction and air resistance as a force which slows things down or prevents them from starting to move;*
KS2: 2d – *when objects are pushed or pulled an opposing pull or push can be felt;*
KS2: 2e – *how to measure forces and identify the direction in which they act.*

Light and Sound

KS1: 3a – *identify different light sources including the Sun;*
KS1: 3b – *that darkness is the absence of light;*
KS1: 3c – *that there are many kinds of sound and sources of sound;*
KS1: 3d – *that sounds travel away from sources and get fainter and they are heard when they enter the ear;*
KS2: 3a – *that light travels from a source;*
KS2: 3b – *that shadows are formed because light cannot pass through some materials;*
KS2: 3c – *that light is reflected from surfaces;*
KS2: 3d – *that we see things only when light from them enters our eyes;*
KS2: 3e – *that sounds are made when objects vibrate, but vibrations are not always directly visible;*
KS2: 3f – *how to change the pitch and loudness of sounds produced by some objects;*
KS2: 3g – *that vibrations from sound sources require a medium through which to travel to reach the ear.*

The Earth and Beyond

KS2: 4a – *that the Sun, Earth and Moon are roughly spherical;*
KS2: 4b – *that the position of the Sun appears to change during the day and the effect this has on shadows;*
KS2: 4c – *that the Earth spins on its own axis, and how day and night relate to this spin;*
KS2: 4d – *that the Earth orbits the Sun once each year, and the Moon takes approximately 28 days to orbit the Earth.*

Energy

- Electricity only flows when there is a complete circuit of conducting material for it to flow around.
- Insulating materials resist the flow of electricity.
- The amount of electricity which can flow in a circuit (the current) depends upon the battery (the voltage) and the materials (the resistance) in the circuit.
- Bulbs, switches, buzzers and other components in a circuit may be represented in a circuit diagram using agreed symbols.
- Some objects produce light and some reflect it.
- Some objects obstruct light, causing shadows, and some let it pass through.
- Objects can be seen because of the light which they either produce or reflect.
- Light normally travels in a straight path; mirrors can reflect light, changing its direction.
- Eyes are light detectors; we see because light from objects enters our eyes.
- Sound spreads out from a source, travelling in all directions at once and gradually becoming fainter as it spreads.
- Loud sounds can travel further than quiet sounds.
- Sound is produced by objects which are vibrating.
- Objects of different sizes and shapes vibrate at different rates and give sounds of different pitches.
- Ears are sound detectors; we hear when sound vibrations enter our ears.
- Sound travels through solids, liquids and gases, but travels in some substances more easily than in others.

Earth and beyond

- The Sun, the planet Earth and the Moon are roughly spherical.
- The Earth turns on its own axis, so we have day and night, with each complete turn taking 24 hours.
- The Earth is held by the gravity of the Sun and so it orbits the Sun, taking one year to complete an orbit.
- Because the Earth's axis is tilted, some parts of the planet receive more light and heat at certain times of the year than others, giving us the seasons.
- The Moon is a small, planet-like body which orbits the Earth, taking one month to do so.
- The apparent shapes of the phases of the Moon are due to part of it being in shadow and the fact that we see it from different angles at different times of the month.
- The Earth is only one of the planets in our solar system.

This is a huge area that can be subdivided into a number of topics for different age ranges in a progressive scheme of work.

Work on the physical processes (Sc4) is a good vehicle for practical work of all kinds (Sc1, discussed in Chapter 3). Experiments and investigations can be directed and managed fairly easily, effects are often immediate, and such tasks are good for practising data handling, recording, searching for patterns and other skills and processes. Forces and energy are also fundamental to work in design and technology, so there is an opportunity here for cross-curricular links.

Forces and motion

This is such a large area that in many schools teachers are likely to subdivide it and integrate parts with broader cross-curricular topics. For example,

Area	Topic
Forces and their Effects	Toys, Bridges, Houses and Homes, Making Life Easier, Things Which Help Us, Machines
Forces and Motion	Moving Around/On the Move, Bicycles/Cycle Training, Transport, Visit to a Railway Station, Traffic Census
Friction	Moving Around, Slipping and Sliding, Best Buys (e.g. Training Shoes)

Very young children need to develop an appropriate vocabulary for describing and classifying forces in the world around them such as pulling out trays or pushing doors closed or twisting doorknobs and taps. The classroom and school environment can be a source for a Forces Hunt in which they learn not only to recognize and classify different forces but also to use the appopriate vocabulary. A forces table could be set up with objects and toys that involve different forces. Various sources of forces should be experienced: human forces in action, pushing, pulling and twisting and natural forces such as the wind blowing litter around. Our dependence on forces should also be illustrated. Observation and direct contact would allow children to explore forces at work in toys or in means of transport like push-chairs and bicycles.

Older children could explore the effects of forces of different magnitudes. They should be introduced to force meters so that they can feel directly what a range of forces is like, for example, 1N compared to 10N compared to 100N force. This leads into work on gravity and movement. Ideas to do with fair testing and control of variables fit in well here. The movement of toy cars on slopes may be investigated and the effect of the weight of the car, the angle of the slope and the type of surface on the ramp can all be explored. Using force meters the effects of pulling blocks of different masses on different surfaces may be investigated, leading into work on friction and using machines to help us do jobs more easily.

Relevant contexts should be provided for these kinds of activities so that the children can relate what they are doing to the real world. Work on friction could be to do with choosing the best training shoes for running on sports day.

Starting with stories and rhymes is always useful with young children. Traditional tales like *The Three Billy Goats Gruff* or musical rhymes like *London Bridge is Burning Down* can lead to work on bridges and structures and forces. With older children, introduce simple biographies of people like Galileo and Newton to help humanize the subject.

Magnetism and electricity

Magnetism tends to be treated as a topic on its own with opportunities being provided for younger children to investigate different kinds of magnets, see what objects they attract and determine the relative strengths of magnets by counting the number of paper clips or pins each will pick up. Older children can determine the materials through which magnets will work and find the limits of thickness. They might also make magnets by stroking steel knitting needles with a magnet. Activities using plotting compasses can be linked to work in geography. Electromagnetism may be introduced once the children have appropriate experiences of electricity. Designing and making games and toys which use magnets is an interesting challenge for older Key Stage 2 pupils in design and technology.

Electricity as a topic needs to have good foundations. Very young children need to acquire the underlying concepts of push and flow in order that they can make sense of analogies. Water play in the nursery and reception class starts this off, pouring water through funnels and tubes and using mechanical pumps provides useful early experiences on which to build. With older children, extend the experiences with other examples such as water flowing in gutters and streams and sand flowing in egg-timers. The water circuit can then be introduced with appropriate vocabulary. Young children can make simple electrical circuits, rearranging and testing the components in different combinations. Older children can then convert the three-dimensional circuits into two-dimensional circuit drawings and begin to design and make their own circuits and predict effects. They can explore which materials conduct electricity and apply their ideas, designing and making such things as traffic lights, motor driven buggies and lighthouses. With older KS2 children, the central role of electricity in our lives may be explored, perhaps through a visit to a power station to link ideas to electricity in the home and to matters of safety. Introduce people from the history of science, like Gilbert, Volta and Edison. Look for stories which have a relevant theme.

Mechanical energy

Because of its abstract nature, energy is a difficult concept to introduce to primary children. Toys are a useful teaching device, allowing children to explore directly the idea of 'something waiting to change'. Mechanisms can be examined to identify what the components do and work in design and technology can draw on this.

Light

Like magnetism and electricity, light tends to be treated as a topic in its own right. Sometimes it is combined with colour and linked to art work. However, these topics can be difficult for primary children because they can often be treated in an abstract way. Concrete examples, analogies and appropriate hands-on experiences are all crucial to effective work on light. Start from relevant events in real life such as a power cut or winter illuminations. Younger children may observe themselves in mirrors and spoons to see the effect of flat and curved surfaces. Reflectors and shiny things in the classroom, school or home can be found. Provide opportunities for older children to experience and explore the properties of light. Challenges like, *Can you get the torch to shine round a corner?* can start discussions. Periscopes and kaleidoscopes can be introduced. Patterns and regularities can be explored so that children can construct the rule that the angle of incidence equals the angle of reflection in their own words. Colour leads to a lot of cross-curricular opportunities and to matters beyond the classroom such as road safety (for example, *the best colours to be seen*).

Sound

Young children love making sounds (or perhaps noise) and this can be a starting point for their science work. By exploring simple musical instruments, they can be introduced to the sorts of sounds they can make, the source of the vibration and the relationships between size and pitch. This can be built upon in KS2 with work on vibrations and pitch, and investigations of different materials for transmitting or absorbing sound. This can lead to the manufacture of home-made musical instruments in design and technology.

Earth and beyond

Earth and beyond is not a topic that lends itself well to first-hand, practical activities, other than things to do with shadows. However, it is an excellent vehicle for discussion, imagination and the use of secondary source materials to gather information. Remember that the children you teach will not be able to remember a time before the space age. Within their lives space probes, people travelling in space shuttles and views of the Earth from satellites are all part of everyday life. A short extract from a relevant science fiction film or television series will set the scene for one of the most popular topics in primary science, *Space*. Children love to talk about it and tell you their ideas, although some may be wildly inaccurate. However, the idea of what it is like in space and what we would need to do to live there can provide a focus for discussion and finding out the children's ideas. Demonstrations with model globes and the children themselves acting out the movements of the planets can help them to organize and consolidate their ideas. Children can be asked to keep records of what the Moon looks like at night and a large chart may be maintained at school. Prediction may be used to fill the gaps on the chart for nights that are cloudy. Scale models, stretching across the classroom or school hall, may be constructed drawing on art skills to paint the features of the planets. Such information can be downloaded from the Net or from one of the many CD-ROMS on the subject.

SUGGESTIONS FOR FURTHER READING

If you would like to explore further some of the issues touched upon in this chapter, the following books should be of interest to you.

Carey, J. (1995) *The Faber Book of Science*, London: Faber and Faber
John Carey is not a scientist, but a professor of English with an interest in well-written and comprehensible accounts of science. He has brought together in this book over one hundred readings, spanning the world of science past and present. Many relate to the physical processes and are worth reading. For example, for Earth and beyond, look at 'Galileo and the Telescope' (pp. 8–16) to read Galileo's own views almost 400 years ago and compare them with Isaac Asimov's views on 'Black Holes' today.

Farrow, S. (1999) *The Really Useful Science Book*, 2nd edition, London: Falmer Press
The basic ideas of science are introduced at a level suitable for primary teachers to help them meet the requirements of the National Curriculum Order for Science. Section 4 covers ideas related to physical processes and the Earth and beyond, supplementing those ideas explored briefly in this chapter.

Newton, D.P. and Newton, L.D. (1987) *Footsteps into Science*, London: Harcourt Brace Jovanovich
This is a set of 64 workcards and a teachers' guide, designed for use with KS2 and middle school pupils. Each card has a brief biography of a scientist, some suggested related science activities and some cross-curricular ideas. People like William Gilbert, Isaac Newton and Alessandro Volta are included.

7 What Do We Mean by Key Skills in Primary Science?

You may have heard about *key skills*. In essence, they are the *generic* skills that cross subject boundaries and are useful for life. They cover the following areas:

- application of number (numeracy skills);
- effective communication (communication skills);
- use of computers, etc. (information technology skills);
- improving one's own learning performance (study skills);
- effective interaction with others (skills for working with others); and,
- meeting needs and solving problems (problem solving skills).

(QCA, 1999, p. 8)

You will see that many of these key skills are directly relevant to primary science. Of particular importance are numeracy, communication, IT and problem solving skills.

In this chapter we shall begin by looking at problem solving in primary science and how it links to Sc1 activity. How to support and develop children's communication skills and links with literacy will then be considered. Finally, the use of ICT and numeracy will be explored.

PROBLEM SOLVING IN PRIMARY SCIENCE

Problem solving is not a subject; it is an approach or a way of thinking and working. Nor is it new to primary education or specific to any one curriculum area. As an approach, it fits well into the area of science. When problem solving, children are required to apply their basic and scientific skills in new contexts. They use higher order thinking skills, like inferencing, analysis and evaluation. They are given opportunities to develop social skills of cooperation and communication through their group work and discussion. Problem solving activity involves children in:

- dealing with difficult situations;
- overcoming obstacles;
- bringing about desired effects;
- resolving puzzling questions; or,
- getting required results.

Problem solving as an approach is useful in science because it involves processes of thinking and doing for some specific purpose. It is a means by which children can acquire, practise and demonstrate scientific skills and knowledge.

In Chapter 3, scientific investigation was discussed. As a teacher you should be aiming for the children to go beyond investigation to the point where they recognize problems for themselves and design and carry out their own investigations to solve them. Problem solving, while involving many aspects of scientific investigation, is a more complex process incorporating other skills. It requires of children active mental as well as physical participation and can be very effective in helping to build lasting understanding. To generate a solution to a problem, children need to recall prior knowledge and experiences, identify those that will be useful and transfer and apply them to new situations.

Children usually find well-organized problem solving exciting and stimulating. During problem solving, they have a sense of responsibility for their own learning and become self-reliant. This makes them feel independent and they gain self-confidence and self-esteem. They also learn to cooperate as team players in a group. They are strongly motivated to make their own decisions and persevere with the task to reach a solution. Problem solving also develops creative and critical thinking because the children have to think for themselves. The former involves looking at the problem from various angles and generating a variety of solutions. The latter requires reflection on experience, and informed choice to reach decisions.

You will find that planning for problem solving is not as straightforward as it might sound. First, you need to provide relevant contexts to which the children can relate. Work by Juniper (1989) indicates that you also need to be:

- *Decisional:* You need to think clearly about the purpose of the activity.
  (For example: What is the aim? How much control of the situation do you want to take? To what extent is the problem new to the children? How much freedom of action do you want to give them?)
- *Procedural:* You need to establish clear priorities in the organizational details to be considered.
  (For example: You need to think about targets and outcomes, progression in skills, knowledge and understanding, differentiation and support for individual needs, equal opportunities and links across the curriculum.)
- *Solutional:* You need to arrange the situation so the children have sharp and precise targets.
  (For example, if the children cannot reach a solution or if the route is tortuous, frustration develops and this can be demotivating. The children must have had the prerequisite experiences to make achievement possible.

They need to know what constraints are upon them in terms of time, resources, ways of working, recording methods, and so on.)

- *Generative:* You need to identify ideas and materials which can carry over from the present into future activities or problem solving sessions. (For example, ideas, hints, suggestions, resources can all provide cues and support transfer.)

Task 7.1 Contexts for problem solving	Problem solving is more meaningful and effective if embedded in real-world contexts. This was discussed earlier in relation to making science education relevant.

Think of some safe, real problems from around the home, the school or the neighbourhood that you could give to the children as problem solving activities in science. Choose one of them, and describe it briefly in terms of the needs identified above by Juniper. Use the headings:
- *decisional;*
- *procedural;*
- *solutional; and*
- *generative.*

COMMUNICATION AND LITERACY

Good communication skills are fundamental to success in most areas of life and are useful in most contexts in which children and teachers find themselves. It is:

> . . . absolutely essential that these skills are fostered across the whole curriculum in a measured and planned way.
>
> (NCC, 1989, p. 3)

Communication is both a mental and physical activity. It is valuable in the context of science because both teachers and children can learn something from the act of communicating. From the teacher's perspective, effective communication skills enable you to:

- provide a role model for effective communication;
- introduce new scientific vocabulary at appropriate times;
- create opportunities to explore the children's ideas more fully;
- note the gaps in their knowledge;
- identify the strengths amd weaknesses in their understandings; and,
- scaffold the learning that is taking place.

The children, on the other hand, learn to:

- make sense of their experiences, clarifying them and knit them together;
- sort their ideas into a logical order, sequencing events and deciding what is important and what can be ignored;
- produce structures or frameworks to represent the overall experience and synthesize their ideas;
- develop and use appropriate scientific vocabulary in different contexts and apply various language skills; and,
- step back to examine experiences from different perspectives and reflect upon them.

Task 7.2 Language and vocabulary problems in primary science teaching	Science has its own specialized vocabulary and terminology. How and when to introduce particular words and terms is left to the judgment of individual teachers, although the National Curriculum Order for Science does point the way.

Choose three commercially produced primary science schemes which have either books or workcards intended to be used by pupils.

Think of a science topic, perhaps one that you will be teaching on your next school placement. In each scheme, look for the material on that topic and read it through. Identify any specialist language being introduced and used (particular words or phrases, for example). Also look for:
- the density of the information given;
- the length of the sentences used;
- the clarity of the instructions and explanations;
- the use of abstract concepts;
- the use of analogy and metaphor;
- the use of illustrations to support the text.

Choose one of the schemes and re-write a section or activity of text in a way which suits the needs of the pupils you will be teaching.

You should view communication activities within science as part of the overall learning experiences being offered to children. It is not simply a way to collect evidence that opportunities for learning were provided and outcomes achieved. In particular, you need to think about how the children in your class can communicate and record effectively in science and how the literacy hour can be used to support the development of scientific thinking.

Children communicating and recording in science

One of the priorities for science education is to provide pupils, at all stages, with appropriate opportunities to communicate and interpret information. A requirement of the National Curriculum Programmes of Study for Science is that pupils should be taught to express themselves clearly, both in speech and in writing, to use scientific vocabulary appropriately and to use a variety of methods to present ideas and information. Carefully planned and controlled methods of recording can satisfy this requirement.

Why should children record during their science activities?

There are a number of good reasons to justify why children should record in some way what they are doing in science. To begin with, there is the argument of *accountability*. Increasingly, as a teacher you will feel the pressures of accountability to other colleagues, the headteacher, the governors and to parents. It is not unreasonable to feel that it is only by having plenty of children's work in exercise books and on display that you can be seen by the outside world as doing your job. This in turn is related to *credibility*, which is to some extent the converse. Some teachers may feel that they are somehow failing in their role if the children's books or folders are not filled with regular, weekly doses of 'what was done in science this week'. This can also be related to the third justification, that of *record keeping*. If children record their science work each session, then you have a convenient running record of science coverage and, possibly, their progress.

These arguments all focus on advantages for you as the teacher. From the children's point of view there are equally strong arguments related to supporting the development of their science skills, knowledge and understanding. Recording may be a *necessity*. Some form of recording may be an integral and essential part of that activity. For example, the children may be required in some way to record pulse rates of the members of their group during different physical acitivities and then later turn these results into a graph from which they can draw conclusions. Further, by recording in different ways during their science activities under your direction, they gradually *practise* and become skilled at the different methods. Later, they can select independently the ones which are most appropriate for the task in hand when carrying out full investigations and meeting challenges. If children record their science work, they should be thinking more deeply about it and internalizing the ideas. Thus recording acts as *reinforcement* for their learning and concept acquisition. It may also *stimulate* further science work, through replication of activities or the use of findings to raise new questions for investigation.

Children's recording – is it necessary?

All of the earlier justifications assume that children should record. Is recording always necessary? In some instances, the answer to this question should be: *No*. Children do not need to record everything they experience in their science work. Recording can occasionally be unnecessary, inappropriate and a waste of time. Recording is pointless if it is not fulfilling a worthwhile educational role. It becomes a time consuming chore, particularly when the same method is used over and over again. Under such circumstances less able pupils can become frustrated by their inability to record in the manner required. On the other hand, the more able children quickly go through the motions and become bored. In both cases, the end result can be that pupils become disenchanted with their science experiences and negative attitudes develop.

This does not have to be the case. There is a compromise. If children are required to record during the science activities with which they are involved, it is essential that the type of recording is matched to the type of science activity going on as well as to the needs and abilities of the children themselves. To be able to do this, you need to make available a variety of recording methods and the children need to have access to and develop facility with this variety over time. The aim is that eventually children will select for themselves the most appropriate method according to the nature of the science task, activity, or investigation.

How should children record their ideas?

There are several ways in which children can be asked to record in science. They vary with the age and ability of the children, but if they are introduced to the range and given opportunities to practise them in different contexts, they become competent and independent, adding to their communication repertoire. These ways can be loosely grouped as written, graphic and other records.

Written records

Free writing about science activities

The first stage in the writing process will be to encourage the children to describe in their own words what they did and perhaps generate some kind of explanation for what they found. Oral questioning by you will help guide and structure this process. In the case of the youngest children, or with those less competent at writing, you could ask questions and note what the child says about the science experiences, perhaps annotating pictures. As the children grow older and their writing skills develop, they can begin to do this for themselves. At first, accounts are likely to be descriptive and detail out of sequence. Again, discussion and oral questioning can guide and focus attention on what is important in developing understandings in science: *What did you already know about . . . ? What did you think might happen when . . . ? What did happen? Can you think of a reason why that happened? If we did this again with . . . what do you think . . . ?*

Structured worksheets

A shift from oral to written questioning can take place once children's reading and writing skills develop. Structured workcards or worksheets focus children's attention on what is relevant and encourage them to answer questions, make predictions, enter descriptive observations, give numerical data as results, put forward ideas or reasons for what they have found and generate some conclusions. Worksheets may be stored in files or glued into work folders, making the addition of related work or supplementary material possible. They can also go into portfolios as a part of the assessment evidence.

New technologies

The use of new technologies in general, and information and communications technology (ICT) in particular, is an aspect of the whole curriculum skills base to be developed with children of all ages. Hardware and software are so variable that the emphasis needs to be on children's general capabilities for using ICT skills in different contexts and for different purposes. There are numerous opportunities to use computers in science. The more obvious ones are word processing, spreadsheets, databases, processing to produce graphs and other presentations. Using information sources on CD-ROMs, and sensing the environment with I.T. controlled sensors should also be introduced with KS2 pupils.

Collective class display

Children's experiences should be shared. Class displays in the classroom, a corridor or in the main hall enable this sharing and valuing of experiences. Displays should be produced by the children themselves, be attractive and if possible interactive. Whenever possible, work in three dimensions as well as two. At the end of each week, work may be collected from two or three children (different ones each time) until the end of the topic when a full class display can be produced and presented.

Selecting appropriate methods

Which type of recording is suitable for children of different ages and abilities? The answer is that there is no hard and fast rule. Each has to be considered according to the task in hand. The degree of teacher support will also determine which can be used and when it can be used. However, Figure 7.2 summarizes a range of methods available and gives an indication of suitability for children at different stages. Very loosely, they are classified according to reading ability.

- Key Stage 1 – non-readers and those in the early stages of learning to read.
- Lower Key Stage 2 – readers who still need support, lack speed and confidence in reading or with limited comprehension skills and intonation ability.
- Upper Key Stage 2 – competent readers, fast, independent, who read with comprehension and intonation.

Science and the literacy hour

Few people would argue against the idea that children need to acquire good literacy skills and that such skills enable them to access the curriculum. Literacy skills are normally defined in relation to reading and writing and a literate person in any society is a person who can read, write and speak at a level suitable for a variety of purposes. Most teachers know from experience that children develop skills in relevant contexts,

	Write-ups	Work-sheets	Questions	Pictures	Diagrams	Cartoon strips	Before-&-after	Graphs: non-standard	Graphs: standard	Record-ing	Drama	Model making	Photo-graphs	ICT	Class record
1. Accountability	LU	LU	LU	IL	LU	U	L	IL	LU	ILU	LU	ILU	ILU	ILU	ILU
2. Reinforcement	LU	LU	LU	IL	LU	LU	ILU	IL	LU	-	-	ILU	ILU	ILU	ILU
3. Part of science	LU	LU	LU	IL	LU	-	L	IL	LU	-	ILU	ILU	-	-	ILU
4. Skill development	LU	LU	-	IL	LU	-	-	IL	LU	LU	LU*	ILU	LU	LU	ILU
5. Replication	LU	LU	-	L	LU	LU	L	IL	LU	U	-	ILU	ILU	-	ILU
6. Teacher credibility	LU	LU	LU	IL	LU	U	-	IL	LU	ILU	LU	ILU	ILU	-	ILU
7. Children's records	LU	LU	LU	-	U	-	-	-	LU	-	-	ILU	-	-	ILU
8. Stimulation	-	LU	LU	IL	U	U	I	IL	LU	U	ILU	ILU	ILU	LU	ILU

Figure 7.2 Methods available for children to record in primary science

I = Infant / KS1; L = Lower Junior / lower KS2; U = Upper Junior / upper KS2; * = social skills and the idea of relevance has already been introduced in Chapter 2. Children first learn to speak and then they learn to represent (write) and interpret (read) these utterances in the form of written symbols. The constancy of such representations and interpretations is governed by rules of language that also form part of the children's learning. In an attempt to raise standards of literacy, the National Literacy Strategy (DfEE, 1998) has been included in the curriculum offered by primary schools.

> Literacy unites the important skills of reading and writing. It also involves speaking and listening which, although they are not separately defined in the Framework, are an essential part of it. Good oral work enhances pupils' understanding of language in both oral and written forms and of the way language can be used to communicate. It is also an important part of the way pupils read and compose texts.
>
> (p. 1)

For most primary age pupils his has resulted in a discrete area of experience dominating the first part of the morning: the *Literacy Hour*. Although the literacy hour cannot be used specifically to teach science, the converse is true. Literacy can be improved through areas of the curriculum such as science. The National Literacy Framework requires children to develop skills and strategies involving:

- giving directions;
- demonstrating and modelling;
- scaffolding;
- explaining;
- questioning;
- investigating ideas;
- discussing and arguing;
- listening to and responding;
- instructing and guiding; and
- exploring.

These all have a place in science. Parkin and Lewis (1998) argue that,

> Science has its own literacy, its own vocabulary and forms, which a child needs to understand in order to develop as a scientist and as a literate person.
>
> (p. 5)

This produces two separate but connected targets for developing literacy and science:

- developing the literacy *of* science: using science to develop appropriate vocabulary and various recording conventions, particularly writing; and,
- developing literacy *through* science: using science as an area of experience to promote literacy skills.

Parkin and Lewis suggest that the cooperative teaching of science and literacy will foster the development of both.

> This is fully in keeping with the views of Ofsted, which recommended that: . . . schools should ensure that literacy and numeracy are supported by and developed in science, pupils are given insufficient opportunity to communicate scientific ideas in writing, particularly where activities are based on worksheets; and many opportunities for developing and using literacy and numeracy in science should be exploited.
>
> (Ofsted, 1998, p. 3)

Such opportunities include:

1   using science language for specific and defined purposes;
2   using stories and rhymes which have science-related themes;
3   examining science non-fiction text;
4   supporting varied approaches to children's recording and communicating scientific ideas and findings; and,
5   use of ICT in science contexts.

Using science language

Science has its own language and this can often cause problems for children. Some words have different meanings in science to everyday life. For example, think of how we use words like weight and materials in those contexts. Other words have precise meanings, for example digestion and reflection, but can be used loosely or inaccurately. Children bring common-sense understandings and experiences to their use of such words. As their teacher, you should model orally the correct use of such vocabulary. Opportunities to talk about science and listen to television programmes can also help extend children's experience. Finally, the use of written word banks and science dictionaries can support children's accurate use of words.

Task 7.3 Scientific vocabulary	Go through the NC Order for Science for KS1 and 2 and for each sub-area (e.g. Green plants as organisms, . . .) make a word list of those words that tend to be used only in science.

Make sure that you are clear in your own mind what each of them means.

Identify words that have a common, everyday meaning as well as a special scientific use or words that have several meanings.

For a topic that you are currently involved in on a school placement, think about the scientific words that you will use with the children. Try writing explanations for some of the key words. Write exactly what you would say to the children.

What approaches might you use in the classroom to help the children to use science language appropriately?

Using stories

The use of children's fiction may play a large part in the literacy hour. There is no reason why this fiction cannot have a scientific focus. Alternatively, story time at the end of the day can have the same approach. Think about stories from:

- *Children's literature:* There is a wealth of literature available, much of which has elements of science in it. For example, some tried and trusted fiction includes Ted Hughes' *The Iron Man* and *The Iron Woman* (materials), Alan Garner's *Elidor* (electricity) or Clive King's *Stig of the Dump* (pollution). It is worth spending an hour or two in a book shop browsing through the stocks and compiling a list to suit your children's interests and abilities. Such stories (or extracts from them) may be used as starting points for children's questions and investigations. For example, Pamela Allen's *Who Sank the Boat* is an excellent introduction to the problems of floating and sinking and can be used successfully with Reception age children or Year 6 children, depending on how you develop the investigation. Alternatively, children may use their scientific ideas to finish off a story.
- *Stories from history:* The lives of scientists and people from the past can be used to introduce ideas in science and simultaneously show scientists as real people with feelings and a life outside of the laboratory. They can also be used to break down the stereotypical image of scientists as white, male, bespectacled, bearded, bald and in a white coat. This could lead to setting up investigations to replicate in simple ways what some scientists in the past did and discovered.
- *Contemporary issues from the media:* Real and relevant starting points for topics may be extracted from something happening in the world today. Cuttings from local newspapers about a proposed building site or new town by-pass may link to work on structures and forces or the local environment and ecosystem balance. A video snip from a children's news programme about floods and hurricanes in another part of the world may link to work on weather or environmental issues. Cuttings from newsapapers may stimulate fruitful debates about issues like Dolly the sheep (genetic engineering), deodorant sprays (ozone depletion) and food labelling (genetically modified crops), particularly with older KS2 pupils.
- *Children's own stories:* The stories do not have to be created outside the classroom. Sometimes the children can use their science ideas and experiences to create stories that can then be read to their class or acted in a model theatre in D and T.

Examining non-fiction texts

Non-fiction texts are usually used on an occasional basis, dipped into rather than read from cover to cover. This means that children need skills like using contents and index pages, skimming, scanning and recognizing what is relevant. They are often supplemented by other forms such as diagrams, tables and graphs. Children need to understand how to 'read' this form of information, too.

Task 7.4 Using stories in science	Visit a local bookshop and compile a list of children's fiction which you could use for the science topic you are teaching on your next school placement.

Look through some local newspapers and cut out articles that have a scientific interest and which you could use with your class. Add them to your resource file.

Identify someone from the history of science who worked in an area related to your school topic. Compile some biographical details and write a script that you could use with the children in your class. List some activities that you could carry out with the children to illustrate her/his work.

Task 7.5 Reading for a purpose in primary science	Reading textual materials that have a scientific content is one aspect of developing pupils' communication skills. Reading can be done in many different ways in the classroom, depending upon the ages, abilities and prior experiences of the pupils.

They might:
- Listen to the teacher read from a 'big book' while at the same time following the text;
- Take it in turns to read aloud from a common text (sometimes called a round-robin approach);
- Read the text aloud with a partner or small group;
- Read the text individually and in silence.

What are the advantages and disadvantages of each of the above? Think of it both from the point of view of the teacher and of the pupils. From what you have observed in schools, what kinds of reading activities have you met in science lessons? Are there others not listed above?

Supporting varied approaches to recording and communicating

You need to introduce children to a range of approaches to recording and communicating effectively in science. This has already been discussed in detail in this chapter.

Using ICT

Issues of information retrieval and effective communication apply to the use of computers and other similar technologies in the same way they apply to pencil, paper and textbooks. CD-ROMs and software packages may be used as tools to promote literacy. This is the focus of the final section of this chapter.

SCIENCE AND NUMERACY

With the government's current focus on raising standards, there has also been the introduction of a National Numeracy Strategy. The DfEE (1998) defined numeracy as knowing about numbers and number operations. As well as developing an ability to solve number problems, including those involving money and measurements, children are expected to become familiar with:

> . . . the ways in which numerical information is gathered by counting and measuring and is presented in graphs, charts and tables.

(p. 2)

Clearly, it is in this last aspect that links with science have most to offer. Numeracy skills may be developed and practised in relevant scientific contexts throughout the primary school. Investigations which generate data for recording, manipulation and interpretation use numeracy skills. At the same time, numeracy supports the search for patterns and relationships, so crucial for underpinning the construction of conceptual understanding. Therefore data handling in science is a critical area for children for both numeracy and science. Science investigations are a major source of numbers. In your teaching you will need to:

- Ensure that the children's mathematical experiences match what is needed for the science investigations.
  (Check on pupils' earlier experiences in mathematics to make sure their prior knowledge is adequate.)
- Make the mathematics content of the investigations explicit for the children.
  (At the start of the investigation, discuss with the children the kinds of data they will collect and remind them of the things they need to think about.)
- Provide appropriate measuring equipment for generating data.
  (Check that the equipment is available, functioning properly and that the children know how to use it.)
- Provide models and examples of recording and handling data.
  (Give the children some practical exercises in recording and data handling.)
- Help children to search for and learn to recognize patterns in tables, charts and graphs.
  (Model how to search for patterns in tables, charts and graphs, and how to read the patterns and trends and to draw conclusions. Invented data can often do this better than real data, at least initially.)
- Support database and graphing skills, perhaps with the use of ICT.
  (Children can waste a lot of time trying to create tables, charts and graphs when this is not the object of the exercise. Some excellent software packages are very user-friendly and can help the children to create clear graphs and reach the goal of looking for patterns in the data quickly.)

INFORMATION AND COMMUNICATIONS TECHNOLOGY

Commerce and industry now depend on computers, from banking and stock control to payroll processing. In the home, information services like Ceefax, Teletext and

Task 7.6 How confident are you at using ICT?

Read through the following and decide where on the rating scale you fall.

Use: 5 = Very confident/no problems at all
       4 = Confident/occasional problems I can usually solve
       3 = OK but sometimes need to ask for help
       2 = Not very confident/often need help
       1 = Will not use it at all/not at all confident

 1 Videorecorder ....
 2 Videocamera ....
 3 Film strip/slide/carousel projector ....
 4 Overhead projector ....
 5 Making transparencies for the OHP using ICT ....
 6 Photocopier ....
 7 Computers – range of hardware platforms ....
 8 Computers – level of technical capability ....
 9 Concept/overlay keyboard ....
10 Word processing ....
11 Data handling ....
12 Spreadsheets ....
13 Data-logging ....
14 Desktop publishing ....
15 CD–ROM ....
16 Authoring packages (like Hypercard or Toolbox) ....
17 The Internet ....
18 E-mail ....
19 Graphing calculator ....
20 Scanner ....

(max. proficiency = **100** points)

How well did you do? Use your score to work out a personal action plan to develop and refine your ICT skills and competences.

telephone systems, entertainment centres, cooking and washing appliances are often subject to computer processing to varying degrees. It is hardly surprising that information technology has to have a place in children's education.

It is the DfEE's belief that:

> Using the Internet can motivate children, improve subject learning, reading skills and much more.

> (Logan, 1998, p. 25)

Most schools have a co-ordinator for ICT who usually works closely with the subject co-ordinators. You should find that there are several sources of help and ideas for using ICT in science. The important thing to remember is that hardware and software varies from school to school. You will need to develop general ICT skills to allow for these differences (see Higgins and Miller, 2000). This book is concerned only with the use of ICT in the context of primary science. So what does ICT have to offer science and vice versa?

Information technology and science

ICT in its broadest sense includes not only computers, but also other technologies like tape recorders, videorecorders, fax machines, photocopiers and cameras. The role of ICT in industry, commerce and our daily lives is so great that its place in the science curriculum seems self-evident. However, its utility is not the sole justification for its inclusion. After all, there is much that is useful that does not have a place in a child's education. What does ICT offer?

- ICT is a legitimate part of science, a tool to aid thinking and working.
- ICT skills are potentially useful for acquiring scientific knowledge and under-standing both in and out of school. It has the potential to extend the com-petence of an individual in many facets of life in the home, at work and in leisure. Since these are often science and technology related, information processing and handling skills have a wider application.
- In developing ICT skills, children are encouraged to develop logical thinking, problem solving abilities and information-finding capabilities, all valuable in science.
- There is a need to develop a critical awareness of the role of ICT in science. It is important to know its strengths and weaknesses, not only what it can and cannot do but also what it should and should not do. ICT is a tool to achieve ends, not an end in itself.

ICT in schools is not delivered solely through science. Its cross-curricular potential is recognized in the National Curriculum and it is one of the clusters of skills identified within the programmes of study for all National Curriculum areas. For example, in science the requirement is that:

> Pupils should be given opportunities, where appropriate, to develop and apply their information technology (IT) capability in their study of science.
>
> (DFE, 1995, p. 1)

In the programme of study for Key Stages 1 and 2 that has become known as Sc0 (the requirements to be applied across Sc1, Sc2, Sc3, and Sc4) it states:

> 1. Systematic enquiry
>   Pupils should be given opportunities to . . .
>   (d) use IT to collect, store, retrieve and present scientific information.
>
> (DFE, 1995, p. 2 and p. 7)

So how do schools use ICT? As a starting point, you need to find out the different ways in which teachers use ICT in science. There are a number of uses to consider including:

- word processing and general communication skills;
- accessing information on CD-ROMs;
- data handling and presentation, spreadsheets and data bases;
- sensing the environment;
- modelling, games and simulations;
- using the information superhighway.

Task 7.7 Using information and communications technology in primary science	Discuss with your class teacher and/or with the science co-ordinator the use of ICT in primary science lessons. In particular, consider the advantages and disadvantages of the use of ICT. Focus especially on: • what we mean by ICT; • the variety of ways ICT might be used;

- the learning and behavioural outcomes from the use of ICT;
- the range of hardware available and the skills needed to use it;
- the range of software available and the time needed to become familiar with it;
- teachers' personal levels of competence in ICT;
- children's general skills in using ICT;
- time management and the use of ICT;
- the organizational issues that arise from using ICT in science.

Prepare a 250 word position statement in defence of the use of ICT in primary science and discuss it with your class teacher.

Word processing and general communication skills

A common use of the computer is as a word processor, a means to record, extend and communicate findings in science. The computer organizes and presents text in forms that are different to those the children are able to produce by hand. Illustrations can often be taken from a bank of pictures stored by the software or drawn on the screen using a software package's draw facility and integrated with the text. Children may compose and record their findings individually or in groups. They can then present them to another child or group to edit. This encourages discussion, helps clarify ideas and leads to explanations and raising questions for further investigation. A class newspaper could serve as the end product of their activities.

Very young children may need the help of an amanuensis – someone to type in information. Some schools use peer tutoring sessions for this purpose with older pupils taking responsibility for a younger child. Overlay or concept keyboards are also supportive in this respect. They operate with simple word processing packages like *Folio* or *PromptWriter*. Concept keyboards are useful for recording with young children or less able pupils as they call for little or no reading and writing skills. Using a grid, the teacher programmes the overlays with words, pictures or symbols to suit the individual topic under study. The overlay is then placed on the keyboard. Pushing a square on the grid (a word or picture, for example) triggers a command representing that keyword or idea which then appears on the screen. Hence, text or stories can be constructed. Although this may restrict the communication of scientific experiences to basic descriptive writing, it can be used in conjunction with a conventional computer keyboard.

Older pupils might learn to construct memo boards on the computer to store and retrieve their own files as they work with them. Simple desk top publishing packages can be introduced so that reports can be enhanced with illustrations and format and layout variations.

Task 7.8 Using your ICT skills to design science resource sheets	For a science topic of your choice, design and create a task/activity/work sheet for pupils of a specified age. Use as many of your ICT skills as you can.

Try the sheet out with a small group of children. How do they respond?

Evaluate your sheet. What could you do to improve it?

Accessing information on CD-ROMs

One of the strengths of computers is the quantity of information that can be stored both in the computer's own memory and on discs. Whole encyclopaedias, complete guides to the human body and tours around our solar system are all possible with the computer. CD-ROMs allow children to interact with the programme.

Task 7.9 CD-ROMs in primary science	If the school where you are on placement has a computer with a drive for CD-ROMs, have a look at the packages that are available for science. List the packages. What age ranges

are they for? What aims and targets do they support? How does your class teacher or the science co-ordinator normally use them?

If you can, set up the computer to use one of the packages and have two children use the computer during a science lesson. Observe them as they do so. What problems (if any) do they encounter? How do they actually use the computer? What kind of interaction takes place between the children? What kind of help did you have to give?

Read through your notes and evaluate the session. What were the advantages and disadvatages of using the computer in this way? What could you do to make more effective use of CD-ROM packages?

Through CD-ROMs, the computer can support the teacher in developing know-ledge and understanding because it can act as instructor, demonstrator, guide and questioner. However, it is important to remember that a computer is only ever as good as the way it has been programmed; nor can it respond to a puzzled look (at least, not yet) and does not replace a teacher. Young children need to interact with real people.

Data handling and presentation: spreadsheets and databases

The computer is particularly adept at storing and sorting large quantities of information. When children carry out surveys or collect a lot of data, the advantages of information technology is immediately apparent. At its simplest, the procedure might be to use a simple word-processing package to design survey sheets and create organized lists of the observations or results. These could be saved and later retrieved for the addition of more data. For example, the children could design an observation sheet for checking the birds that visit the school field between 9.15 am and 9.45 am each morning. Are they different to those that visit between 1.00 pm and 1.30 pm each afternoon? The data can be entered in a data base and accumulated. The children might use software which identifies the birds for them and provides information such as appearance, size and feeding habits. Later, results could be automatically collated and charts and graphs produced for a presentation.

Data handling also requires the search for patterns and interpretation of the data to reach conclusions. The data can be qualitative and quantitative. In the process, the children learn about measurement and quantities, and explore numbers using spreadsheets which helps with mathematics and graph work. Since children must demonstrate their ability to do this in scientific investigation, the application of science skills like classification, observation, prediction and interpretation to information stored and classified in a database is an excellent extension of those same skills used in practical activity sessions. Dispositions like curiosity and perseverance may also be enhanced.

Branching database programmes can help children observe and classify objects by appearance. Programmes like *Animal, Vegetable, Mineral* encourage the children to structure their thinking into logical sequential steps and ask appropriate questions.

By using electronic floor turtles (or their equivalents) and LOGO-type programs children can also master their control of variables as in scientific investigations. Initially, they can use pre-prepared programs but once they have been introduced to the idea of variables they can begin to vary values and change the program themselves. The outcomes can be clearly seen and it is easy to predict and check the consequences of changing variables.

Data logging sensing the environment

A key function of information technology is to provide automatic and rapid measurement of the environment and items in it. In the real world, the children will experience electronic sensors which switch on street lights as dusk approaches and devices which sense movement and sound an alarm. In the kitchen, electronic timers on a cooker or the microwave oven tell them when food is ready to eat. The central heating system switches on and off in response to the changing temperature in the house. The videorecorder tapes their favourite programme when they are out. Even programmable toys use various kinds of information handling and sensing devices.

Using sensors to measure, collect and display data in investigations is a major application of computers in science. Data Harvest's *Ecolog* and Philip Harris's *First Search* are two familiar sensor packages used in primary schools. Sensors detect all kinds of changes in our environment – the passage of time, temperature change, light intensity, noise or movement. All are aspects of change which primary children are likely to measure and record and information technology allows them to do so with accuracy and ease. Programmes and the related hardware allow the children not only to sense their environment but also to feed the information into the computer's database, analyze it and prepare graphs and presentations to show the changes. These experiences of electronic control lead into their applications in new contexts, particularly in design and technology in meeting needs and solving problems or in the control of various products.

Modelling, games and simulations

Modelling or simulating a process or event is an important application for the computer in the classroom. Initially, the children can see that it has this potential through adventure programmes and games such as *Granny's Garden* or *The Rainforest Journey*. Such programmes set the activities in imaginary contexts with which the children can identify and they become actors in those contexts, drawing on their existing knowledge and understanding, acting on the information they receive and making decisions. Some programmes model real systems and environments, like the house central heating system or a pond or wood ecosystem. These are particularly useful for allowing children to explore the effects of human influences on those systems or environments.

Using the information superhighway

The Information Superhighway usually refers to a huge worldwide network of computers (the Internet), the information the networks carry (the World Wide Web or WWW), and the ability to use the network to communicate with others (usually through electronic mail or e-mail). The Internet is made up of thousands of clusters or regional networks scattered around the world that can communicate with one another. The Web is not the same as the Internet. WWW refers to the sites of information carried on the Internet. Browsers are pieces of software that enable you to view the WWW on your computer and navigate your way through the information. This is so vast that there is a need to limit the children's attention to a few good WWW sites for science. Some suggestions are listed in *Appendix 1: Help and Information* at the end of this book.

One of the best ways to show that you understand something is to explain it to others. Similarly, one of the best ways to help children construct their understanding in science is to encourage them to explain their ideas to others. Normally, this is done in the classroom through children communicating with one another, orally and in writing. Often the teacher discusses their ideas with them, raises questions and even challenges their thinking. Using the computer and the information superhighway involves the children in electronic communication: communication with other computers in other schools, industries, communication centres and other countries.

Choosing which software to use

In some ways choosing software for use in science is no different to choosing a good book to use with the class. As a teacher, you want the software to do a number of things:

- to communicate successfully;
- to use effective teaching strategies;
- be an interesting and worthwhile alternative to other ways of working.

At the same time, there are important differences between a piece of computer software and a book. For example, a book is deaf to the response of the reader, while the computer can enter into some form of dialogue with the user, depending upon the software. However, a book needs no introduction or instruction manual on how to use it, it can be borrowed easily and it does not need a power supply. It also tends to be much more portable and tolerant of abuse than the computer. The physical differences between textbooks and computers tend to conceal a common purpose, that is to support effective teaching and learning. It is, therefore, useful to forget the physical differences between the two and focus on judging the software as you would a textbook. Think about things like the level at which the language is pitched, the choice of vocabulary, length of sentences and even the font used. What about the effectiveness of the illustrations? Are real photographs preferable to cartoon characters? Do the characters move? There is also a need to consider the kind of learning which is supported: is it the recall of facts, procedures, understanding or application in new situations? However, the differences between the two cannot be ignored. If a book is opened at the wrong page the mistake is easy to remedy. What happens if a wrong key is pressed? Does the system crash or does the child have to sit through screen after screen of information before returning to where he wants to be?

The use of television and video recordings

ICT can be interpreted in a broader sense than merely applying the use of computers but, as with computers, there are varying degrees of competence. For example, can you use an overhead projector? Can you adjust the OHP so that the image is in focus and not a trapezoid? What about if the OHP bulb blows – can you change the bulb? You might be competent at sending e-mail but can you send file attachments. Photocopying A4 pages is fine, but what about multiple copies of double-sided A3 reduced pages?

Television and the associated videorecorder is frequently used in schools. The use of TV and video greatly increases the breadth and range of experiences you can offer the children in science. It is possible, however, to become too dependent upon it. The children become passive observers of a time-filler. Some justifications of ways in which you can use TV and videorecordings effectively are:

- to capture the children's attention and set the scene;
- to cover and sum up broad chunks of content quickly and succinctly;
- to support understanding through analogies and examples not readily possible in the classroom;
- to make a learning goal more forcefully or spectacularly;
- to illustrate or compare scientific ideas;
- to stimulate questions and discussion;
- to enable re-play of ideas.

If a teacher uses a videorecording or television programme, the lesson should still be interactive. The reasons for the use of television and video must be clear to you as the teacher.

Task 7.10 Using television programmes and video recordings	Check your local newspaper or television guide to see what primary science programmes are being broadcast over the next few days. If possible, arrange to record one of them. If this is not possible, see whether your placement school has any broadcasts on tape which you could watch.

Watch the programme. What role does it serve in support of teaching and learning? Note:
- how the programme makes the science explicitly relevant;
- which key scientific ideas are being developed;
- the opportunities for practical activity and scientific investigation which arise from the programme;
- the language used;
- the resources used;
- the teaching methods and approaches used.

Think about how you would use such a programme as part of your primary science programme for half a term. What would your targets and outcomes be? How would it meet National Curriculum requirements?

Talk to your class teacher or the science co-ordinator about the use of television and videorecorded materials in primary science.

SUGGESTIONS FOR FURTHER READING

If you would like to explore further some of the issues touched upon in this chapter, the following books should be of some interest to you.

Association for Science Education (1998) *IT in Primary Science*, Hatfield: ASE
This is an illustrated and accessible guide to using computers in primary science. It contains over a hundred ideas for science activities, an extensive section on sensors and helpful descriptions of word processing, databases and spreadsheets. There is also a glossary and a review of sensors, software and resources available.

Parkin, T. and Lewis, M. (1998) *Science and Literacy: A Guide for Primary Teachers*, Nuffield Primary Science Series – Glasgow: Collins Educational
The *Science and Literacy* strand of the series links primary science to the National Literacy Strategy. This teacher's guide explains how literacy teaching and primary science can be combined effectively. The guide is supported by practical examples drawn from the Nuffield scheme and provides ideas, photocopiable activities and writing frames to help children develop their skills in science writing and reading.

Primary Science Review (1998) *Literacy and Numeracy Through Science*, Special Issue, No. 53, May/June 1998
This special issue includes useful articles on approaches to literacy through science, measurement, representations of scale and data handling.

PART 2

Your Science Teaching and Learning Base

Introduction

The mere existence of science as a body of knowledge and as a way of thinking and working is not, in itself, enough to justify its inclusion in the primary school curriculum. Only a fraction of children we teach will grow up to become professional scientists so we cannot argue that we must prepare them for a career in science. Therefore, why teach it?

There are a number of reasons. First, science is very well suited to the aims of primary education. The children *do* science, that is, they are active participants in scientific exploration, investigation and experimentation. Procedural competence is as important as conceptual knowledge. The skills and processes they practise and acquire and the traits encouraged in science are of general value in dealing effectively with the environment in which we live. Observing, weighing evidence, reaching conclusions are all important skills for life, not just for science.

Second, through science children gain knowledge and understanding of the world in which they live. Since science impinges on us all, an awareness of its nature and ways of working helps us to understand both the scientific society and the biophysical environment in which we live. Armed with such knowledge and understanding, we can make rational and reasoned decisions about them. Our scientific understanding and capability can be beneficial, benign or detrimental to varying degrees. Thousands of years ago, the effects of a small community chopping down trees for shelter and fuel and leaving waste materials behind as the by-products of their lives was of little consequence. Today, the destruction of rain forests, the pollution caused by industries and a population explosion can create environmental disasters. Everyone needs to be aware that a lack of understanding of science and its unwise application can have unexpected, sometimes serious, ramifications as well as benefits. At the same time, decisions should be humane. Science explains events in our biophysical environment and helps us to control them.

Third, science as an area of experience fulfils human needs. It provides interest, stimulation and challenge, involving people in meeting needs and solving problems.

This results in explanations of how things work and understandings of why things happen. Science is relevant to all of us, pervading all aspects of our lives, although this relevance is not always made explicit (Newton, 1989). In the primary school, science lends itself well to cross-curricular and integrated experiences, traversing traditional subject boundaries and using a wide range of skills and abilities. As such, it can be motivating for children who have a wide range of needs and abilities.

Finally, active participation in science activities and experiences may help to foster positive attitudes and beliefs about science and the scientist. There is evidence that children as young as 6 years of age have already developed a stereotypical image of scientists as male, white, bearded, balding, with spectacles and a special coat. They tend to place their scientists alone in laboratories, surrounded by glassware and chemical apparatus. Furthermore, the introduction of the National Curriculum does not seem to have made much difference to this image (Newton and Newton, 1998a). Children need to be introduced to science as an area of experience which is suitable for men and women and for people from all cultures and societies.

Task P2.1   Justifying science in your classroom

Imagine that you have to teach the following topics to your class:

- Growth (Y1, 5–6 years)
- Moving around (Y2, 6–7 years)
- Forces and motion (Y4, 8–9 years)
- Photosynthesis and green plants (Y6, 10–11 years)

For each topic, think about how you would respond to a pupil who says, 'This is boring – why are we doing it?'

How would you make the topics *explicitly* relevant? What would you do to avoid it being perceived as boring?

Ask your class teacher how s/he makes some of the more conceptually challenging or more abstract topics relevant.

What would you say to a parent at a parents' evening who says to you, 'Why is my child wasting time doing science when there's all this literacy and numeracy to do?'

There are many opportunities for science activity in the primary classroom. Your task as the teacher is to plan for and help the children to use such opportunities to achieve the aims identified above. What you are aiming for is summed up well by Ofsted in their *Handbook for the Inspection of Schools* (1996).

> Where teaching is good pupils acquire knowledge, skills and understanding progressively; the lessons have clear aims and purposes. They cater appropriately for the learning of pupils with differing abilities and interests, and ensure the full participation of all. The teaching methods suit the topic or subject as well as the pupils. The conduct of lessons signals high

expectations of all pupils and sets high but attainable challenges. There is regular feedback which helps pupils to make progress both through thoughtful marking and discussion of work with pupils. Relationships are positive and promote pupils' motivation.

(Ofsted, 1996, Part 4 Guidance: Quality of Teaching)

Task P2.2 Why teach science to primary children?	Think of the reasons for teaching primary age children science? You may be able to add more to the list given above. Turn your reasons into *aims*, by writing: 'Science is taught to primary age pupils in order to . . .'

When you are in school, preparing for your next teaching practice, look at the school's policy statement for science.
- Which aims are stated in the policy statement?
- Which aims did you see being translated into practice by your class teacher when s/he taught science?
- What are the aims for your teaching practice?
- Which of the aims do you think might be a problem for you when teaching science?

Identify any difficulties you might have with aims and discuss them with your school mentor.

The Department for Education and Science publication, *Science 5 – 16: a statement of policy* (DES, 1985), identified ten principles for good practice for planning and supporting the teaching of science. These are:

1	breadth	6	continuity
2	balance	7	progression
3	relevance	8	links across the curriculum
4	differentiation	9	teaching methods and approaches
5	equal opportunities	10	assessment

These criteria can serve as a checklist for you when thinking about your teaching and the learning you want to occur. As a teacher of primary science, you will need to ensure that the different aspects of science are planned for and offered to all the children in your class with these criteria in mind. This is the focus of the next five chapters, the science teaching and learning base you need to be effective in the classroom.

8 What Do We Mean by Progress in Learning in Science?

In this chapter, we will begin to look at the pedagogical knowledge and understanding you will need to secure pupils' progress in science – in other words to help them to learn. The principles underpinning progress in learning in science are the same for any area of experience. They are concerned with:

- the curriculum planned;
- the learning experiences offered;
- progression and continuity through those experiences.

As a teacher of primary science, you will need to match the learning experiences you offer the children with what you judge to be appropriate to their needs, abilities and interests, all within the framework of the National Curriculum Order for Science.

> Matching involves attempting to get the degree of challenge and success right – for many of the pupils for much of the time, at least. It means seeking to provide opportunities to consolidate and extend existing ideas and skills. Better matching will lead to better progression.
>
> (Keogh and Naylor, 1993, p. 125)

The importance of such match, and the lack of it with respect to planning for science in the primary classroom, was discussed by HMI (DES, 1978) and reiterated in the Non-Statutory Guidance offered by the National Curriculum Council in 1989.

> Providing appropriate learning experiences . . . requires careful planning and sensitive teaching by teachers with a broad understanding of science and the ability to match the work to their pupils' capabilities. Activities must challenge all pupils and, at the same time, provide them all with success at some meaningful level.
>
> (NCC, 1989, p. A9)

This suggests a three-sided partnership:

- you as the teacher: the quality of your planning, organization and choice of methods and approaches;
- the children as learners: what they bring to the learning situation; and,
- the science content: of the National Curriculum and its place in the broader curriculum framework.

Each of these might be expected to contribute to progress in children's learning. In planning for teaching and learning in primary science you will have to deal with a dynamic organism (the school as an organization) shaped by and in turn shaping the context in which it functions. The shape and direction of the curriculum is not only the product of the intentions of planning at central and local government levels. It is also influenced by an array of other factors over which planners have no control. Pupil numbers, especially with falling rolls, generate financial constraints. Public opinion, such as the falling standards debate, results in a focus on teacher accountability and credibility, perhaps leading to teaching only what is seen as important. A blind faith in scientism — an undue trust in measurable performances and objective procedures — ignores the non-measurable aspects of teaching and learning, the value-added dimension. These forces will all influence the decisions you take at both school and classroom level.

In this chapter, we look particularly at the concept of curriculum and children's learning in science and how these relate to the progression.

THE CURRICULUM FOR SCIENCE

The concept of curriculum in education is used in a variety of ways, from a very broad general term to encompass everything a school does to the very narrow specific term describing an educational activity designed for an individual child at a particular time in a particular area. Historically, schools have established curricula (content area courses) through which pupils progress with increasingly complex and precise learning experiences, often culminating in tests or examinations. This fits with the origin of the word curriculum, from the Latin *currere*, meaning 'the course to be run'.

Eisner (1979) provides a useful interpretation of the concept of curriculum.

> The curriculum of a school, or a course, or a classroom can be
> conceived of as a series of planned events that are intended to have
> educational consequences for one or more students.

(p. 39)

The key words here are *series, planned* and *consequences*. 'Series' suggests that you will need to identify more than one step or stage in the learning process to be taken in order or sequence. 'Planned' identifies your aims or purposes for the experiences to be offered. 'Consequences' indicates that no matter what you intend, the total learning experience is likely to be greater for the child than that which was offered. Since children differ in social and cultural backgrounds, prior experiences, and aptitudes and interests, the curriculum offered might be identical for all but that received can never be identical. What children actually learn will inevitably be different from and wider than what teachers intend to teach. While planning is important, what is equally important is the quality of those experiences. To be an effective teacher you will need to recognize and value the learning process that the children use instead of simply evaluating or assessing the outcomes.

When thinking about the curriculum for primary science there is a clear balance in the content between skills and processes to be developed and the body of knowledge to be acquired. You will need to offer a broad and balanced curriculum through which the children are constructing both procedural and conceptual understanding. The criteria for good practice identified by HMI (1985) define breadth and balance.

All pupils should be introduced to the *breadth of science*, both in terms of the natural and physical sciences and also science as a way of thinking and working. Experiences need to support the development of skills that underpin science as a process. They also need to support the acquisition of conceptual understanding: the facts, ideas and generalizations that underpin science as a body of knowledge and which explain living things, materials, forces, energy and Earth and its place in space.

Since all pupils are required to study science throughout their school lives, the programmes designed to achieve this must reflect a *balance of the major components of science* and also make provision for all pupils to have access to these components. The National Curriculum Order for Science selects *Life Processes and Living Things*, *Materials and their Properties* and *Physical Processes* to represent the major components of conceptual knowledge and defines the skills to be practised in *Scientific Enquiry* (formerly *Experimental and Investigative Science*). Each should be given a fair and reasonable representation in activities. Through conscious planning, equal weighting must be given to the development of skills as well as to the acquisition of concepts in science. This orientation is important for the way it manifests itself in the classroom situation and its consequences in terms of learning opportunities.

First, the planning, teaching and learning would generally be activity-centred, requiring pupils to draw on prior skills and knowledge to identify new problems for inquiry. Such problems might be given by the teacher or identified by the children (collectively or individually) during their activities. Second, the teaching strategies used require you as the teacher to do more than simply generate questions for investigation (or help the children to do so). Once embarked on an investigation, the teacher needs to use a variety of strategies, such as questioning, to direct children's attention to levels of thinking they would be unlikely to use without such support.

> The teacher has a positive role to play in cultivating 'the higher mental abilities' by virtue of the tasks provided in the curriculum, the materials that are used, and the kinds of questions he or she raises while teaching.
>
> (Eisner, 1979, p. 54)

Task 8.1 Is there a tension between Sc1 (skills and processes) and Sc2, 3 and 4 (knowledge and understanding)?	In the 1980s, there was a debate about *process* versus *content*. To what extent do you think teaching methods and approaches influence the balance of the science taught?

While you are in school, keep notes on the science lessons you observe. Record the following information:

- the content focus of each lesson;
- the different methods and approaches the teacher used;
- how frequently these methods were used.

The following list might help you organize your ideas. Look for:

- teacher giving children information;
- teacher dictating notes;
- children copying from chalkboard/worksheet/book;
- class discussion about the topic;
- teacher guided question-and-answer session;
- group activity (non-practical);
- group practical activity following workcard/worksheet;
- group practical activity (open-ended investigation);
- other (you describe).

Make an estimate of the balance between Sc1 (Scientific Enquiry) and Sc2, Sc3 or Sc4 (knowledge and understanding).

Which methods and approaches emphasized facts (conceptual knowledge and understanding) most? Which emphasized skills and processes (procedural knowledge and understanding) most?

Is there such a thing as a correct solution? If so, what do you think it is?

LEARNING IN SCIENCE

As a result of the wealth of data from well-documented projects, there is a lot known about how primary teachers teach and, to a lesser extent, how children learn as reflected in achievement scores. However, less is known about how children learn in the sense of the achievement of real understanding. In his book on learning in primary schools, Pollard (1990) suggested that there is a need to identify more explicitly how learning takes place and to recognize how teachers may affect young children's learning. He focused on three views of teaching and learning.

1   He considered *listening*, with didactic formal presentation of information and passive receptivity of the learners. This, he said, emphasizes the learning and recall of factual knowledge but ignores the vital element of understanding. That factual recall has a place in teaching and learning he acknowledged with a caveat.

. . . children can and do learn much from listening to adults providing the adult's offering is appropriate for the learner.

(p. 7)

In other words, learning must be meaningful and connect with the knowledge and understanding already owned by the learner.

2   Pollard next considered *doing*, in which the emphasis switches to direct experience whereby the learner interacts directly with people, events, artefacts and places. The learner is seen as actively constructing his or her understanding through interaction and the teacher's role becomes one of providing or encouraging activities to stimulate such interaction in a secure learning environment. This approach builds very much on the work of cognitive psychologists like Piaget.

3   Both listening and doing incorporate aspects of language, but the third mode described by Pollard has language at its focus, that is, *discussing*. Under the psychological umbrella of constructivism (the view that meaning and understanding are constructed) it gives priority to discussion and exploration of ideas by debate or argument as a major vehicle of learning and in which learning is negotiated between the participants of the process. In this mode, the influence of others on the construction of knowledge and understanding is acknowledged.

Any theory of learning that identifies the integral role of prior knowledge in the construction of new knowledge and understanding can be termed 'constructivist'. What seems to be particularly important in this approach is that adult support for children in the development of their thinking skills is valuable with appropriate interventions to promote and extend children's understanding beyond the point they could have reached unaided. Such support is referred to as mental scaffolding for learning. Scaffolding can be described as the process used by the teacher to enable the children to carry out a task, solve a problem or achieve a goal that would be beyond the child if not helped. Scaffolds can be oral or textual, in the form of the social interaction that occurs between the teacher and pupil or between pupil and pupil, and also between high-quality surrogate teachers like textual materials or computer software and the learner. The construction of effective scaffolding depends upon:

- the teacher's sensitivity to and skill in recognizing what children already know and understand;
- the teacher's awareness of the social and cultural context that influences each child's willingness and motivation to learn;
- the teacher's knowledge and understanding of what constitute appropriate learning experiences for the child; and,
- the teacher's ability to organize and deliver these.

When thinking about teaching and learning, Eisner (1979) suggested that:

Learning is a humble thing compared to teaching. To teach puts one in a superordinate position, to learn in the position of a subordinate.

(p. 86)

Planning a coherent, progressive and continuous curriculum is one thing. The National Curriculum Order provides a framework on which you can build and the QCA (1999) Scheme of Work provides one model that can be adopted. It is relatively easy for teachers to sit together to produce such a document or decide upon a commercially produced scheme which suits their needs. Delivering it is a different matter. It has to be translated into practice at the classroom level. This seems to be the logical next step which is much harder to take, as indicated by Cullingford (1989):

> For whilst the debate about the curriculum centres in the end on the nature of teaching, the essential question will always be about the nature of learning; not what is given to children but what children receive.
>
> (p. 3)

Planning for learning therefore involves more than simply planning what set of science experiences should be offered to children in your class. It requires identifying the knowledge, skills, concepts and attitudes children should understand or develop. This means you will need to be aware of how children learn generally, how they learn within subject disciplines, what other experiences they have had, and what your role or function will be in encouraging that learning. As John (1994) suggested,

> Tasks can thus be seen as mechanisms by which teachers begin to develop cognitive activity in their pupils according to subject area. The completion of the tasks provides the teacher with evidence about both the extent of the learning and the efficacy of the task itself. Tasks are therefore selected because of their ability to promote learning in a manner which the teacher intends. In this sense they are highly personalised constructions which relate to the teacher's knowledge of his or her subject, classrooms and pedagogy.
>
> (p. 11)

One of the most thorough research studies of classroom tasks is that of Desforges (1985). He has shown that there are four main types of task which you can consider when planning for progression and continuity in learning experiences:

- incremental tasks to introduce new skills or ideas;
- restructuring tasks which require the child to invent or discover an idea
- enrichment tasks that involve the child in applying familiar skills or ideas to new problems or situations; and,
- practise tasks that encourage the use of new skills in familiar problems or situations.

As mentioned earlier, teaching and learning cannot be divorced from the subject content. Does the nature of the subject itself impose specific interpretations or particular demands for planning on the teacher? Does science require that certain areas of knowledge or experience be offered before others? The National Curriculum indicates that this is the case with its linear model of Level Descriptors. As Colin Conner (1999) suggests in his discussion of progression:

> The introduction of the National Curriculum increased the importance of progression, since it assumes that it is possible to organise and sequence learning and therefore assign levels to children's achievements.
>
> (p. 141)

However, he goes on to emphasize that such a hierarchical approach must not be seen as cast in concrete. Such a hierarchy of learning may not be appropriate for all learners in all curriculum areas at all times. In science we are not always progressing from simple to complex, from concrete to abstract, from easy to difficult. There may be cycles within each step of progress a child makes. Progression does not imply an automatic increase in demand of the learning tasks that are given to the children in line with their increasing ability to respond to similar tasks. In the framework for inspection of schools, Ofsted inspectors are reminded that they have a responsibility to evaluate and grade children's progress:

> . . . on the basis of the quality of pupils' learning in lessons and over a period of time, drawing on the pupils' current work and any past work which is available.
>
> (Ofsted, 1998, p. 12)

Learning in science is a combination of both physical and mental activity, ranging from active participation in science investigations to more apparently passive activity such as observation, where mental rather than physical activity is taking place.

> Essentially [learning science] involves children finding out about something through their own actions and making some sense of the result through their own thinking . . . when we observe, all of us pay attention selectively to some things rather than others and we try to make sense of what we find as we take in.
>
> (Harlen and Jelly, 1989, p. 5)

This 'making sense' act is one of trying to connect the new information from observation or investigation to existing knowledge and understanding they already possess.

> When children explore [observe, investigate, experiment . . .] the ideas they have about . . . things afterwards will be different from the ideas they had before they had the encounters.
>
> (ibid., p. 6)

Theories of learning in science are currently dominated by constructivist perspectives in which the learners actively construct their own knowledge. Constructivists suggest that children may already have naive ideas about phenomena before we begin teaching them. Meaningful learning can only occur through the development of existing knowledge and understanding and not by simply imposing meaning from outside. Therefore, learners use their existing knowledge to interpret new information in ways which make sense to them. Teaching needs to start with the children's own ideas and teachers need to take their pupils' initial conceptions seriously. This has obvious implications when thinking about progression. Research into children's ideas, what ideas and conceptions they hold at different ages and patterns of progression in those beliefs and ideas is important. It can help you question assumptions about children's learning and guide your practice about what to do and why to do it.

PROGRESSION IN LEARNING

There are two uses of the word *progression*. First, there is progression in relation to a course or programme of study, planned for a group such as a class or a year group and covering a long period of time. The second use describes progression in planned experiences offered to individuals in order to develop particular skills, knowledge and understanding. The two are related although not interchangeable. Programmes of study in science should support increasing levels of skill, knowledge and understanding. This is generally what is thought of as progression. Matching experiences to the needs of individuals in order to ensure this progression is generally thought to be both feasible and desirable and yet it is no easy task. If you cannot do this, it may seem to indicate a problem with you rather than with the ideas under study.

There are certain assumptions that underpin matching and progression through learning experiences. First, the notion assumes that the level of demand of a learning experience can be assessed reasonably accurately. Second, it assumes that the level of development of children can be assessed with equal accuracy. Finally, there is the assumption that learning experiences can be designed that will match these two and, consequently, prove effective. However, the time and effort to do this would seem to outweigh the outcomes since children, contexts and subject matter all vary. Children do not come to new learning experiences with empty heads. Judgements about how meaningful and demanding any task is will be depend upon knowledge of the whole learning situation and the prior knowledge and experiences of the individual pupils. Their performance on activities will change according to contexts and emotions. Nor do children operate constantly at the same uniform level. Any prediction of their future performance can, at best, be no more than tentative, since it will be affected by numerous other factors, such as linguistic and mathematical demand, social interaction skills and general physical and emotional states. In other words, since such matching can only ever be loose and approximate, time and effort would seem to be better spent on more general and global strategies for individual, group and class progression.

A concept associated with progression is *continuity*. The primary school phase of children's education is very varied. If what has been achieved at each stage is not to be lost, then links are needed between the stages to ensure continuity. Most schools will have structures in place to aid the transition from one phase of education to the next. These are often concerned with reducing children's worries about such transitions, but that alone does not bring about continuity.

Prior to the National Curriculum, primary teachers usually had complete autonomy over classroom organization and management, resource availability and use and the curriculum. Such autonomy sometimes resulted in a lack of continuity and progression in the educational experiences of pupils in general and in science in particular. Anecdotal accounts which illustrate this are frequent in my own experiences of working with primary teachers. For example, it was not uncommon to find in September and October many teachers with a science topic of *Autumn*. The children, whether 5 or 11, would be gathering seeds for chocolate box seed collections and fallen leaves to make wax crayon rubbings. The latter would be cut out to make leaf trees for display, accompanied by some painting and creative writing about autumn. This would be seen by the teacher as science. Throughout the school year, topics like *Autumn*, *Ourselves* or *Water*, would be covered several times in the same school by different teachers.

This, in itself, was not the problem. Such an approach is at the heart of a concentric curriculum in which topics and experiences are re-visited, building upon what has gone before and using children's developing skills and broader knowledge base. The problem is that in these examples the approach was unsystematically concentric. The necessary building on prior experiences did not always occur. The experiences being offered to children of different ages were sometimes identical and often took no account of prior learning. There was little thought given to progression in content and skills, according to the needs and abilities of the children. In these anecdotes this task match was not happening. Consequently, the science curriculum lacked coherence and there was unnecessary duplication or serious omission of experiences.

Hierarchically structured learning tasks that target the learning and behavioural objectives to be achieved can also be useful, especially when specific facts and skills are desired. This seems to meet National Curriculum demands and allows lessons or activities to be planned and structured in a sequential and progressive way. In the past the emphasis has been on learning separate and quite often unrelated facts. Such facts were usually acquired by rote-learning. This does not mean that such facts, in the forms of laws, definitions or principles, are unimportant. They are important but knowledge of these alone does not necessarily equate with knowing why. The important thing here is being able to connect the facts and ideas in order to develop understanding by building upon (but not necessarily accepting uncritically) prior knowledge and established ideas.

> If scientific activity is seen as developing understanding . . . Ideas will be explored rather than accepted and committed to memory and alternative views examined in terms of supporting evidence.
>
> (Harlen, 1992, p. 2)

This was also stressed by White (1988) who emphasized the crucial role of children's earlier experiences and prior knowledge:

> Learning is not the simple absorption of knowledge but the construction of meaning through the individual's relating things seen and heard to things already known. Learning is active – not passive.
>
> (p. 19)

Thus learning is often a process of examining and modifying existing ideas rather than simply absorbing new ones. This process is one in which the child goes through a sequence of steps: observing; searching; linking; checking; changing; and, learning. The actions which occur in each of these stages are summarised in Figure 8.1.

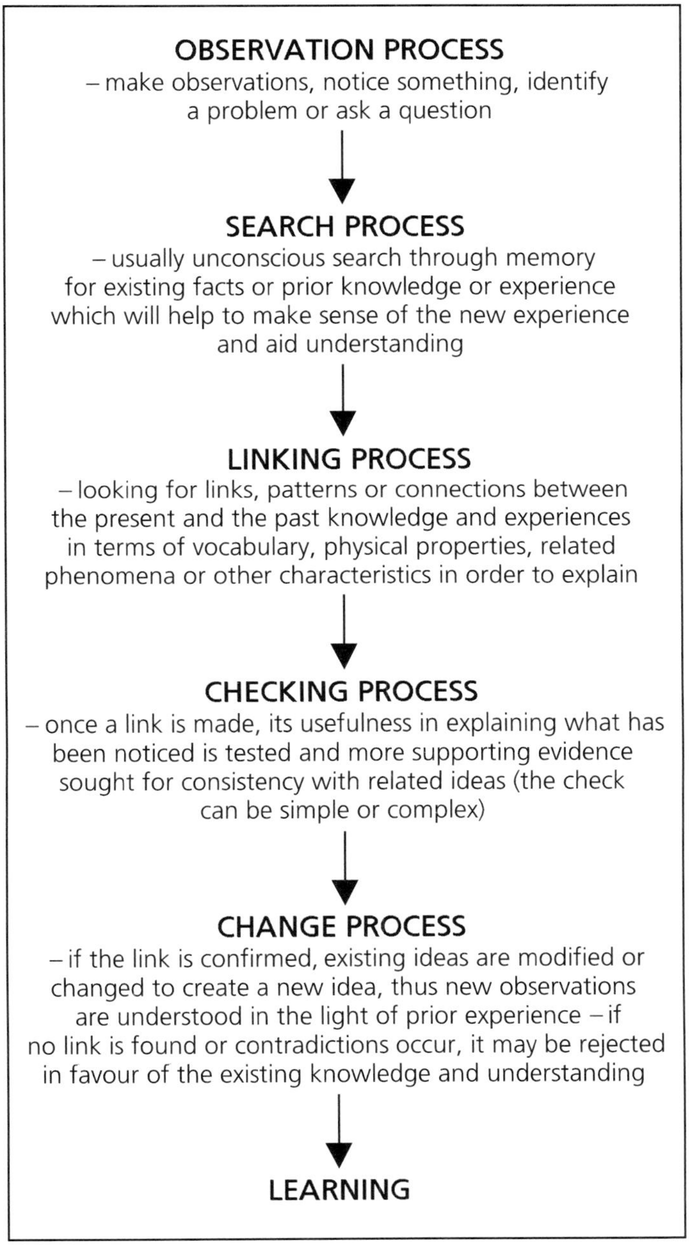

OBSERVATION PROCESS
– make observations, notice something, identify
a problem or ask a question

↓

SEARCH PROCESS
– usually unconscious search through memory
for existing facts or prior knowledge or experience
which will help to make sense of the new experience
and aid understanding

↓

LINKING PROCESS
– looking for links, patterns or connections between
the present and the past knowledge and experiences
in terms of vocabulary, physical properties, related
phenomena or other characteristics in order to explain

↓

CHECKING PROCESS
– once a link is made, its usefulness in explaining what has
been noticed is tested and more supporting evidence
sought for consistency with related ideas (the check
can be simple or complex)

↓

CHANGE PROCESS
– if the link is confirmed, existing ideas are modified or
changed to create a new idea, thus new observations
are understood in the light of prior experience – if
no link is found or contradictions occur, it may be rejected
in favour of the existing knowledge and understanding

↓

LEARNING

Figure 8.1 How does learning come about? The process of learning

Young children bring with them ideas which they have formed in the everyday exploration of their world. They can be tenacious in their hold of these ideas despite being confronted with contrary evidence (Osborne, 1985). You will need to acknowledge the existence of these ideas and take account of them in developing scientific experiences. The Science Processes and Concepts Exploration (SPACE) project based at the University of Liverpool, has explored young children's ideas and some techniques for assessing them. The team found that children's ideas:

1   emerged from a process of reasoning about experience, rather than from childish fantasy or imagination;
2   did not stand up to rigorous testing against available evidence;
3   sometimes required additional evidence to be made available if they were to be tested;
4   were influenced by external information (such as the media, peers and significant adults); and,
5   were often expressed in terms that sounded scientific but when explored were unsound, ill-defined and inconsistent.

That learning in science involves changing ideas also helps to explain why telling children things or providing information in other ways (for example, through text) does not necessarily lead to learning in the sense of cognitive changes in a required direction. If the information does not link with existing ideas the children will continue to use their own ideas to explain things for themselves despite, in some cases, being able to recite the accepted knowledge. To know what, how, when, where and who does not always mean to understand why.

Planning for learning in science requires that you will provide opportunities for progression in learning so that children can build understanding. This means teachers must be aware of the progress children make or can be expected to make in their learning. What is their starting point? What prior knowledge, skills, understandings or experiences do the children bring with them? Where are they going? What does the teacher hope they will learn or achieve? What can the teacher do to facilitate this development?

PROGRESSION IN PRIMARY SCIENCE

Learning, in the sense of developing understanding, is fundamental to the concept of progression. In the document, *Science 5 – 16: A Statement of Policy* (DES, 1985), one of the ten criteria for good practice in science education is progression. It was defined as:

> . . . courses being designed to give progressively deeper understanding and greater competence, not only within individual schools but also over the compulsory period as a whole, whatever the age of transfer between schools may be.
>
> (p. 10)

What goes on inside children's heads is the crucial issue. The important question is, what is *progressively deeper understanding*?

As mentioned earlier, progression and continuity are closely related. Indeed, they are often regarded as synonymous since the achievement of one often means the achievement of the other (Keogh and Naylor, 1993). However, continuity is teacher-focused and those involved, both within and between schools, share views on the curriculum content and the order of its delivery. On the other hand, progression is pupil-focused and relates to the forward movement through a sequence of learning targets designed to match needs and abilities. It is progression in learning by pupils.

Having established a centrally controlled National Curriculum for Science, the principle of continuity both within and between schools ought, in theory at least, to be achieved. Progression is more problematic since learning is more complex involving, at times, regression as well as achievement. Teachers' selection of learning experiences for pupils have to take such complexities into account. The meaning of the terms 'understanding' and 'competence' in the government's definition of progression will need to be defined and understood by primary teachers. To ensure progression in ways of thinking and working in science (Sc1) and in knowledge and understanding of science (Sc2, 3 and 4) teachers should plan carefully the courses offered. But an examination of the science curriculum is not enough to ensure progression. It is also necessary to consider how children grow and develop mentally.

Implicit in the structure of the National Curriculum is a mechanistic model of learning which assumes a linear progression. It is also assumed that there is enough common ground between sequences in children's learning so that an hierarchical model is a useful way of recording attainment. As a consequence, it was considered possible to define Levels of Attainment and Level Descriptors. These assumptions are increasingly being tested and challenged (Hughes, 1996). One of the main themes explored by Hughes is that of pupils' understanding and the extent to which it progresses both within and across the subject areas. In his introduction, he states,

> The issue of progression has been made particularly salient by the ten-level scale underpinning the National Curriculum, and the associated need to draw up models of progression within each attainment target and each subject.
>
> (Hughes, 1996, p. xv)

Research does indicate evidence of pupils becoming more knowledgeable within particular domains. For example, Simon, Brown, Black and Blondel (1996) found progression in pupils' understanding in terms of them becoming more knowledgeable about forces. As part of the same research project, the work of Millar, Gott, Luben and Duggan (1996) also found evidence of learners becoming more knowledgeable about the nature of the domain of science investigation. They concluded that there was some progression in terms of pupils' understanding of how evidence is used in science, but, as Hughes's pointed out, what is not clear from these findings is the nature of the relationship between these two kinds of knowledge. Does pupils' learning progress in a linear manner? In the work cited above, a linear and evenly spaced development was not apparent. Hughes concluded that:

It is perhaps not surprising that this research has identified some clear areas of progression in pupils' understanding – one would, after all, expect learners to become more knowledgeable as they grow older. What is more surprising, however, are occasions when it appears that no real progression is taking place – or even where pupils' understanding appears to go backwards rather than forwards. There are at least two occasions . . . where the authors have pointed out what they consider to be significant gaps in key areas of pupils' knowledge or understanding.

(p. 194)

He also identified a common point emerging from all the studies,

. . . that there was often greater variation within particular age-ranges than across them.

(p. 195)

Pollard (1990) asks the question:

Does the attempt to create linear programmes of study really reflect the diverse patterns of children's interests, development and capacities?

(p. 41)

His question is particularly important in that it has implications for the way primary teachers approach their planning and control the learning in their classrooms. How do you plan for progression at the level of the class and for each individual within it?

HMI, in their surveys of schools in the early years of the National Curriculum, found that almost all schools visited had revised schemes of work to meet National Curriculum requirements (DES, 1991). The schemes included aims and objectives, teaching methods, resources, and interpretation at a general level of programmes of study and attainment targets. However, very few had identified the means by which progression was to be secured and achievement assessed and recorded at a more specific level. To provide support for this, the QCA schemes of work were developed. They are not statutory but guidance documents.

It seems to be obvious that your planning should take account of the need for progression in skills, knowledge and understanding of the individual pupils, for,

Where the best learning takes place, it is built upon what the children already know, can do and understand, and therefore relates to the children and their previous learning.

(Humberside LEA, 1991)

This also has implications for continuity and cross-phase liaison.

The purpose of liaison is to lead to better continuity; the purpose of achieving continuity is to lead to better progression in learning.

(Keogh and Naylor, 1993, p. 134)

For this to happen there must be mutual recognition of the special responsibilities of each phase. There must also be appropriate channels of communication between schools to ensure that the work in science in the earlier years of schooling is acknowledged and built upon.

Task 8.2 Progression, continuity and liaison in primary science	What do the two terms – progression and continuity – mean for you? In what ways do they overlap? How are they different?

Discuss with your mentor how the school plans for progression and continuity in science. Link these ideas to what you know about long, medium and short-term planning. Look at the school's long, medium and short-term plans for science and identify the progression and continuity embedded in them.

How does the National Curriculum Order for Science support the notions of progression and continuity? Construct a flow diagram to summarize progression in science as a process and science as a body of knowledge. What is it that is progressing?

How does continuity relate to this?

Why do you think liaison between staff teaching in different key stages, phases or even schools matters? What strategies might be used to encourage liaison?

A genuine progression in terms of understanding and conceptual development is difficult to achieve (Pennell and Alexander, 1990). The National Curriculum has not made the primary teacher's task easier in this respect. While the prescriptive contents of such documents might make it possible for teachers to plan what to teach, the documents do not specify how to teach that content. Perhaps more important, the existence of a National Curriculum does not guarantee what the children will learn as a result of the experiences.

Conner (1999) concludes his report with a number of important messages about progression.

1   Progression is not necessarily age related.
2   Not all learning is hierarchical in nature and some areas need to be revisited regularly in contrasting ways to ensure the understanding is fully established.
3   Dialogue with children about their learning is essential. Putting their ideas into words provides evidence of their level of understanding.

For you as a teacher, reflection and evaluation are crucial steps in monitoring learning and making decisions about the next steps.

The principle of progression is not a simple case of planning what teachers' teach with each class. This is a part of the process, but perhaps the lesser part. The real need is progression in what children learn, what they know, what they can do and understand. Teachers need to be able to plan for progression in this much more difficult area and yet, if they do not really have any guidance in this respect it is not surprising that, as the HMI survey found, this dimension is sometimes ignored.

> Curriculum plans describe the intended experience for pupils. However what children learn depends on the interaction between the plans, the teacher and the pupils. Matching and, therefore, progression in learning must take this interaction into account.
>
> (Keogh and Naylor, 1993, p. 125)

Until fairly recently, there was an assumption that children could only learn when they were 'developmentally ready' (Mills, 1988). This assumption and the concept of 'readiness' to which it led is now questioned and a more positive view of children's abilities and potential is more widely accepted.

A number of important ideas have been introduced in this chapter on progression. Many of them will be developed in more detail in the subsequent chapters.

SUGGESTIONS FOR FURTHER READING

If you would like to explore further some of the issues touched upon in this chapter, the following books should be of some interest to you.

Hughes, M., (ed.) (1996) *Progression in Learning*, Clevedon: Multilingual Matters
In his book Martin Hughes brings together the latest research on progression in learning across a range of curriculum areas and age groups.

Keogh, B. and Naylor, S. (1993) 'Progression and continuity in science' in Sherrington, R., (ed.) (1993) *The ASE Primary Science Teachers' Handbook*, London: Simon and Schuster
This edited volume brings together a number of articles on issues related to primary science and is worth looking at generally as well as for the section on progression.

9 What Do We Mean by Teaching for Understanding?

DOUG NEWTON

In this chapter, we will continue to consider how you, as the teacher, can ensure your pupils' make progress in scientific skills, knowledge and understanding. We look, in particular, at what we mean by developing understanding.

UNDERSTANDING

Understanding is about getting a handle on things, grasping the point, getting the message. But what do these mean? Generally, they refer to what we do when we make mental connections between facts, concepts, ideas and procedures. These connections establish relationships, such as, when the force pulling on a bowstring doubles, the distance it moves doubles. They describe patterns in data, such as the way the temperature levels out at 0°C as ice below this temperature is warmed through its melting point. They relate the stages in a natural process, like transpiration in plants. They are the reasons for a particular sequence of actions, as in separating a salt and sand mixture. We use understanding to refer to a variety of different mental activities. There is the need to understand words and sentences such as, *evaporate* and *melt* and *Can you make a fair test to see which glove is the best for a cold day?* Here, there has to be connections between the sounds and their meanings. There is a need to understand a situation, as when faced with grasping the variety and abundance of life in a pond. Particularly important in science is the need to understand the reason why there are fewer predators than prey, as this is often the reason we teach science in the first place.

The ability to make mental connections is innate. However, children may not always make the connections you want. At times, even adults see connections where there are none, as when the astronomer Percival Lowell thought he could see canals amongst the marks on Mars' surface. Children may not make connections at all or with sufficient precision unless you focus their attention on what matters and support their thinking. Making connections may be an innate ability but it can also be demanding. When it is, we have to reduce the demand to a level that the children can cope with and can benefit from. We all have difficulty trying to juggle several things in our minds at once and this applies even more to children. Familiarity with many of the ideas we have to use has made some thinking easier for us, even automatic, but children have not had the advantage of this experience. This has to be considered when planning support for understanding.

| **Task 9.1 Quantity versus quality in science** | What does it mean to be 'good at science'? Ask this question of the children in your class. Find out what counts, for them, as important in science. Is it being able to do activities and investigations? Is it something to do with getting the answer |

right? Is it remembering all the facts? Has it anything to do with understanding relationships between things?

Ask the children what they think we mean by 'understanding' when we are thinking about science. What does this tell you about children's conceptions of what counts as understanding in science?

What strategies can you use to help children to construct their understandings in science?

How can you help them to understand what we mean by understanding?

DOES UNDERSTANDING REALLY MATTER?

If all that counts is giving the 'right' answer, then it does not matter if children do not understand? All they need to do is memorize the information and reproduce it on demand. But understanding is a frequent target in science teaching (and of all teaching). This is because understanding has more to offer than memorization. It can:

- satisfy needs like curiosity about why the world is the way it is and help a child relate to the world;
- help a child learn new material because it provides a framework to tie new information to;
- make learning durable and accessible – what is understood often lasts longer and is recalled more readily;
- make children's performances flexible – they are more likely to think product-ively in novel situations, solve problems and find new ways of doing things;
- help to manage information which is not well organized and which may sometimes be of doubtful quality, such as that offered by the Internet.

What understanding has to offer is very significant for the child. Ultimately, it enables the child to make sense of the world and to make rational choices in life. Unfortunately, understanding is not always a central concern. Acting against it is the quantity of material to be covered, the need to think of ways of making it understandable, the mental effort required by the children, and the impending tests. Nevertheless, understanding is so valuable that it is worth every effort. At the same time, teaching in ways that support understanding will make your job more interesting and more satisfying. But first, what is understanding in science?

UNDERSTANDING IN SCIENCE

As already suggested, there are several kinds of understanding in science and some need our particular attention. These include:

1   conceptual understanding;
2   situational understanding;
3   causal understanding; and,
4   procedural understanding.

Conceptual understanding

This is what we expect when we say a child understands, for instance, *energy*, *elasticity*, or *respiration*. Each of these is a scientific concept and each involves other concepts. For example, *energy* might be underpinned by the concept of 'something waiting to change'. We would expect this to have meaning for children, to relate well to what they already know, and to link with particular instances of 'something waiting to change', like a coiled spring or inflated balloon. The child would know what happens when these change – the spring uncoils and the balloon deflates – and see links with what these changes might be made to do, such as launch a toy rocket or make a small buggy move. The point is that components of the concept of *energy* would be related to what already has meaning for the child, that is, to the child's prior knowledge. In turn, they would be related to each other to form a coherent whole.

Situational understanding

This kind of understanding could occur in both conceptual and procedural understanding. You set up some situation and the children must grasp what it amounts to and what is significant in it. Suppose, for instance, you want to show reflection of light from a mirror. You set up a large plastic mirror and shine a torch on it. The torch is covered by some black paper with a hole in it to narrow the beam of light. A spot of light is reflected from the mirror to the classroom wall. The majority of children will easily perceive the mirror, torch and paper and their relative positions. However, they also need to realize that the colour of the paper is not particularly important as long as it does not let light through and, similarly, that the mirror is plastic is not of significance. What is significant is that the spot of light on the wall came from the torch and 'bounced' off the mirror. They need to connect the three mentally for an understanding of the situation. Often, we assume that the connection is obvious but it need not be for someone who sees it for the first time. When such situations are described in books, the connections may be more difficult to grasp. In this example, illustrators commonly draw in the path of the beam of light as though it can be seen in order to help the child. But, after such a picture, what does a child make of the real thing? We have to be sure that a child understands situations as we intend them to because this is commonly how we present new phenomena to them.

Causal understanding

A causal event is when there is some change in a situation. While we want children to know that one thing leads to another, we often also want them to understand why. This means we want them to connect an initial situation with a final situation by a causal link. For example, when they connect a torch bulb to a battery, the bulb glows. If it is left for a long time, the bulb becomes dimmer and dimmer. Why? What is the cause? The children have to grasp the situation and the change. Next, they must bridge the gap between them: first the bulb was bright, now it is dim. They may suggest that a flat battery is the cause. What does that mean to the children? Is it just a statement they have heard, without meaning? Is it well-founded in some prior knowledge so that it makes some sort of sense to them? Causal links are particularly important in understanding the world and, often in simple terms, figure a lot in our teaching.

Task 9.2 Understanding cause and effect in primary science	One of the fundamental relationships in science which children need to understand is that of cause and effect. Do the following activity in school when you have been working on an appropriate science topic with your class, either with a small group of children or with the whole class.

1 Give the children a list of causes and a separate list of the matching effects, but randomly arranged.
2 Ask the children to work in pairs. They are to sort the two lists and match each effect to its cause.
3 Having matched cause and effect, the children are now asked to write their reason for each choice.

Discuss the choices with the children. In the light of this discussion, what teaching points emerge that inform your subsequent planning?

Procedural understanding

In science, we often expect children to be able to understand ways of doing things, particularly in connection with practical work. First, they have to comprehend the sequence of activities but this does not mean that they know why they are doing them. Procedural understanding is when they know the reasons for what they do. This is more than being able to remember the words you said; it requires them to know what each step is for and why the sequence is in the order it is. Again, like conceptual understanding, it should be underpinned by and linked with well-founded knowledge.

Understanding through practical activity

The kind of understanding we want to foster shapes the kinds of activity you will provide in science lessons.

- *Providing experience to support conceptual understanding*
  We might provide direct experience of some phenomenon, effect or event in order to help us support children's conceptual understanding. For instance, we may want children to experience the way that friction results in heat. The children are given erasers and rub them vigorously on paper then touch their noses with the eraser to feel the heat. This experience is some of the raw material that helps children develop conceptual understanding. The aim is to embed new knowledge firmly in experience. It is not sufficient to provide experience and assume that concepts will develop adequately on their own. You will still need to support the process and monitor the quality of understanding that is constructed.

Understanding in a practical activity can, and often does, involve conceptual, situational, event, and procedural understanding. While our intention might be to focus on one of these, others often cannot be ignored. Understanding why the Sun casts shadows on the side farthest away from the Sun, for instance, might be explored with a small torch and cut-out figures made from card. Concepts such as *light* and *shadow* are involved. Less obvious are other concepts which are likely to be relevant such as *straight line*. The situation itself has to be understood: there are the parallels between the Sun and a person and the torch and the cut-out; there is the appreciation that light is travelling from the torch to the cut-out, even though it cannot be seen if the air is clear; and there is the shadow which is an absence of light. Finally, there is the all-important causal link to be established between the absence of light and the obstruction of the cut-out. At an elementary level, the property of some materials, like card, to obstruct light might be accepted as a sufficient cause. With older children, we might expect more. Why, for instance, does the light not curve around the card so that there is no shadow? The cause is, of course, that light travels in straight lines.

At times, you will draw on the children's prior experience to develop conceptual understanding. On other occasions, you will want to control that experience, or provide new experiences and may choose to do that with practical, hands-on activity. However, science teaching within the National Curriculum also involves developing an understanding of scientific investigation.

● *Providing experience to support understanding in scientific exploration and investigation*
Activities intended to explore or develop conceptual understanding may also lead to investigations. The one to do with light and shadows, described above, is an instance. Such activities involve a number of kinds of understanding and, to be effective, all should be monitored. When developing investigation skills and understanding, attention is directed to an understanding of why the investigation has the form it does. For example, young children may devise an investigation to find the best place in the classroom to grow cress. They will, of course, need some conceptual understanding of what *grow* means, they will need to know that cress is a plant which does grow, that some kind of soil is beneficial for growth and that they will need to provide water. Unless the task is to be a somewhat random one, they will also need to have some ideas about what promotes growth so they can predict places they think are likely to be good, bad and indifferent.

Note that some prior knowledge makes the investigation more likely to be a success. Sometimes, this prior knowledge will be based on informal, out-of-school experience. The children develop their own ideas about the world and so the investigation allows the children to test them. Sometimes, you will have supplemented this informal experience with conceptual understanding and exploratory activity in lessons. Together, these enable the children to make predictions for testing.

During the design of the experiment and its execution, however, the children will reveal their understanding of scientific investigation through the procedures they adopt. Do they use the same kind and amount of soil in each pot? Do they provide the same amount of water for each one? In other words, do they control variables and make a fair test? Can they explain why they do these things? How will their measurements provide the information they need to decide which place is the best? To understand what, how and why they are doing things is the point of this exercise. As a bonus, the activity may also support the development of other kinds of understanding, such as conceptual understanding.

UNDERSTANDING THROUGH OTHER ACTIVITY

There is a tendency to think that only practical activity promotes understanding. Certainly, practical activity can be very valuable in this respect, particularly if you press for what underpins what the children are doing, but it is not the only useful activity that you can provide.

One such activity is discussion. This may be between you and the class, you and a child, or between children themselves. Discussion which involves explaining and giving reasons is particularly useful because it obliges the children to go under the surface, to develop their communication skills, and justify what they think, propose or conclude. Another activity can be reading or listening to a story about science, provided that more than passive reading and listening is involved. Drawing and writing, too, are important because they make the children bring together half-formed understandings and render them coherent. Do not assume that an understanding is well-formed and secure because it has been shown in one context with prompting by you. Support it in other ways so that it develops. Understandings are not fixed; they may half-form, form, and re-form at deeper or wider levels. In understanding the cause of the shadow, for instance, two possible levels were mentioned. Moving from one to the next often needs more experience and time. Returning to an understanding from different directions is a useful way of supporting this development.

In all activity, practical or otherwise, it is important for the child's mind to be actively engaged as well as the hands. To ensure this, you will need to press for higher level thinking, going beyond the facts and descriptions of the science to what underpins it.

THE ROLE OF PRIOR KNOWLEDGE

As you see, children's prior knowledge is important in understanding science. It serves several, overlapping functions:

- children have to draw on it to help them grasp what they are expected to understand,
- children construct connections between the bits and pieces of the new information but also relate it to what they know already; if they succeed in making a coherent structure and integrating it with their prior knowledge, there is an understanding which could be deeply meaningful and long lasting,
- children's prior knowledge is not confined to facts about the world, it also includes ideas and theories about how the world works; these help them understand the world and make predictions about it (often useful for testing in investigations).

Do not assume that children's ideas about the world are always wrong, faulted and hinder learning. A lot of their prior experience may be adequate for the purposes you have in mind. Some may be simple and easy to rectify: birds live in nests all the year around, for instance. Some erroneous ideas are less specific and may take a little more effort, for instance that all wild animals are dangerous. Although, logically, it should take only one non-dangerous example to negate this idea, in practice a large number of cases may be needed so that the rule, 'all, except that one', does not develop. Other ideas may be deep-seated, well integrated and actually work in the child's world but, scientifically, they are inadequate. For instance, a child may believe that a continuous push is needed to maintain an object's motion. In the child's world, this is what experience teaches and it predicts quite adequately the kind of action that is needed to keep a bicycle going along a level road. Nonetheless, a rocket's engine can be switched off in space and the rocket will continue to cruise along at the same speed unless it meets something else. On the Earth, friction opposes every action, in space it is often negligible. Such ideas or misconceptions, as they are often called, can be difficult to overcome. You need to know, therefore, what children bring with them to the lesson. It will help you plan what to do next.

<table>
<tr><td>**Task 9.3 Children and science**</td><td>Discuss with your class teacher or mentor the strategies he or she uses to encourage children to recall prior knowledge and understanding in science.</td></tr>
</table>

Ask two or three young children from the Reception or Year 1 class to recall some of their science experiences. What sort of things have they been doing in science? What does 'science' mean to them?

Repeat the questions with children from the middle of the school (from Year 2, 3 or 4) and with older primary children (from Years 5 or 6).

Compare their answers. What does 'science' mean to children of different ages in primary school? What sort of things do they remember doing in science?

WAYS OF FINDING OUT CHILDREN'S KNOWLEDGE AND IDEAS

There are various ways of finding out what children already know, understand, and misunderstand. Some have to be indirect because ideas about how the world works may not always be at a conscious level. Some children may not have the vocabulary or be able to describe adequately what they know or think. However, you might begin with the direct approach.

- Ask the children to think of a recent event or relevant scenario and introduce it to the children, perhaps as a short anecdote to set the scene and focus minds on the topic in hand. Intersperse this with some exploratory questions relating to vocabulary, facts and understanding, making sure that you include the latter but also be prepared to explore unexpected areas, too. For example, when intending to introduce some work on electricity, you might show a torch that you have found no longer works and ask, 'Who knows what this is? What is it for? What is this part called? What is a bulb? What does it do? Can you draw what it looks like inside? What is inside the torch? What is a battery? What does it do? Why do you think it won't work?

- Show the children an event and have them write an explanation. You examine their explanations for clues about their underpinning ideas.

- With older children, have them draw a concept map, linking facts, objects and ideas with one another, as in the example in Figure 9.1. The children will need to be shown what one is and how to construct one but, once learned, concept mapping can be used regularly for this purpose (and also as an indicator of developing and changing understanding). You should bear in mind that this form of assessment is rough and ready rather than precise, and it often helps to have children explain their maps.

- Have children draw a sequence of diagrams to show how they would do something. This can reveal procedural misunderstandings.

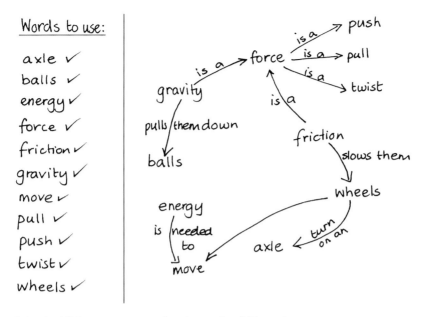

Figure 9.1   A child's concept map for the topic of 'Forces'

- An indirect approach might use a practical task, such as, 'See if you can make this bulb light. There are lots of electrical bits and pieces – more than you need – have a go'. You observe actions and listen to the children's talk and hence deduce what underpins what they do. In this approach, the children's knowledge and theories reveal themselves through their actions and the explanations of those actions and it should be used as a matter of course during the teaching of a topic to detect misconceptions and misunderstandings. (Compare this with miscue analysis in English).

CHILDREN'S MISCONCEPTIONS

Children can bring with them a wide range of misunderstandings and faulty frameworks for understanding the world. Their ideas come from direct experience of the world: their play, toys, helping adults, and from school. Other experience which supplements this comes from comics and books, the television, and computer games. For instance, in A.A. Milne's *Winnie the Pooh*, the bear is shown with a balloon that has been blown up by breath from the lungs. As a result Pooh floats off, dangling from the balloon. The problem is that balloons filled with air actually sink to the ground. Those which do float are filled with a gas that is lighter than air, such as helium. Telling children about hot air balloons, blimps and airships can simply add to the confusion unless some ground clearing is done first. In this case, the children could be given a balloon, asked to predict what will happen then try it for themselves.

Practical experience like this will also need to be supported by explanation and discussion about the 'silly book-writer who did not know any better'.

While children can have a wide variety of misconceptions, some of them are fairly common so can be anticipated. Here are some:

- people are not animals, they are in a group of their own;
- the body is hollow inside or is full of blood;
- plants get their food from the ground;
- plants are green and have soft stems; this means that trees are not plants;
- dissolving is a kind of melting;
- there is nothing around us;
- air exists only when it is moving, as in a draught;
- anything which is hollow will float;
- white or brightly coloured objects and mirrors give off light; in a dark room, you would be able to see if you had one of these;
- we see things because light comes from our eyes;
- words somehow pass from one person to another like a ball thrown across a room;
- electricity comes from a battery to a bulb and lights it; it is consumed there; and no other wire is needed to go back to the battery;
- heat and temperature are the same;
- there has to be flat parts on the earth for us to stand on.

Nevertheless, do not assume that children's prior knowledge is worthless and should be ignored. The aim is to develop it, revise it, and connect new knowledge with it.

LINKING SCIENCE WITH THE REAL WORLD

It is easy to say that children should be mentally active and engaged in what they do. How do we achieve that?

First, children have a natural curiosity about the world which is to our advantage in science. Show them something new and they want to know more about it, try it out, and become competent in doing things. Linking science with technology helps in this respect. Learning about why things move, for instance, is an opportunity for children to practise what they have learned. This makes learning more concrete and meaningful and gives a real sense of achievement when a buggy first moves in the way planned.

Second, we can catch children's attention by observing what interests them and by developing a topic from it. This draws on existing interests and popular activities, such as collecting things. For example, the children could be asked to *Make a collection of as many different seeds as you can.*

Nevertheless, there are things that must be taught which may fall outside these opportunities. In any case, there has to be some real reason why we teach any topic to a child, so why not tell them? The point is that we should point out the relevance of science to everyday life. Inevitably, the applications of science are what tend to come to mind. The vacuum cleaner, television and household lighting are what justifies teaching electricity. This is true, in part, but there are other reasons for teaching about electricity and, if utility was to become the basis for the curriculum, it would become difficult to justify many topics in many subjects. Instead, we must look at why science is relevant in a broader sense.

Science is relevant because it satisfies human needs. These include personal needs such as curiosity, wanting to know why things are as they are, and satisfaction at understanding something. They also include, of course, the utilitarian aspects of science, what science has contributed to in the material world. This generally relates to health, homes, transport, food and water supply, materials, exploration, and communication. However, these applications can have adverse as well as positive effects on the world and our lives, so we have congestion from traffic and poor air quality in some places, for instance. There is also a need for us to understand and relate to the world and science has contributed to that. It has provided a world view which is very different to, say, that of people in the Middle Ages. This can make it difficult for us to relate closely to how people of earlier times felt. Knowing that our views are not like their views is a start.

How do we make these explicit to the children so that they know why science is important to them? With young children, the emphasis should be on doing science and being a scientist. The child is given opportunities to explore, test ideas, find out and tell about the scientific world. The aim is to satisfy personal needs like those of the scientist described above and to draw them into consciousness with questions, such as, 'What did you like about that?' The topics need to be embedded in real world events that are meaningful to the child, so that Water might begin with Washing Day, for instance. Some environmental problems may also be broached with young children. For instance, there are stories about the rain forest and the effect of people on wildlife (e.g. *Rain Forest*, by H. Cowcher, Picture Corgi). Similarly, pollution as dirty water, a litter-ridden playground, or as smelly air can make useful discussions and exploration opportunities. Why, for instance, does a plastic cup last so long so it blows around the playground week after week? There are also opportunities for children to relate to the living world and behave responsibly in it. When studying minibeasts, the need to care for and about them should be introduced and the children should be involved in their release back into their habitats.

Older children will not, of course, cease to be curious so this need should not be ignored. However, increasing maturity, knowledge and experience make other things possible. They can have simple case studies of scientists and try simple activities related to their work. Stereotypical images of the scientist as a bearded, bespectacled man in a white coat, working alone in a laboratory with bottles, flasks and chemicals can develop early and be reinforced by cartoons on television and pictures in comics, as shown in Figure 9.2. Apart from being somewhat off the mark for much of science, it also gives the wrong message about opportunities for girls. Look for biographical stories about women and non-Western scientists to give some balance and include stories that tell of scientific work outside the laboratory. This gives you a good lead into discussing attitudes, values and beliefs in science.

Figure 9.2   A stereotypical view of a scientist

| Task 9.4 Attitudes, values, beliefs and primary science | Discuss with your class teacher how primary science can be used to develop particular attitudes, values and beliefs. What does each of these terms mean in the context of primary teaching and learning? How can they be introduced |

in the context of primary science? Draw a table with three columns, as follows:

Attitudes	Values	Beliefs
......	......	......

In each column, list five examples of an attitude, value or belief which you would hope to encourage in primary science.

What problems do you think you might encounter when you try to introduce such attitudes, values and beliefs to children?

SUGGESTIONS FOR FURTHER READING

If you would like to explore further some of the issues touched upon in this chapter, the following books should be of some interest to you.

Edwards, D. and Mercer, N. (1987) *Common Knowledge: The Development of Understanding in the Classroom*, London: Routledge
This easy to read and informative book introduces the idea of knowledge construction in the context of science. It develops the discussion by reference to many examples drawn from the interactions between teachers and pupils in the primary classroom.

Newton, D.P. (2000) *Teaching for Understanding*, London: RoutledgeFalmer
In this book, Douglas Newton brings together research findings and common sense, to provide a succinct summary of what counts as understanding in different domains and how teachers can support learners in their construction of understanding.

10 What Do We Mean by Strategies Which Will Support Understanding?

DOUG NEWTON

Much of what has been said in the previous chapter leads directly to the focus of this chapter, how to develop and support pupils' understanding of science. When thinking about strategies to support teaching for understanding in science, there are two simple rules to remember:

- *Be clear what understanding you want before you start*
  If you know what you want, you will be able to monitor progress in achieving it. You will be sensitive to the children's errors and what they indicate and will be able to focus your attention on the task of achieving your understanding aims. Having decided what you want children to know and to understand, list some key questions that you will ask to check for understanding. These will help you focus clearly and will assist in assessing the quality of the children's learning.
- *Plan your approach beforehand*
  As teachers, we understand the cause of shadows, the springiness of trapped air and how to interpret food webs. There is always the risk that what seems obvious to us is overlooked in our teaching. Be sensitive to this risk and respond to signs of incomprehension. At the same time, do not imagine that because you tell all, understanding must follow. Understanding is something that the children have to do for themselves: you cannot do it for them; they have to work at it. But you *can* and *should* support them as they try to understand.

One general principle to bear in mind is that *mental activity* can foster understanding. This activity, however, must be such that it seeks to connect pieces of knowledge into coherent wholes and connect them with the reasons for things. There are many kinds of active learning. Unfortunately, this is sometimes taken to mean only practical exploration and investigation (Sc1). Practical work is a valuable tool but active learning can also mean making a prediction, working at an explanation, seeking out the reason for something, answering a why question, writing a summary, and much more. Exploration and investigation can support the development of both conceptual and procedural understanding. Alone, they are often insufficient. The child will benefit from a blend of active learning strategies and from your questions while they work. Some questions might legitimately be factual, others will be to do with understanding: Why did you do . . .? Why did that happen? What would happen if . . .? Some important strategies are centred on explanation, talk and discussion, scaffolding children's thinking, having children apply their knowledge and understanding in relatively new situations, using information and communication technologies (ICT) and, of course, hands-on, practical experience.

SOME STRATEGIES TO SUPPORT CHILDREN'S UNDERSTANDING

Bear in mind what has been said earlier. Children may come to the science lesson with no prior knowledge of the topic in hand; they may arrive with knowledge you can draw on; and they may bring with them ideas that are inappropriate and which hinder further learning. You need to know the state and nature of their prior knowledge and ways of doing this have already been described. You should also set the scene and direct the children's thoughts towards the topic in hand. You might do this through, for instance, an artefact, a picture, an anecdote or story, questions, a hobby, or a game. Within this you are also likely to have ensured that the relevance of the topic has been made explicit and will have planned the general structure of what you want to cover and how you will do it so that the children are interested. Nevertheless, within that general structure, there are still some unanswered questions. In particular, how will you make what you plan to do effective in supporting understanding?

Explanation

When explaining how something works, why it is the way it is, or the reason for something happening as it does, provide concrete structures that the children can use to think with. For example, when attempting to make the point that there are such things as life cycles, choose a specific instance such as the frog or butterfly and set that out in a form which makes the cycle obvious (Figure 10.1). Since you are likely to want to establish a generalization about life cycles, you should add other examples to this, but not at the outset. The aim is to establish the idea *then* extend it. Finally, to make it clear that not all animals follow this pattern, you might provide a structure for a mammal or bird, where metamorphosis does not take place in this way. In short, the concept is introduced with an example, developed and widened and then its limits pointed out.

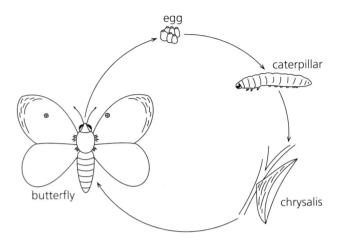

Figure 10.1   Life cycle of a butterfly

Models

Providing concrete structures like this is known to be very supportive and often memorable. Models can have the same effect. For example, some young children think that water comes from walls, quite literally. The tap is simply a device which is plugged into the wall and the water drains out through the tap. The sight of a damp wall can reinforce this idea. Of course, ripping out the pipes behind the tap and tracing them back to the water supply is not a practical option. Instead, a model, as in Figure 10.2, may have to be used to illustrate the real state of affairs. If this can be followed by a visit to the washroom to point out the pipes and the water tank, all the better. The model and real world will then be connected.

Analogies

Analogies also are conceptual structures that can support understanding. They behave something like models and give the children something to think with that is easier to handle than the real thing. For example, the child's world stretches away from them to the horizon and has hills and valleys which are significant bumps and hollows but we tell them that the Earth is a sphere, and a fairly smooth one at that. Having the children truly grasp (as opposed to agree to) the insignificance of the bumps and hollows in the scale of things is not always easy. Using the analogy of an orange can help. An orange has bumps and hollows which can be seen even without a magnifying glass but the orange still looks relatively smooth from a distance. If a hollow was the valley where our town is, a really strong magnifying glass would be needed to see the town, let alone the people in it. The immensity of the Earth in comparison to the heights and depths of mountains and valleys is broached with the use of a concrete, visible object that the children are familiar with.

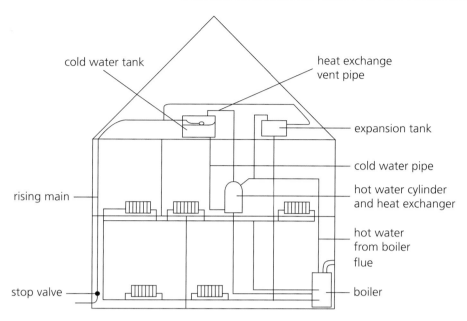

Figure 10.2   Model of a house hot water system

Other examples of this kind are in comparing the insect's hollow proboscis with a straw, the skull with a crash-helmet, and bones with card tubes. In the same way, we might use the way a ball bounces off a wall as an analogy for the way light reflects from a mirror. Knowing the way the ball behaves allows the children to predict what will happen in the case of light. It used to be assumed that young children could not think analogically but that has been shown to be unfounded. What is important is that what you use for the analogy has to be well-known to the children and the children need to know what they are supposed to do with it. Even in the ball-bouncing analogy for the reflection of light, although we can assume that children have played with a ball, they may not have noticed the effect you are interested in or, more likely, it may not be in their consciousness. You should remind them with the real thing what happens and what part of it is relevant before using the analogy.

Analogies can also change someone's perspective on some aspect of the world. For instance, Torricelli compared living at the bottom of the atmosphere with living at the bottom of the ocean. The analogy brings out some striking parallels: in the ocean are fish swimming around while crabs walk about on the seabed; in the 'ocean' of air there are birds 'swimming' around while we walk about at the bottom of this ocean. Just as water presses down on the crab, so the air presses down on us. A fish near the surface, with less water above it, has less pressure on it than one near the bottom. Similarly, when we climb a mountain, the air pressure decreases. After meeting this analogy, it changes how we think of the air around us and our relationship to it. It is no longer a vague and disconnected material but a body in its own right. We now live in that body, in a particular place, rather than simply with it. Science is often about acquiring new perspectives and seeing things in a new light so children need to have conceptual structures that help them do that and they need to talk about and with them so that they become a part of their thinking about the world.

All talk with young children should, of course, be considerate. That is, it should use words and structures children can grasp readily. For instance, use a chronological sequence when explaining; it often helps children grasp an event or set of instructions more easily. At the same time, do not leave gaps in an explanation believing that what you leave out is obvious. Either tell all or better, ask the children what happens next. While you will have to use scientific vocabulary, try to begin with simpler terms, then pair them with the scientific terms, and finally use the latter alone. For instance, you might begin talking about 'push apart', then 'push apart: the proper word is repel', then 'repel, remember that means push apart' and, finally, 'repel; what does that mean?'.

Discussion

Discussion is, by definition, a two-way affair. An element of discussion is often present in explanation when children seek to clarify something or you check that they are follow-ing what is being said. Here, while you may be steering the course of the discussion and have particular ends in mind, children are intended to make a very significant contribution. For instance, an outcome might be an explanation, a justification or a design for an investigation generated by the child with your guidance. However, for a discussion to be fruitful, children need to know how to engage in it and they need to be suitably seated so that discussion is facilitated. Some teachers prefer a circle but other seating may work well for you. Whatever physical arrangements you use, establish it as a routine. Finally, the children need some basic rules about speaking, listening, responding, turn-taking and respectful behaviour to one another.

Suppose the intention is to open up and explore the topic of *Clothes* with young children, leading to the properties of the fabrics used for garments with different functions. You might begin with a picture of people in different kinds of weather and ask the children what time of year each is and what the differences are they can see. The next key question could be: Why do people wear different things at different times of the year? Do they wear different things? What is best to wear on a cold morning? What makes it best? You might have some fabric samples and pass them around to examine. Which is their favourite? Why? Would it be good to wear on a warm day? Why? Magnifying glasses might be passed out at this point for a closer examination of the fabrics. What does waterproof mean? Why do you think this one is waterproof? How could we test it like a scientist to see if it is really waterproof? The children's collective responses and their evaluation of each lead to a design for a simple experiment which compares the fabrics for this property. The children now do the investigation and could be gathered together again for a concluding discussion about what they found. Their new knowledge might now be extended by a discus-sion of what things they might use the waterproof material for other than for clothing, asking for justifications of their choices.

During teacher-led discussions of this kind, you will also have the opportunity to *model* your thinking. This is when you respond to a question or are faced with a problem and think out aloud for the children. For example, a light bulb will not come on in a simple circuit so you begin, 'Let me see, now. Both wires are on the battery and the battery is a new one. I wonder if the bulb is OK. Let's hold it up to the light. Yes it looks OK, there's the filament all in one piece . . .' This lets the child see *and* hear the non-random, step-by-step process which underpins the fault finding process. On the next occasion, you have them do the same thing and talk it through aloud in that way while you listen. A different situation is when demonstrating a practical procedure: 'Now the first thing I should do is . . . because . . . Hmm. It hasn't moved much. I'd better change the ruler for one with millimetres on it, that would suit it better. Next, I must be sure I keep it fair so I'll . . .' Notice how you demonstrate the reasons for the actions and hence show the children that the reasons are important. Similarly, when exploring a causal link, you might say. 'Oh, look! That must be *because* . . .' This modelling serves several functions. First, it lets the children know there is a rational basis for things and that this is what matters. Second, it lets them hear thinking processes 'in action' and brings them to awareness so you can discuss them. Third, it provides a pattern for them to follow (or, probably more precisely, for them to follow in reporting on their thinking).

Discussion can also take place on a child to child basis. Young children who have practised discussion with your support may try it on a small group basis. However, you will need to provide a structure for them to work to, at least to begin with. You could break down a discussion into steps and the children are given one step at a time to discuss. Activities for this purpose are described below, under Scaffolds. There is, however, a danger you must be aware of with pupil–pupil discussion in science. Science is not a subject of arbitrary understandings. We aim to develop children's understanding in the direction of the understandings accepted in science as a discipline. While this may develop as hoped in a child–child discussion, it is also possible that misconceptions will be propagated. A vocal and popular child who believes that a fruit floats if it has hollows for its seeds could disseminate that idea widely. This means that group discussions of this nature need to be monitored or, at least, checked in a plenary session when ideas are aired.

Practical work

As mentioned earlier, practical work in science can serve several functions and sometimes more than one at once. You need to be clear what you want the practical work to do. If your aim is to develop conceptual understanding, you may have the children produce some effect simply to experience it, speculate on its causes, and generally discuss how it relates to other things. For instance, they might try out various kinds of magnet on things around the classroom to learn what a magnet is and can do. You may include in it some measurement and focus the children's attention on the patterns in the data and the relationships they suggest. The children, for example, dip a magnet in a bowl of paper clips and count the clips on different parts of the magnet to illustrate that certain parts of the magnet are more significant than others.

If, on the other hand, your intention is to develop investigative skills and procedural understanding, you might design an activity specifically to develop understanding of the control of variables. You might ask, for instance: Which material would be best to use on the floor where everyone seems to slip as they come in? In essence, you want the children to test a variety of surfacing materials such as, cork, carpet, vinyl and concrete. The test they are to carry out has to be fair so they need to control the variables. You may have the children open up the situation through discussion and then plan their investigation. As a result, we would want to see their understanding of variable control improve but, at the same time, it is likely that their understanding of the properties of materials would also benefit. While the follow-up discussion would include a review of fair testing, it should also include a review of this new knowledge to ensure that it is well integrated with existing knowledge.

Since an investigation seems to offer two gains for the price of one, could you always begin a topic with an investigation? The answer is that it depends on the topic. If it is one that the children already have some reasonably well-founded knowledge about, then you can use this to develop ideas for testing. At the same time, the children will have enough subject background to draw on in their planning. As a result, they may develop both practical and conceptual understanding. If, on the other hand, the topic is one for which there is not a great deal of background knowledge, its absence appears to hinder progress and little is gained. In this situation, conceptual understanding should have priority and, once there is a foundation, can be developed into investigations.

Communicating science

It is sometimes said that you never really understand something until you have to teach it. Why should that be? When we are forming our understanding, we tend to be satisfied if we capture the main relationships and make a more or less coherent structure. The problem is in the more or less. The inconsistencies and loose connections make themselves apparent when we have to explain that something to others. Faced with the need to do it, we address those areas and attempt to improve the coherence of our understanding. It is the same with children. Have them talk about their ideas and conclusions and they become aware of the gaps in their understanding. Since talk is a fast-flowing form of communication, some children may stall when they meet a difficulty and dry up. After all, they do not want to make a fool of themselves and others are waiting. Sometimes, they may be able to make good their understanding with a little backtracking, especially if they can think on their feet.

Writing on the other hand, is a slower, more private process. It allows the mind time to think about the gaps and inconsistencies and resolve them. Writing about science need not be simply a report on what has gone before. Understanding at the end of writing can be better than at the outset *provided that* the topic you have given the children to write about needs understanding and not simply a recall of facts. You may need to ask about such facts but, to support understanding, you should also ask for explanations, justifications, reasons, predictions and applications of knowledge.

Writing is not always essential as tasks and pictures can allow a child to exercise understanding. They might, for instance, draw a strip of pictures with labels to describe what they show about a procedure. You may also provide information in words or pictures which require organizing or explaining. The constraint is that they should call for relevant mental engagement.

STRATEGIES

There are a number of specific strategies which you can use in your science lessons to support understanding.

Games

Some of the things you do to support understanding can be turned into games. For example, after orienting the children towards the topic in hand, you could divide them into groups of about four and have them recall what they already know with a dice game. Give each group a sheet of paper, a pencil, a die and each takes a turn to throw it. They respond to particular tasks according to the number which comes up. Prepare cards with the task lists as follows:

1   Think of one thing you know about the topic. Write it on the sheet of paper and put a circle around it. Collect one point.
2   Think of a question you would like to ask about the topic. Write it on the sheet of paper and put a circle around it. Collect two points.
3   Think of one thing you know about the topic. Write it on the sheet of paper and put a circle around it. Collect one point.
4   Miss one go.
5   Think of one thing you know about the topic. Write it on the sheet of paper and put a circle around it. Collect one point.
6   If there are fewer than two circles on the paper, miss a turn. If there are two or more circles then think of a way in which any two are connected. Draw a line between the two and write why they are connected along the line. Collect three points.

Each child has one minute to respond to the task. Note that, in this game, one task appears several times. This is to ensure that there is a press for sufficient elements of prior knowledge to enable other tasks to occur.

Graphic organizers

A graphic organizer is a picture, chart or diagram that helps children structure their ideas and thinking. Usually, the children work on the sheet, completing parts in the order given. They can be designed for planning and executing an investigation, for making sense of a lesson, and for collating and sorting ideas about a topic into some sort of order. Figure 10.3 is an example. Such organizers can also show fairly quickly when children have missed the point of something or have a misconception.

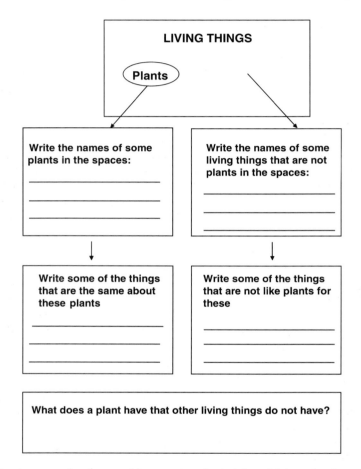

Figure 10.3 An example of a graphic organizer for helping children develop conceptual understanding of plants

Questioning

Every teacher believes in asking questions and often asks a lot of them. To support understanding, questions need to be shaped to that end. This means that the questions you ask should support children's thinking at different stages in their understanding. As an example, suppose you want children to understand a situation, such as the way friction makes it difficult to move something. Possible steps in the sequence might be as follows:

- **Orienting children towards the topic**

  Show the children a picture of horses pulling logs from a forest. Ask questions about the picture in general so they tune in to it. Include one or more **focused questions**, such as, 'What is the horse doing?' 'Does it look easy?' 'Why do you think it looks hard?'

- **Eliciting prior knowledge**

  You can move from the first step straight into this one with focused questions of the kind: 'Have you ever tried to pull something along the ground?' 'What was it?' 'Was it hard to do?' 'What do you think made it hard to do?' 'Is there anything that would make it easier?' 'Why does this make it easier?'

- **Developing additional experience**

  On the basis of the children's responses, suppose you decide that they need additional experience. You have ready a range of surfaces of different thicknesses and some blocks of wood, each with a string attached. The children feel the surfaces to begin with, talk about 'rough', 'smooth', 'catchy' and 'slippy' and look at them with a magnifier. Focused questions during this time might include: 'Why do you think it is slippy?' 'If the horses had to pull logs over giant sheets of sandpaper like this, would it be hard to do? 'Why?'

- **Making a prediction**

  At this point, you might introduce the wooden blocks. 'We don't have any logs but I've got some wooden blocks. We don't have any horses but we do have you. You can be the horses.' Now you ask your focused question: 'Suppose you were a horse and had to pull your log over these things, which do you think would make it the hardest work?' 'Why do you think that?' 'Which would be the easiest?' 'Why do you think that?' 'So, that's what we think will happen. How can we test our idea?'

- **Planning an experiment**

  Focused questions could include: 'What should we do first?' 'Why is it better to do that first?' 'How are we going to make our test fair?' 'Why does that make it fair?' 'Is there anything else we should do to make it fair?' 'How do we know if we are pulling each block with the same pull?' 'Why does that help?'

- **Pulling things together**

  Following the practical activity, you will need to check that the children have arrived at an adequately founded conclusion. Focused questions might include: 'What were we trying to find out?' 'What did you find?' 'Was it what you expected?' 'So, if we want an easy life, what is it that matters when it comes to dragging things along?'

- **Naming concepts**

  You now want to extend their vocabulary with the word, 'friction'. Focused questions here check for prior knowledge, ask for examples of how the word is used, and have the children use the word in the context of the experiment and horse picture, for example, 'Why do we say this sandpaper gives more friction than that kitchen foil?

- ## Applying and extending

    The concept is now applied in new contexts. Focused questions could include: 'Remember that day when it was icy?' 'How many of you fell over?' 'Was that because there was a lot of friction?' 'Why do you say that ice didn't have much friction?' 'What kind of shoes might make it better?' 'Could you have a lot of friction between your shoes and the ice?' 'Why did the caretaker spread sand on the ice?' 'When do we want there to be very little friction. Tell me one time when it would be useful if we did not have a lot of friction.' 'Why is that useful?' 'When would it be useful to have very little friction?' 'Why do we want very little friction on the slide in the playground?' 'Why does it have so little friction against our clothes?

In practice, you might tackle a topic like this in a different way but the point is that, however you choose to do it, the questions are tailored to each step and are aimed at making the children think about reasons for things and causal links. One of these focused questions needs a particular emphasis. Asking for a prediction is a particularly useful question because it makes children organize their ideas and use them to reason with. Their prediction may then be put to the test.

Bridging

Bridging is when you link new understanding to existing understanding. It may be used when what is to be understood does not immediately relate to anything the children know. It is also useful when what they are to understand is counter-intuitive. In essence, it is the building of a series of mental connections (bridges) from what is known or intuitively accepted to what you want the children to understand. For example, suppose you want the children to understand what happens to the water in a wet cloth when it dries, that is, the process of evaporation. Evaporation is usually an invisible process and you could end up saying the equivalent of, 'Take my word for it'. You can do more with bridging.

First, find or arrange something to show evaporation that is reasonably obvious. For example, put out a bowl of warm water on a cold morning. 'Smoke' will be seen coming from the bowl. What is it? Put the bowl close to a cold window. The window will mist over and begin to run with water. The 'smoke' drifts from the dish, onto the window and turns back into water. We cannot always see the water leaving the dish. Have the children breathe outside and note their visible 'breath'. Repeated indoors, it is invisible, but it is still there. They test that by breathing on a cold window and see it mist over. What would happen if we left the dish long enough? What happens to puddles in the street? They disappear because the water slowly drifts away. Take a wet cloth and hang it out on a cold day. The water vapour will be seen leaving the cloth. Hold the cloth near the cold window and see the water mist. When water drifts out of things in this way, we say it has evaporated.

The above sequence is, of course, expressed in condensed form and would take a little time to develop. In comprises a bridge from evaporation from a bowl of warm water, to visible and invisible water vapour in breath, to street puddles, to the drying of a wet cloth. Another example illustrates the way a surface pushes up on an object when the object is placed on it.

First, the children bend an eraser and see how it springs back to its original shape. They can also feel its push. Next, they push down on a springy board. They see the board bend and also feel the upward push on their hands. They now place a heavy pile of books on the board and see the board bend just as it did for them. The board must be pushing up on the pile of books just as it did on them. What happens when we put the books on a table? Does the table bend, too? Use a polished surface and shine a torch at it so that a reflection is cast on the ceiling. Have the children push down hard on the table. They will see the reflection move as the table top bends. Now they place the books on the centre of the table and the reflection will move again. The table bends, just like the springy board, so the table must be pushing up on the pile of books. We may not always see the bend or the squash of tables, chairs and floors because it can be microscopically small but they resist and push back just the same. Here, the bridge is from the eraser, to the springy board to the table.

Supporting understanding might seem daunting. However, it is unlikely that you would need to invent everything you want to do in a lesson from first principles. Draw on existing resources, such as published materials, and your science co-ordinator's advice. Published materials may not provide you with all the support for understanding you want but could give you ideas for things to do. Around these, apply the strategies suggested above. While supporting understanding can be demanding, it is also very rewarding when you are successful.

SUGGESTIONS FOR FURTHER READING

If you would like to explore further some of the issues touched upon in this chapter, the following books should be of some interest to you.

Newton, D.P. (2000) *Teaching for Understanding*, London: RoutledgeFalmer
   In the later chapters of his book, Douglas Newton brings together research findings to provide a succinct summary of how teachers can support learners in their construction of understanding.

White, R. and Gunstone, R. (1992) *Probing Understanding*, London: Falmer Press
   The aim of the book is to describe a variety of ways in which teachers can assess understanding across a range of subjects and at all levels of education. Implicit in it are strategies for exploring and supporting the construction of understanding.

11 What Do We Mean by Effective Planning of Science?

It is vital for the all-round development of the whole child that skills, knowledge, understanding and attitudes are identified, planned, monitored and assessesed. Planning will be a crucial dimension of your work as a teacher. It is also just one step in a cyclical process which involves assessment and reflection. You should appreciate by now that having a good knowledge and understanding of science is not enough to teach it successfully. You also need to have a good knowledge and understanding of the teaching and learning processes that will help the children develop skills and construct their knowledge and understandings. In this chapter, we will look at planning for effective teaching and learning in science, bearing in mind the needs of all pupils. Earlier, the ten criteria for good practice in primary science were introduced (DES, 1985). In this chapter, we will begin to look in detail at some of these criteria, since they relate directly to effective planning.

PLANNING FOR PRIMARY SCIENCE

When planning for science there are four particular criteria you need to think about: *breadth, balance, continuity* and *progression*.

All pupils should be introduced to a **breadth** of scientific experiences. Such experiences need to support the development of a knowledge and understanding of science as a process, a way of thinking and working and the skills which underpin that process. They also need to support the acquisition of conceptual understanding, the facts, ideas and generalizations which underpin science as a body of knowledge, and enable explanations of phenomena.

Since science is a core area of the curriculum, most pupils are required to study it throughout the period of compulsory schooling. Therefore, the science education programme planned to achieve this needs to reflect, at each key stage, a **balance** across the major components of science. The National Curriculum Order for Science states that contexts derived from the knowledge and understanding of *Life Processes and Living Things*, *Materials and their Properties* and *Physical Processes* should be used to teach pupils about the methods which underpin Experimental and Investigative Science. Through careful planning, equal weighting must be given to the development of skills and the acquisition of knowledge and understanding.

Programmes of work in science education should be designed to support the acquisition of greater levels of skill, knowledge and understanding in science. The complex matter of **progression** was discussed earlier.

Finally, the primary school phase of children's education is very varied. In some local authorities, children transfer from first to middle schools when they are 8 or 9 years of age. In other areas, the system involves a move from infant to junior school at age 7 years, and then a further move to secondary school at age 11 years. There also exist schools where the children stay through the primary stage in one school, although the internal organization of the school might have clear stages. Indeed, these stages are highlighted by the National Curriculum itself with its key stage changes at ages 7, 11 and 14 years. The consequence of this mix is that, if what has been achieved at each stage or in each school is not to be wasted, then links are needed between the schools or stages. There is a need to plan for **continuity** both from class to class, phase to phase and school to school. Most schools have structures in place intended to aid transition from one phase of education to the next. These are often concerned with reducing to a minimum the emotional disruption that such transitions can cause children. The National Curriculum Orders make it essential that curriculum continuity is also supported. Some strategies which are often used include:

- Visits by older pupils in the infant, first or primary school to the next school they will attend. They could be involved in some science activities while they are at the same time becoming familiar with their new environment.
- Visits by pupils in the first class of the new school which the pupils will be attending to work alongside the older infant, first or primary school pupils, perhaps in a peer tutoring capacity. This can work well for practical science activities.
- Science fairs, involving all the schools in the area, with common themes or investigations so that children can talk to one another about what they are doing and share experiences.
- Joint staff meetings to share ideas, consider common issues such as planning, record keeping and assessment and, possibly, to organize some joint in-service training time.

To achieve breadth, balance, continuity and progression in the science curriculum, school staff use a variety of planning stages, usually described as long-term, medium-term and short-term planning. Most local education authorities have produced guidelines for schools on preparing long, medium and short-term plans. Although these terms apply to the requirements of all areas of the National Curriculum and religious education, the focus here is obviously the science curriculum.

Long-term planning for science

Long-term planning for science is usually a whole school process, led by the science co-ordinator. It provides an overview of the science experiences planned and must fulfil a number of needs. It should:

1   address the general organization of all the science work to be undertaken in the school;
2   relate directly to long-term cycles of teaching and learning in science, for example, science in the early years or overlapping two-yearly blocks or a whole key stage;
3   identify the science focus for the major areas of experience that provide a coherent curriculum for the children;
4   ensure the science curriculum is broad and balanced, and provides continuity throughout and between phases, stages or schools as well as meeting the needs of the children;
5   address the development of scientific skills, concepts and attitudes;
6   give maximum autonomy to teachers to devise medium-term plans within the agreed framework and enable them to develop and use children's personal interests, current events and other relevant opportunities.

In most schools, the long-term planning will already be in place. As a student or a newly qualified teacher you will probably be given a copy of the science policy statement with its broad overarching aims, links to other relevant policies (such as the school's assessment policy) and the long-term plan for science. This will tell you, usually in the form of some master timetable, what areas of science you will be covering with your class at a particular time of year. Figure 11.1 gives you an example of a long-term plan for a typical primary school.

Medium-term planning for science

Once the long-term plan has been constructed, groups of teachers often work together at the next level of planning. This really shifts the focus from an overview of the school to a more detailed overview of your class within a particular phase. Medium-term planning should:

1   evolve directly from the long term planning for science;
2   address all the science work to be undertaken by a group of children in a class or a year group over a lengthy period of time like a term or a half-term;
3   describe the organization of science in terms of what is to be included, the main learning experiences to be offered and how they are to be organized, all at an undifferentiated level;
4   identify the relevant parts of the Programmes of Study and Attainment Targets of the National Curriculum Order for Science to be covered;

| | Class/ | AUTUMN TERM | | SPRING TERM | | SUMMER TERM | |
	Teacher	1st Half	2nd Half	1st Half	2nd Half	1st Half	2nd Half
Pre-Ks1	Nursery	Senses	People who help us	Colour	Weather	Food	Seashore
	Reception	Harvest / Fruit and Vegetables	Time/Day and Night	Weather	Water	Growing Things	• Ourselves as Animals
KS1	Year 1	Day, Night & Seasons	Birds as Animals	Transport & Movement	Sound and Communi-cation	Water - Floating & Sinking	Seashore
	Year 2	Me, Myself & My Family	Light and Colour	Water and Dissolving	• Electricity	• Magnetism	Seasons & Growth
Lower KS2	Year 3	Houses & Homes	Ourselves - Body and Health	Senses	• Air	Plants and Soil	Seasonal Changes
	Year 4	Colour & Camouflage	Hot and Cold	Ourselves and other Animals	Homes	• Cookery & Changes	• Sound and Music
Upper KS2	Year 5	• Rocks and Fossils	• Changes of State (SLG)	• Magnetism	• Forces and their Effects	• Exploring Environments: the Local Wood	•
	Year 6	Air and Flight	Water & Flotation	Transport & Communic-ation	Electricity in our homes	Colour & Light	Water & Flotation

Two teachers have mixed age classes (Y4/5 and Y5/6); to work a three-year rolling programme between them.
• Additional topics to give breadth and balance and to ensure NC requirements are met.
As far as is feasible, teachers still have at least four of the topics they like to teach.

Figure 11.1 Long-term planning: a school programme for science (from Newton and Newton, 1998b, p. 122)

5   identify through assessment the range of levels of skills, knowledge and under-standing in the science experiences within the class or year group;
6   involve children as far as possible in the planning process so that they can begin to take ownership of their own learning.

Medium-term planning is where you, as an individual teacher, begin to focus on the needs of your class within the specified areas of study. The planning is much more detailed, often culminating in a scheme of work for a half-term or whole term science topic. Teachers often begin this stage by brainstorming the topic to identify what *might* be included in the scheme of work. Then the ideas are sorted into a progressive structure which shows the broad aim, a sequential development of skills, concepts and ideas, assessment targets and methods, and resource needs. An example of a scheme of work for a topic on *Clothes* is shown in Figure 11.2.

Task 11.1 Putting across ideas in science – medium-term planning	Choose a primary science topic that you might teach on a school placement.

1 Identify the knowledge and understanding that under-pins the topic and is important for you to put across to children of a specified age.
2 Sort your ideas into a sequence of steps which represent the order in which you want to introduce and develop the ideas.
3 For each step, identify those aspects that would benefit from some sort of concrete input. This could be a visual aid – artifact, poster, slides, television programme, chalkboard work – or it could be a practical activity of some kind.
4 Identify the different ways you might organize and manage this sequence of lessons.
5 What would be your main resource needs?
6 Link what you have produced to the National Curriculum requirements to show how you are meeting these.

Short-term planning for science

Once again, when you go into school on a teaching practice you may well find that the medium-term planning has been completed and you are expected to translate it into more detail at the daily or weekly level. Short-term planning is very much at the level of what will be done next week or tomorrow in science. It should:

1 evolve directly from the medium-term planning for science;
2 address all the science work to be undertaken by the children in a class or year group over a short-term period like a day or a week;
3 use the results of prior assessment to address the needs of the individual children in the class;
4 describe the science activities to be undertaken, including:
   - timing (date, day, time, approximate length of the lesson/activity . . .)
   - pacing (approximate length of each part of the lesson/activity . . .)
   - class organization (whole class, group or individual work . . .)
   - teacher focus (teaching whole class, working with groups . . .)
   - resources needed (what, when, where . . .)
   - how the work addresses the NC Programmes of Study
   - main learning and behavioural objectives (or targets)
   - organization for differentiation (by task, outcome, support . . .)
   - main assessement targets

Topic: ....*Clothes (Keeping Warm)*...................................   Class: ......*Y4*.......

Date/term: ....*Spring term, first half (5 weeks)*...................................

Time: ...*Thursday afternoons, 1.15–2.35 pm (1 hr 20 min.)*...................................

Aim(s): *By the end of the programme, most children will:*
1. *recognize that temperature is a measure of how hot or cold objects are;*
2. *be able to use thermometers to measure temperature;*
3. *be able to identify which materials might be good insulators;*
4. *investigate insulators and record results;*
5. *apply this knowledge to our choice of clothing in cold weather.*

Week	Targets and Outcomes	Activities
1	*Sense of touch as temperature measure.* *Thermometers for accuracy; using thermometers.*	*Ice cubes in hands and bowls of warm water; compare inside and out.* *Exploring how thermometer readings change; taking temperatures and recording results.*
2	*Keeping ourselves warm; insulators.* *Temperature as a measure of how hot or cold something is.*	*Clothes we come to school in; observing fabrics and fibres with hand lenses.* *Generating questions for investigation.*
3	*Applying ideas in new contexts – setting up and carrying out an investigation into insulators.* *Recording results and using evidence.*	*Investigating insulators (directed)* *– the best scarf* *– the best gloves/mittens* *– the best socks* *– the best coat.*
4	*Continuing investigations from week 3; groups identify their own approach and procedures to investigate the insulating properties of newspaper, bubble-wrap, etc.*	*Investigating insulators (free choice)* *– investigate which of the given materials would keep a homeless person warmest.*
5	*Explaining ideas and applying them in new contexts.* *Class record / display*	*Group activities* *– designing an outfit for a winter holiday; justifying choice; presentation to class.*

Figure 11.2 Medium-term planning: a scheme of work

5   allow for evaluation and reflection to inform future planning;

6   ensure that over the long term the balance of the activities (in terms of targets) matches those identified in the long-term plans for science.

Short-term planning is usually completed using a lesson planning proforma. Your college or university will probably have provided you with examples. A planning sheet that I find particularly useful for sorting the main elements of the planning is shown in the Teaching Ideas Sheet in Figure 11.3. A structure like this helps you to clarify your objectives or targets and aspects such as support for understanding and the balance between Sc1 and Sc2, 3 or 4.

Task 11.2 Using a teaching ideas sheet

Thinking about the sequence of lessons you planned in Task 11.1 above, choose one lesson and complete a teaching ideas sheet for it.

Write a script for your own dialogue. Now imagine you have your class in front of you. Use a tape recorder and record about 15 minutes of your lesson as you use your script to guide you through your exposition.

Listen to the recording. Ask yourself:
- *Have I introduced the topic in an interesting way?*
- *Are my examples appropriate to the children's needs and interests?*
- *Do I make effective use of my voice?*
- *Do I use questions appropriately?*
- *Do I pause long enough for children to absorb information and construct a response?*
- *Do I explain new ideas and vocabulary clearly?*

Evaluate your exposition and write down five things you could do to improve it.

MATCHING ACTIVITIES TO CHILDREN'S NEEDS

When planning your science lessons and activities you will need to keep the notion of quality in mind. A learning activity of high quality is one which:

- consolidates the development of skill(s) or the construction of knowledge or understanding or enables the children to take the next step in their learning of a skill or concept;
- results in learning in science that can be used and applied in new contexts;
- is a coherent part of the learning process, contributing to and supporting other learning activities in science and, perhaps, across the curriculum;
- is seen by the children as being relevant to their development and is thus motivating;

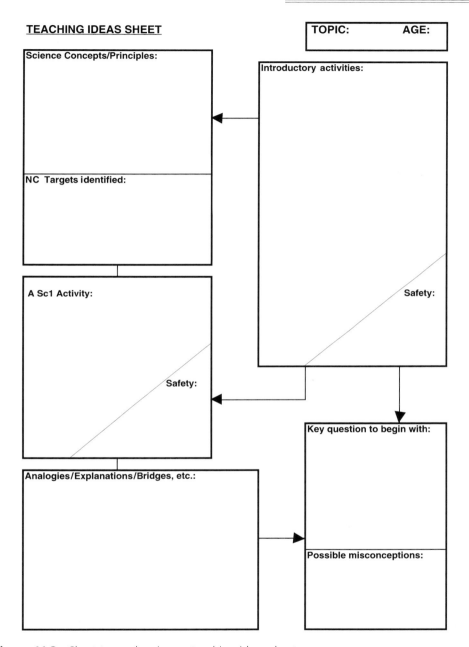

Figure 11.3 Short-term planning: a teaching ideas sheet

- is differentiated to match the assessed needs of the children as part of the progressive development of their scientific skills, knowledge and understanding.

To do this, you will need to think particularly about the individual needs of the children and the differences between them.

> **Task 11.3 Children with different needs in primary science**
>
> While you are in school, try to arrange to have a talk with the school's SENCO (special educational needs co-ordinator). Find out as much as you can about the school's SEN policy and how it is implemented throughout the school and across the curriculum. Ask her or him for some ideas on how to recognize different needs amongst the pupils you will be teaching.
>
> Ask your class teacher what strategies he or she uses in science to support children with different needs so as to ensure they receive maximum opportunity to achieve their potential.

DIFFERENT NEEDS AND DIFFERENTIATION

Children are different from each other. Teachers will tell you they have taught the same age group for ten years but no two classes have been the same. Not only are there physical variations in what the children are able to do, but the variety of learning needs in terms of intellectual ability can be large. The Cockcroft Report (DES, 1982) referred to the seven-year spread of ability in any primary classroom. This means you could have some 8 or 9-year-old children in your Y4 class who are still working at the level of 5 or 6-year-olds while others are at the level of 11 or 12-year-olds. To cater for these different needs and abilities, you will have to *differentiate* in some way. In essence, the intellectual and practical demands made by science education should be suited to the abilities of all pupils allowing the highest possible standards to be achieved by the most able pupils while catering for the needs of those pupils unable to reach those standards. At the same time, it should provide the essential experience of a broad and balanced science programme for all pupils. So how can you do this?

What can be differentiated?

The first thing to say is that differentiation means different things to different teachers. You can differentiate almost anything. In other words you provide something different for different children according to their needs. So you can differentiate:

- by content – provide different tasks/activities in science for different children;
- by outcome – have different expectations from the same task/activity;

> **Task 11.4 Differentiated teaching**
>
> Ask your teacher to identify a child with learning difficulties in your class who you can observe in detail across a range of science lessons and activities.
>
> As you observe the child, make notes on what she or he does. Focus in particular on:
> - the general level of interest shown by the child to each lesson;
> - how the child participated in each lesson in terms of asking and answering questions, interacting with other children and contributing to the lesson;
> - how often the child was on task and off task;
> - the quality of the child's written work;
> - the quality of the child's investigative work and his or her level of skill;
> - how the child behaved when he/she encountered difficulties;
> - how independent the child was; and,
> - how the teacher responded to the child's needs.
>
> What do your notes tell you about the child's needs? What strategies for differentiation to meet these needs can you use to help this child?
>
> Discuss your ideas with your class teacher.

- by support – provide verbal or written support for some children and not others;
- by resources – limit or structure the resources used by some children;
- by language – adjust your vocabulary to suit different groups;
- by group – have the children in groups by ability, each with specific targets;
- by worksheet – have different workcards/sheets for different children;
- by time – allow less able students longer to complete tasks.

The list could go on. In an ideal world, differentiation would be at the level of the individual child. So in a class of thirty-five children you would have thirty-five separate (differentiated) science programmes running. In the real world, you are unlikely to have the time, the resources or the energy to operate such a system. Most teachers operate the class as three, four or five differentiated groups.

A model for differentiation

There is no single, simple model for differentiation in science. One possible way of working, used by many teachers is shown in Figure 11.4. It starts from medium-term planning in that it focuses on the learning experiences that are central to the whole class, the main skills, knowledge and understanding. In your preparatory planning you will have identified the aims and objectives, content and learning contexts for the whole class. Within this you need to identify the main skills, knowledge and understanding

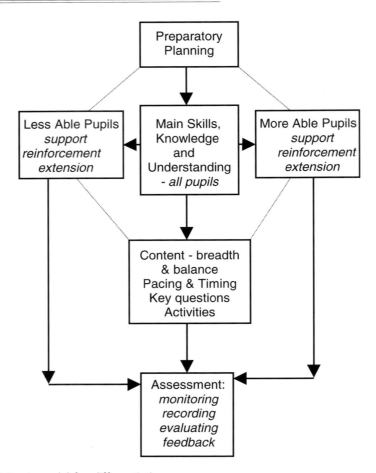

Figure 11.4 A model for differentiation

that *all* pupils must develop. These are to be introduced in some way to the whole class. To do this you need to make judgements about starting points and prior experiences, drawing on assessment evidence and baseline information. You also need to be very clear about what you are doing and why and how you are doing it. You will then need to identify the main route in terms of the breadth of the experiences, pacing and timing, the language you are using to question and explain and the resources you will require.

At this point you will recognize that more than one route will be needed. Some pupils will need support in some way. It may be pupils that are less able or have some sort of learning or physical disability. It may be you must consider the needs of more able children. This means you need to think about at least two groups, one either side of the main route. Your next step would be to identify different levels of activity and experience, perhaps just three. This number is quite arbitrary, and should be a reflection of the needs of the children in your class. However, remember that the more groups you have the harder it is to plan, organize, monitor and assess the different groups. HMI evidence would suggest that with more than five groups this becomes difficult to do. The experiences you select for the different groups should have at their heart the main skills, knowledge and understanding, but be varied in terms of breadth and depth of content, pace and timing, support and reinforcement, and language used. Generally, less able pupils will need experiences which are sharply focused, broken down into small steps or stages, involve simplified or supported language, located in concrete, relevant contexts and enable reinforcement of the learning experiences. The more able, on the other hand, can usually be extended through deeper and more open-ended tasks, in which they take more responsibility themselves for staging the experiences and locating the relevant contexts. They also enjoy using scientific vocabulary. The next stage would be for the different groups to come together to share their experiences, present their findings and draw conclusions. Throughout this process, you would interact with the children in different ways and for different purposes, as discussed in the next chapter. This would include monitoring progress and collecting assessment evidence.

Task 11.5 **Differentiation in** **primary science**	For a topic you will teach on your next placement, choose one of the science lessons. Identify: • the core idea(s) which you want the children to acquire as a result of the lesson/experience;

- the core skill(s) which you want them to develop and use as a result of the lesson/experience;
- the main activity(ies) which you want the children to carry out;
- how you will assess the learning which occurs as a result of the lesson/ experience.

Now think of your class as having three broad ability bands. Assume that what you have identified above constitutes your main or core ideas. How will you present them so that they suit the needs of the less able band (group) *and* the more able band (group). Think about:
- the language you will use (words, sentence length, density of information);
- the concrete and/or abstract ideas you will introduce and how to support these;
- the resources you will use to support the activity;
- the nature and quantity of help/support you can provide;
- how you will make the experience relevant.

Show your plan to your class teacher and discuss it.

Problems with the model

This very simple model has certain weaknesses. For example, all children can benefit from extension and reinforcement activities, depending upon the nature of the experiences. Also, any model of this nature works on the basis of 'averageness'. It assumes that most teachers identify the children in their class who are in the middle of the spread of ability and one or two groups of children either side of these. This, of course, leads to difficulties in how you define and measure the different needs and abilities, what we mean by the middle group (sometimes called 'average') and how you select for the different groups.

One way to deal with this is to start with an open-ended activity for all the children, in order to find out where the children are. Then design a set of National Curriculum related experiences at several different levels to locate the individuals within the class. Adjust the groups so that the children are matched. However, evaluate children's progress regularly and be willing to change the groups so that the children are not fixed in one. Beware of grouping children for science on the basis of English or mathematics results. The three are not directly linked.

Teachers catering for the individual needs of their pupils are likely to make increasing use of open-ended activities, an approach well-suited to raising questions for experimental and investigative science. The nature of science as a process enables tasks and activities to be interpreted at different levels by individuals and groups of pupils and, consequently, different results, conclusions and explanations can be generated. However, such tasks must be planned with the other criteria for good practice in mind, particularly continuity and progression.

Another thing to think about when planning for differentiation in science is how science information and activities are presented to the children. Some general rules when planning the presentation of science information might include:

- plan carefully what new information needs to be presented to all pupils;
- identify what prior knowledge or experiences the children have had and should have in order to build new knowledge and understanding;
- select the most appropriate and relevant way of introducing the new information to capture attention and motivate the pupils;
- plan for questioning by identifying the key questions and the cognitive purposes they serve;
- consider alternative strategies that support understanding, such as the use of an analogy;
- plan appropriate reinforcement and extension activities to support the information being presented in different ways.

Some general rules when planning practical science activities might include:

- introduce new tasks and activities to the whole class beforehand;
- plan structured tasks and activities that are challenging yet achievable;
- keep oral and written instructions or directions simple, so encouraging pupils' independence on task;
- present practical instructions for non-readers in alternative ways, such as through pictures or tape-recorded directions;
- communicate written tasks in an attractive and appealing way, using short sentences, simple vocabulary and illustrations;

- ensure that all pupils are familiar with the science vocabulary for the activities by using wordlists, dictionaries, labelled diagrams or similar forms of support;
- allow mixed ability groups so that there can be peer support;
- use other adults, school auxiliaries, teaching assistants and parents, either to work with other groups of pupils on non-science tasks or to work with a science group (such adults will need precise instructions);
- have expectations appropriate to the pupils' needs, interests and abilites and recognize all pupils' successes.

Task 11.6 Designing differentiated activities for children in science

Look for science materials on working with children with different needs. Relate the ideas you have collected from these sources to what you have heard, read or seen in school.

Either choose an existing worksheet or activity sheet from a commercial scheme *or* design one of your own to suit a current topic. It should be aimed at the children in the class who are identified by your class teacher as having no specific learning difficulties.

Now modify your worksheet or activity sheet to take into account the needs of:
    [a] a more able child who has some behavioural problems;
and   [b] a less able child who has communication problems.

If you can, try out your worksheet with one or two children in your class and evaluate the outcome.

If space in the classroom allows, a system that lends itself well to differentiated activities in science is the *learning centre* or *learning station*. The main purpose of a learning station is to provide opportunites for reinforcement and enrichment of a topic or theme. It enables pupils to work independently or with a friend and explore experiences, ideas of interest and new challenges. Learning stations have the added advantage that they also allow teachers to provide access to resources and materials in a controlled way. A science learning station and how it can be used is described later in the next chapter.

OTHER THINGS TO THINK ABOUT

Three further criteria for good practice are also important when thinking about planning. These are relevance, equal opportunities and links across the curriculum. All of these have already been discussed at some length in earlier chapters and will be mentioned again here to emphasize their importance in connection with effective planning.

Relevance

Science *is* relevant for all of us but this relevance is seldom made explicit. In the primary school, science education should draw extensively upon the everyday experiences of pupils, providing opportunities in relevant contexts to which and with which the pupils can relate. It should encourage children to appreciate how science can be used to meet human needs and solve problems through technological applications of science. It should show the choices and decisions there are to make. Science education should aim to prepare pupils for lives as citizens in an increasingly scientific and technological society.

Equal opportunities in primary science

Science education should provide equal opportunities for all pupils, ensuring that they find tasks and activities relevant and interesting irrespective of their sex, ability, culture or religious backgrounds. In science in particular, the need to interest girls in and motivate them towards the physical sciences is well documented. The popular view that girls are suited to biology while boys are suited to the physical sciences is wrong. With appropriate teaching and motivation, a positive attitude towards both aspects of science from both sexes can be developed. Attitudes are formed at a very early age and are influenced by the home and the media and by experiences in school. In practical activities, if boys and girls are reluctant to work together it might be better to allow friendship and/or single sex work groups. Later, mixed pairs may be introduced, carefully chosen according to what the teacher knows about the children. Eventually, mixed teams may be tried.

The contributions of different cultures can enhance the learning experiences of all pupils. Use the history of science and a study of some of the people involved in the discovery of scientific ideas from all around the world. This may be a way to make science experiences more relevant as well as introducing the influences of various cultures. You should also think carefully about the examples you draw on to explain ideas or to provide practical activities. Ensure that these are culturally balanced, too.

Links across the curriculum

The skills, knowledge and understanding developed in science can be drawn from a wide range of contexts in real life. After all, science pervades most aspects of our lives and so it makes sense to integrate experiences to emphasize this. While science education can be planned to stand alone in the curriculum this does not have to be the case. A cross-curricular approach can be used to integrate experiences. Many of the topics and themes used in primary schools either have clear science starting points (such as *Ourselves*) or have opportunities for science within them (such as *Houses*, where *Materials* and *Structures and Forces* or *Energy* can all be introduced and developed).

Task 11.7 Effective planning in primary science	In this chapter, the emphasis has been on effective planning and in particular, the importance of identifying the main skills you want the children to develop and practise and the main ideas you want them to acquire.

1 For a scientific investigation which you have seen your teacher use or which you are planning to use yourself, construct a skills web. What is the main skill the children are to develop? What other major skills will the children practise? How have you planned to support the children in the development and use of these skills?

2 For the scientific topic of which the investigation in (1) above was a part, construct a spider chart of the key ideas to be covered. What is the key concept or idea at the heart of the topic? What subordinate or base level concepts do the children need to begin with? What are the superordinate concepts that you think might be acquired?

3 When observing your class teacher teaching a science lesson, try to identify the main skills and concepts that underpin her/his teaching. How is the teacher making these clear to the children?

4 After the lesson, and with your teacher's permission, talk to some of the children about the lesson. Choose pupils across the range of abilities. Ask them for their views on what was important about their science work. What were the skills they were using and developing? What were the new ideas they were learning? What do they know and understand now that they did not know or understand before the lesson? Have the children's ideas changed?

SUGGESTIONS FOR FURTHER READING

If you would like to explore further some of the issues touched upon in this chapter, the following books should be of some interest to you.

Edwards, D. and Mercer, N. (1987) *Common Knowledge: The Development of Understanding in the Classroom*, London: Routledge

Primary science teaching and the various theories of teaching and learning that underpin it are discussed at length by Edwards and Mercer. They view education as 'a communicative process' and researched ways in which knowledge (mainly that which forms the content of the school curriculum) is presented, received, shared, controlled, negotiated and understood by teachers and pupils in older junior (9–11 year) classrooms.

Qualter, A. (1996) *Differentiated Primary Science Teaching*, Buckingham: Open University Press

In this book, Anne Qualter explores the nature of differentiation and how it can be put into practice in primary science lessons. She tackles the difficult question of whether it is really possible to provide differentiated learning activities in science for a class of 30 or more primary children. Throughout, her book is illustrated with examples from the classroom to support her suggestions.

12 What Do We Mean by Effective Organization and Management of Primary Science?

In the previous chapter, we considered planning science activities in line with school policy and children's needs. Here, we will look at the need for you to consider certain operational matters in the primary science classroom such as problems of classroom organization and management and the ways in which you and the children interact during lessons. These operational matters are what Kerry and Eggleston (1988) call the nitty-gritty of classroom life. They describe them as the most critical of all issues and point out that,

> . . . classroom processes are not just about the context of learning but about those aspects of teacher behaviour that are labelled 'teaching skills'. They are about effective classroom management; about the ability of the teacher to explain, question and set interesting and demanding tasks; about the teacher's proficiency in providing a variety of learning experiences which pupils see as valuable.
>
> (pp. 78–79)

Such operational matters will be a reflection of your own personal philosophy of teaching and learning, the complexity of the school situation in which you find yourself and the curriculum requirements. One of the major issues you will need to think about is *motivation*. How can you organize and manage the class so that all children want to do science? Part of this relates to effective planning for learning and the match of relevant tasks to abilities to avoid frustration or boredom. Part of it is a consequence of your own attitude towards science and how you organize and manage the teaching and learning situation.

Effective planning, organization and management strategies will help you to reduce or even eradicate motivational problems in primary science. In this chapter we will look at:

Task 12.1 Motivational problems in primary science	While you are in school, observe the children in your class. What are their attitudes towards learning in science? Do they show signs of any of the following?

- disconnection
- disruption
- disaffection
- disengagement
- reluctant compliance
- minimalism
- hard work and diligence
- obsessive drive

Is their behaviour consistent or variable?

Discuss your observations with your class teacher. Has she or he any further information which can help you to understand the children's behaviours?

Ask your class teacher (or the school's SENCO) for ideas on how to motivate the children. For each of the above behaviours, see if you can identify a strategy to help children exhibiting this behaviour.

- organizing children, classroom and resources;
- managing the teaching-learning environment; and,
- being safety conscious.

ORGANIZING CHILDREN, CLASSROOM AND RESOURCES

The organization of primary schools and the classrooms within them varies. Even where schools profess to hold very similar philosophies and aims, the practice is often very different because children, teachers and resources vary. Some aspects of organization are not within the control of the school, for example, local education authority policies on primary education and in-service training support for staff. Often there are internal factors, such as resource allocation and devolved responsibilities that influence practice. These have implications for how you organize your science.

Documentation introducing the first National Curriculum Orders for Science (DES, 1989) recommended that:

> Schools need to organise the work to suit their children, teachers and circumstances. No one organisational model is likely to be equally appropriate to all.
>
> (para. 8.5)

At the same time, the Orders reminded teachers that:

> While organisational flexibility is essential to our proposals, any scheme devised by a school will need to cover all the relevant parts of the Programme of Study and enable pupils to achieve all the attainment targets specified for the key stage.
>
> (para. 8.6)

Science involves the development of both mental and physical skills and activity as well as the acquisition of procedural and conceptual knowledge and understanding. You will need to teach it in ways which support both of these aspects. There are several things to consider, including:

1   possible teaching methods and approaches in science;
2   ways of organizing your classroom for science;
3   the management of the children during science activities; and,
4   the teacher's role during the science activities.

Teaching methods and approaches

When planning for any area of the curriculum, two main approaches are possible. One is to use a subject-focused curriculum in which science is taught as a separate subject. The other is to plan through integrated topics or themes. There are, of course, hybrids of the two.

For a new teacher, there are some advantages in using the subject-based approach for science. First, it is possible for you to plan a programme for science so that it ensures progression in skills, knowledge and understanding running from the reception class to the oldest pupils in the school. Such a programme avoids the unnecessary duplication of experiences and significant omissions in meeting National Curriculum requirements. It also easy for your school's co-ordinator to monitor such a programme and update it in line with new requirements or staff changes. Second, it is possible for you to focus on particular aspects of science within the programme. For example, you may wish to teach for and give practice in particular aspects of investigative work, like using scientific skills in new contexts or applying a range of skills in a more complete investigation. You can also develop a particular aspect of knowledge and understanding in which children have particular interests and strengths. Third, it is easier to plan for and manage the necessary resources and equipment you will need when the programme is clearly structured in this way.

However, there are also several disadvantages to a subject-based approach. The main one is that the science curriculum offered to the children can lack spontaneity and flexibility. The children have little choice in what they do or when they do it. Such a curriculum tends to be divided into slots in which the children are unable to spend longer than planned on tasks because they must move on to the next lesson. Also, opportunities to link curricular experiences can be missed and experiences risk being seen by the children as detached, irrelevant and with little to offer of long-term value. Nevertheless, these consequences can be avoided by careful planning.

The second approach is to plan the science experiences through topics or themes. The terms 'topic' and 'theme' are often used synonymously although some curriculum designers distinguish between the two. They describe a topic as having a clear subject focus which may be extended and integrated with other subjects, for example *The Romans* (History), *Colour* (Art) or *Capacity* (Mathematics). A theme has a more general experiential focus, for example *Communication* or *Shopping*, and all curricular areas may be developed from it. The topic or theme is usually one chosen by you as the teacher. You then apply your knowledge of the children and the topic concerned to identify specific scientific experiences. Many of the topics and themes popular with primary school teachers either focus upon or lend themselves to the development of science skills, knowledge and understanding.

As with the subject-based approach there are both advantages and disadvantages to this approach. First, the topic or thematic approach can promote realistic, integrated learning experiences, drawn from the immediate environment and unifying many areas of the curriculum. As such, it helps to make explicit the relevance of science to our lives and to the world in which we live. Second, it allows freedom and flexibility, providing opportunities for the children to contribute personal interests and ideas and allowing you to respond spontaneously to events which can be used to stimulate learning. Third, it facilitates different ways of organizing practical activities, particularly small group and individual work, that encourage communication and interaction and can reduce demands on limited resources. Finally, it can allow individuals to work at their own pace and level thus supporting a more differentiated programme.

On the other hand, not every topic or theme will contain opportunities for science activities. Given the status of science as a core subject in the curriculum, it is unlikely that you will feel you can spend a half-term pursuing a topic that does not include science. It is necessary to analyse the experiences that topics present and keep detailed records to ensure that all the appropriate elements of the Programmes of Study for Science are covered.

As is often the case, the appropriate solution would seem to be a blend of the two approaches.

Classroom organization

Classrooms can be organized for science in a number of ways. On some occasions you will prefer to have the *whole class* doing science at the same time. At other times this may be more difficult because it makes heavy demands upon resources. On other occasions, it may be a good way to introduce new ideas and demonstrate procedures to everyone. It is also useful for reporting back and explaining or reiterating particular points. If whole class teaching is used in this way, you may need to re-arrange furniture to maximize involvement and contact. This has an added advantage with younger children who need to be close to feel involved and motivated otherwise they may lose interest.

Often children will work on science investigations in *small groups* of perhaps four pupils. This is particularly appropriate when the equipment and resources are in short supply. You can organize the class into workgroups that can be selected in various ways: friendship groups are a good starting point for practical activities as sharing and co-operation can be more easily facilitated. However, such groups will often be single-sex and there may be occasions when co-operation between the sexes is desirable. Friendship groups may also combine pupils who are like-minded and of similar abilities and so there will be occasions when mixed ability workgroups are desirable to encourage peer suppport. In some schools, peer tutoring is taken further by having a fixed time each week when older pupils work with younger ones on a range of practical activities. An extra adult during practical science work is also useful but they must be well-briefed in their roles. With this method of organization you will retain the option of having the whole class do science at the same time.

| **Task 12.2 Using group work in primary science** | Group work can mean several different things in primary science. When you are on school visits, observe your class teacher and, if possible, the science co-ordinator, teaching science. |

Notice how often the children are working in groups.
What purpose are the groups serving?
Do individual pupils within the group have specific roles?
Do different groups work in different ways on the same task?
What is the nature of the 'science talk' in the groups?
Do the pupils use scientific language or do they re-interpret it into everyday language?
If the group is involved in practical activity, how are the resources managed within the group?
How does the teacher interact with each of the groups?
What purpose does her/his interaction serve?
What do you think are the pros and cons of group work in science?

Discuss your observations with the class teacher. Can she or he add any further information to the picture you are building of group work.

When children do science investigations and experiments as a group they sometimes work better if they are assigned roles or special responsibilities. Initially, these can be allocated by you but, as the children gain confidence and competence, they might select who does what for themselves. For example, with a group of four older junior children one could be the chairperson for the session, leading the group, stating the details of the task or investigation and managing the working arrangements. A second child might be the secretary who records the event. A third member might be the one who collects things and puts them away. Another child might be responsible for deciding how and what is reported back to the whole class and for planning the presentation. All members of the group would be involved in contributing ideas and in carrying out the actual investigation. If the group was one which existed for any length of time, the children could rotate the roles from week to week as they moved on to new investigations. Such a structure offers children real opportunities for developing interaction and communication skills and for co-operative decision making as well as for emphasizing the importance of teamwork and feedback.

Sometimes you might decide to have children working *individually* or *in pairs*. In an ideal world, every child in the class would be able to carry out experiments and investigations, practise skills and manipulate scientific equipment individually or with a partner whenever they wished. However, primary classrooms are seldom ideal. If space allows, individual work can be supported by the use of science areas in the classroom. These could include:

- a three-dimensional display area which can be changed regularly and provide stimulus;
- a clean area for activities which require more mental activity, such as reference skills work and writing;
- an area where messy tasks can be accomplished, such as working with water or making equipment using wood and tools;
- a storage area for the sort of materials used in science but common to all classrooms, such as measuring equipment and containers;
- access to a computer and appropriate science focused software.

Obviously such areas are likely to be dual purpose and used for activities other than science. The science learning station is a development of the idea. A learning station is a place where several children can work at one time, using the resources and activities located in the station. Learning stations can be established for any area of the curriculum or for cross-curricular topic work and are designed to support a differentiated approach to teaching and learning. Children select the tasks to do, the order in which they will do them, and work at them at their own pace and in their own way. The time spent at the learning station can be directed by the teacher or left to the children, as can whether the child works alone, with a partner or with other members of his or her group.

At the learning station, the children will find a background display of posters and artifacts, books, pictures, slides and other resources relevant to the topic under study, along with examples of children's work. This should serve to establish the topic, focus attention and motivate the children. Those who are non-readers can listen to information and instructions on a tape-recorder. The station would offer an assortment of resources, workcards or task sheets. These might include:

- *structured workcards or worksheets*, suggesting things which the children might explore and investigate, with some guidance on how to start their investigations;
- *planning sheets for investigations*, to be completed by the individuals or groups to show the nature of the investigation and how it would be carried out;
- *plan-do-review sheets* to be completed by individuals to indicate what his or her contribution to the investigation was and their evaluation of their learning experiences;
- *support, extension and challenge sheets* to be used as needed.

A record book could be left at the learning station for the children to record when they use the workstation, for how long, which cards or sheets have been completed, and any other information related to their work. Simple instructions, on display above the station, tell the children how to use the station, how many children should be there at any one time, how to use equipment and make good missing items or breakages. When setting up the station, you would need to plan for provision, storage and restocking of resources. However, once established, the children themselves can take responsibility for a lot of this. With younger pupils, an adult can help.

MANAGING THE TEACHING AND LEARNING ENVIRONMENT

As with any experience we offer children, it is important that they know what is expected of them. It is also important that your own attitudes towards science are perceived by the children as positive and do not reinforce stereotypes. Once engaged in scientific activities, the children should be allowed sufficient time to complete them. Rushing activities or leaving them to be finished later not only devalues science, it demotivates the children and reduces the quality of the end product. Also, the different rates at which individuals and groups of children work means that supplementary or extension tasks need to be provided as purposeful alternatives rather than as time fillers. You will need to consider:

Managing resources

Furniture: Few primary schools are likely to have a dedicated science room or laboratory. In most schools, the ordinary classroom tables are likely to be used for science activities. Tables need to be washable or covered to protect their surfaces. They should be clear of all unnecessary objects. Traffic routes need to be planned for collecting and returning resources especially if the children are using water or any messy materials. If the children are to set up an investigation which will last longer than the lesson, where it will be located should be decided beforehand.

Resources: One of the biggest management problems that occurs arises from a lack of resources or inadequate access to them. Whatever storage system is used, you would be wise to organize things so that the children can access and return them as needed. This prevents resources becoming yet another task for you to deal with.

There should be all the basic materials needed by the class or group for the task in hand, but there should also be access to a range of common primary classroom resources, such as paper, coloured pencils, measuring instruments, scissors, tapes and glues, plastic containers and recycled materials. These should be of sufficient variety to allow the children's ideas for investigations to be developed. The children should know what is available, where to find and return it, and how to use it.

Task 12.3 Resources for primary science

While you are in school preparing for your teaching placement, make an assessment of the science resources. Remember to include:

- people – the science co-ordinator as well as your class teacher and school mentor;
- textual materials – the books and schemes available for use, as well as library resources;
- audiovisual resources – television, radio, videotapes, pictures and charts;
- the classroom – space, surfaces, display areas;
- information technology – hardware and software;
- equipment – both science-specific (like hand lenses) and cross-curricular (like rulers and containers);
- The environment – the school grounds and the local community.

What are the arrangements for borrowing and using equipment from other classrooms or central areas? When do you have access to things like the television and videorecorder? How do you arrange to take the children outside or to bring a visiting speaker into the school?

Remember that textual resources are also there to help you and provide support in the teaching of science. These may be posters and wallcharts, workcards, worksheets, pupils' workbooks and textbooks. Many schools use a commercially produced scheme; others have developed their own. Textual materials are, in effect, surrogate teachers.

Task 12.4 Teaching with text

From your library, try to obtain a copy of *Teaching with Text* by Douglas Newton (Kogan Page, 1990). The book describes how to choose, prepare and use textual materials for teaching and learning, and many of the examples are drawn from science education.

There are many published schemes available for primary science teaching and most schools have purchased at least one. Does your school use a commercially produced scheme? If so, look at the materials designed for your class.

Does the scheme support the aims and targets of the
National Curriculum Order for Science?
What topics are covered? Do they match National Curriculum requirements?
How is it structured (workcards or textbooks or . . .)?
How does it support different needs and abilities in your class?
What guidance is provided for teachers?
What is the balance between practical and other activities?
What guidance is given for resourcing science activities?
How is assessment linked with the material?
What do your think are the advantages of using these materials?
What do you think are the weaknesses?
How might you use the scheme to support your teaching?

The management of science experiences

Your role in the management of the science experiences is crucial. What exactly will you be doing? This links directly to what you expect of the children. As a general rule, children are more motivated to learn when given a choice in what they do and variety in ways of doing it. They may learn from first-hand experience and through interaction with others. Your role in this process will vary, depending upon the abilities and needs of the children and the experiences to be introduced and developed. At any one time in science you may take on any or all of the following roles.

Leader: As leader, you facilitate discussion in which you guide the children's thinking and ideas, support their recognition of necessary prior knowledge, and provide information, instructions and guidance for practical work as well as new knowledge and experience.

Questioner: As questioner, you use key questions to focus attention on important aspects of the science experience, guide the children's observations, encourage them to make predictions and draw inferences. Questions can also be used to encourage the application of ideas and the evaluation and making of hypotheses with the aim of helping the children to generate their own questions for exploration and investigation.

Task 12.5 Pupils' questioning in primary science	Once you have had a chance to plan and teach some primary science, look back through your lesson/activity plans and consider how many questions you asked. What kinds of questions did you ask? Were you using a full range of closed and open questions?

What opportunities did you give the children to ask questions? Which situations in those lessons could have been used to encourage children to ask questions?

Think of, and try out, some ways to deal with problems like:
- children who are reluctant to ask questions;
- children who dominate question asking;
- children who ask only low-level questions.

Assessor: As assessor, you appraise the ideas put forward during discussions and the questions raised for investigation and experimentation. Through questioning and discussion with the children, you encourage explanation, justification and evaluation.

Challenger: As challenger, you use open-ended tasks and activities to encourage the children to generate the whole process of investigating an idea for themselves. The challenge can come initially by focusing on various parts of an investigation, such as particular skills or strategies, or the use of certain equipment or materials. Gradually the challenge is widened to encourage the children to take full responsibility for planning the experimental work, collecting the evidence and considering it in ways that generate scientific explanations.

Observer: As observer, you stand back and observe the children as they generate their own questions and investigate them. Such observation can also be the starting point of assessment.

BEING SAFETY CONSCIOUS

Safety in primary science should be a paramount concern. It is your responsibility to check that all equipment, materials and practices are safe for the children to use. You should solve any problems or report faults to the science co-ordinator. The Association for Science Education (ASE) produces an excellent handbook on safety in primary school science, *Be Safe!* (ASE, 1990) which is well worth reading. There will also be a general school safety policy with which you must comply. This is likely to draw upon information from the local education authority (LEA), and LEA requirements do vary so you must check them.

Although special clothing is not required in science in the primary school, some activities might need safety glasses or goggles. (These should be available for design and technology work.) If pupils use computers and electronic sensors, then appropriate safety precautions should be taken. A circuit breaker should always be used with all electrical equipment operating from the mains, even if the children are not actually handling the equipment. It is advisable to prepare a summary statement on safety in science, perhaps no more than two sides of A4, which emphasizes the key points and brings together the school's general safety policy, the specific LEA guidelines and the more detailed ASE guidelines.

At some point you are likely to want to take your class out of school. This may be to do some work in the playground or on the school field but if you wish to go to a local park or a museum, for example, there should be very clear school guidelines which you must follow. These will cover matters such as:

- legal requirements and obtaining permission;
- ratio of teachers/adults to pupils;
- matters to do with transport, clothing, food and toilets;
- matters of timing and costing;
- health and safety requirements.

In addition, such visits must be carefully prepared for. You will need to make advance visits, carry out safety audits, plan what the children will do and how the organization and management will work. With visits out of school it is advisable to be over-prepared and very cautious. Try to anticipate all likely difficulties and hazards.

The remaining criterion for good practice that has not yet been discussed in any depth is assessment. Progress in science must be assessed in ways that recognize the importance of thinking and working scientifically and of science as a body of knowledge. Assessment is an important aspect of teaching and learning in science and will be the focus of the next and final chapter in this section.

| Task 12.6 Taking children out of school | Most schools organize at least one visit or trip each year for pupils. If you have the opportunity to organize a science-related trip, what sort of things would you need to think about? |

The visit might be to:

- a hands-on interactive museum;
- an industry and enterprise project;
- a natural science field trip in a local environment.

1   Make a list of the things you would have to do before you take the children on the visit.
2   What would you hope the children would gain from the visit?
3   What would be the major health and safety considerations? How would you address these?
4   Talk to your class teacher or the science co-ordinator about the feasibility of organizing a visit during your school placement. What is the school policy? How does s/he go about this sort of task?

SUGGESTIONS FOR FURTHER READING

If you would like to explore further some of the issues touched upon in this chapter, the following books should be of some interest to you.

ASE (1990) *Be Safe! Some aspects of safety in science and technology for key stages 1 and 2*, Hatfield: ASE
This short booklet provides an excellent summary of what you need to think about in relation to safety in primary science generally and within the context of the separate Programmes of Study.

Sherrington, R., (ed.) (1998) *ASE Guide to Primary Science Education*, Hatfield: ASE
The guide is an edited volume of papers covering major issues which affect the quality of science teaching and learning. It includes sections on curriculum policy, teaching and learning strategies, planning, and management and organization.

13   What Do We Mean by Are the Children Learning?

Teachers are constantly making judgements about what is happening in their classrooms and what the children are achieving. In the first instance, these are likely to be based on subjective impressions. With experience, you will quickly sense when tasks and activities are going well and the atmosphere is conducive to learning. However, there are times when such judgements must be based on a more systematic and objective process of *assessment*.

Assessment evidence can be collected in a variety of ways and for a variety of purposes. However, it is important to remember that assessment produces information that is as much a reflection of the experiences you, as the teacher, have provided as it is of pupils' progress and performance. When the first SATs for the National Curriculum were being trialled with Year 2 pupils, a cartoon in the *Times Educational Supplement* showed a boy offering his very depressed teacher his school report and saying, 'I think you'll find my test results are a good indication of your abilities as a teacher!'. This cartoon summed up the whole business of assessment. It is a complex process which tells teachers as much about what they are doing and how well they are doing it as it does about pupils' attainment. After all, pupils can only achieve what the opportunities provide. Therefore, any assessment of pupils' progress must be matched by evaluation of the learning experiences provided and the teaching and learning strategies employed. Consequently, we need to think about:

- planning what and how scientific experiences are going to be provided for pupils;
- assessing the pupils development of skills, knowledge and understanding in science through the planned experiences provided;
- recording in an appropriate way what has been planned, experienced and achieved; and,
- reporting these achievements.

Assessment is probably one of the most difficult areas of educational activity that you will have to deal with. The whole is a complex package and one that some teachers feel they have not been well prepared for. This chapter will consider the complexity of the assessment process and its inter-connections with other aspects of teaching and learning. A model for assessment will be presented to provide a framework for the discussion.

A MODEL FOR ASSESSMENT

When we think about assessment, we are usually thinking about assessing the progress being made by the pupils in our care. However, the pupils' progress is only a part of the picture. We must also consider the science curriculum offered to those pupils, the teaching methods, approaches and strategies used by you to deliver that curriculum, and the starting and finishing points in the children's learning. In other words, the *what*, the *how* and the *how well*. These questions provide a model for assessment, summarized in Figure 13.1.

The question of planning what to teach in science is not the problem for the teacher that it was in the past. The National Curriculum delineates the 'what' in the Programmes of Study for Science. These are translated into specific learning and behavioural objectives or targets in the detailed level descriptors for each Attainment Target which can be used for assessment. The school in which you work will probably already have long and medium-term plans in place that reflect this. The major task for you is to absorb these into your short-term daily lesson plans, to ensure that appropriate records are kept to show what has been planned and offered to pupils, and monitor progress and achievement.

The question of how to offer these experiences to children is not constrained by the National Curriculum Orders for Science. There is no requirement to approach science in a particular way, to use any one method or to employ recommended teaching strategies. These decisions are left to you. However, with teacher appraisal systems and cycles of Ofsted inspection, a teacher's selection of methods, approaches and strategies will be judged according to their perceived effectiveness. Of course, teachers must be seen to be effective in the eyes of pupils and parents as well. Test results are often seen as measures of effectiveness.

The final question of how well relates to the assessment of pupils' progress. As Harlen (1983) suggested when discussing assessment in science,

> Assessing children's educational development is an essential part of fostering that development, of teaching, so that both short and long-term planning of activities can match the stages reached and provide optimum opportunities for further learning.

(p. 3)

You need to appreciate the different purposes assessment can serve, what evidence would satisfy those purposes, what methods would provide the evidence, the strengths

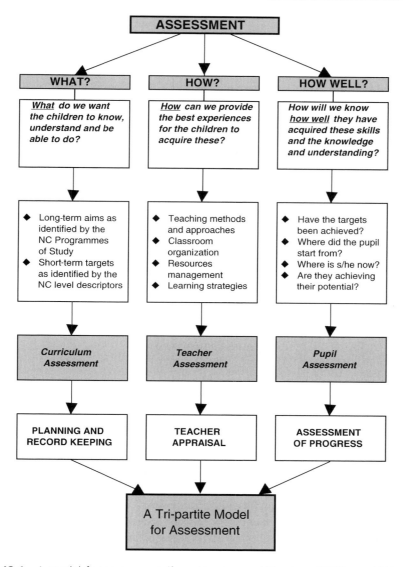

Figure 13.1 A model for assessment (from Newton and Newton, 1998b, p. 139)

and weaknesses of the different methods in different contexts, and how the evidence will be used. This provides four stages for the assessment cycle, summarized in Figure 13.2. The first stage to consider is the question: Why are you assessing? since the answer will shape the remaining stages. The loop is closed in that the end of the cycle, how the evidence is used, should inform the next planning and assessment cycle. At any stage, if there is not a good reason or answer then it is probably not worthwhile continuing with the assessment.

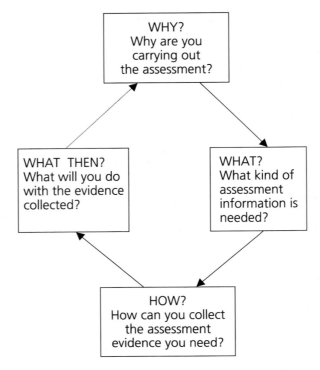

Figure 13.2 Key questions in the assessment cycle

PURPOSES OF ASSESSMENT

You may teach science as part of an integrated, cross-curricular topic, such as *Houses and Homes*. Alternatively, you may prefer to teach it through science activities that are separate from whatever else is happening in the classroom, as with topics like *Magnetism* or *Minibeasts*. Whichever approach you use, you will need to assess the learning of the children in order to ensure that individual pupils are working at the appropriate level for any given programme of study. In this way, the assessment process serves three major purposes:

- evaluation;
- communication; and,
- summation.

Assessment *evaluates* skills, knowledge and understanding and the outcomes can be used formatively and diagnostically. It provides you with evidence that enables you to:

1   match science experiences to individual pupil's needs, interests and abilities;
2   determine what the next step in the learning process should be;
3   plan learning and behavioural targets for your pupils; and,
4   decide on the nature and quantity of the feedback to pupils on their performance and progress.

Assessment aids *communication* by enabling you to:

1   discuss with pupils their progress;
2   advise parents on their child's progress and how it can be supported at home;
3   provide information for the pupils' next teacher on the progress made and the evidence base for those judgements; and,
4   prepare statements about the child's progress to be the basis of discussion with other significant adults, such as supply teachers and educational psychologists.

Assessment *summarizes* children's achievements over time. It provides you with an overall picture of a pupil's progress, indicating what she or he knows, understands and can do. This allows comparisons with the pupil's prior levels of achievement, with those of her or his year group and with the national picture.

METHODS OF ASSESSMENT

Testing the children in some way is the usual method that springs to mind when considering assessment. While various kinds of tests have a major role in assessment, it is not the only method. The principle stated by the Task Group on Assessment and Testing (TGAT, 1987), prior to the introduction of the National Curriculum, is as valid today as it was then:

> The assessment process itself should not determine what is to be taught and learned. It should be the servant, not the master, of the curriculum . . . It therefore needs to be incorporated systematically into teaching strategies and practices at all levels.
>
> (TGAT, 1987, para. 4)

The main strategies for assessing science formatively and diagnostically are:

- observing children at work on their science activities;
- discussing activities with them, during or after the science lesson;
- examining the products of their activities;
- setting specific science tasks.

A fifth strategy which some teachers use is to involve children in their own assessment. Each of these will be considered in turn.

Observing children as they work

Teachers observe children all the time. Such observations are often discrete and check on behaviour, standards, performance and compliance with expectations. From such observations, you gain immediate and detailed feedback on the children's responses to the various activities and experiences and you can respond quickly. Observing children in this way serves a clear diagnostic purpose.

Task 13.1 Observing children as they work

As the children are working on science activities, sit with a group to observe them. Make notes to show:
- how they work with one another;
- individual roles within the group;
- the nature of any interactions between them.

Afterwards, analyse the activity.
1 Was any one person dominant?
2 How much of their interaction was related to science?
3 What ideas were contributed by individuals?
4 What kinds of questions did the children ask?
5 How did you participate in the activity, if at all?
6 How did individual roles emerge?

What does your observation tell you about children's interaction during practical activities in science? How can you use such observation to explore children's ideas and misconceptions?

It is seldom possible to spend very long observing one child or one group of children. The rest of the class will demand your attention too. If there is another adult in the classroom (a parent or a specialist teaching assistant, for example) then this enables you or the other adult to make more structured observations. Dipping into the activity at significant points to observe the children for a few minutes might be possible. A whole activity could be monitored with a particular small group by the adult helper. Photographs can also be useful. Noticing how children do things, not just practical activities, but also writing and discussion work can be a valuable indicator of personal and social development, as well as levels of skill. Such evidence is not apparent when simply viewing the end products of their activities.

Because teachers' memories are not limitless, it is useful to keep a notebook to hand. Allocate a double page per child and note significant events. By dating the entry, a diary-like picture builds up of pupils' responses to the experiences they are being given. Such information may contribute to the broader evidence base.

Good quality, informative observation does not just happen. It needs a degree of preparation. You need a clear focus to avoid being overwhelmed by minute detail. When assessing children's development of skills and ideas in science, the observations must be compared with certain standards or criteria. The whole point of carrying out the observation is to determine children's progress in their scientific development and use the evidence to determine further science experiences. The easiest way to do this when observing children is to start from the lesson targets. The aims and objectives defined in the planning for the science experiences can be turned into assessment criteria.

You will usually have a general aim for the lesson or activity. This is the broad statement of the way in which we want the children to develop as a result of the experience. The National Curriculum Attainment Target summaries provide these general aims for science. The aim will usually be followed by a small number of very specific and precise objectives or targets for the lesson, often written using words and phrases like *Will be able to . . .* , *Will know that . . .* , and *Will understand why . . .* These are all target action verbs that are really stating the learning and behavioural outcomes from the experience. Again, the National Curriculum for Science provides such targets in the Programmes of Study descriptors. Translating specific target objectives into assessment criteria is relatively straightforward. You need to ask yourself a sequence of questions:

1   **What skills do I expect the children to exhibit?**
    The target objectives are likely to be drawn from Sc1, Experimental and Investigative Science for Key Stages 1 and 2 and so the assessment criteria become questions based on the verbs in the targets. For example,
    Is the child able to . . . . . . turn the idea into an investigation into . . . ?
    . . . recognize a fair/unfair test of . . . ?
    . . . describe what was seen when . . . ?
    . . . use appropriate senses to explore the . . . ?
    . . . make careful observations of the . . . ?
    . . . measure accurately the . . . ?
    . . . record results/observations/measurements as . . . ?
    . . . make comparisons between . . . ?
    . . . predict what will happen when . . . ?
    . . . draw conclusions about . . . ?
    . . . explain what was found about . . . ?
    . . . formulate an hypothesis about . . . ?
    . . . design an investigation to find out . . . ?
    . . . manipulate science equipment to . . . ?

2   **What knowledge and information are the children expected to acquire?**
    The target objectives for the facts, ideas and understandings which the child is to acquire and construct are likley to be drawn from Sc2, 3 and 4 (to do with living things, materials, forces and energy). The questions verbs which are likely to be used in the targets again become the assessment criteria. For example,
    Does the child know that . . . ?
    Can the child state the . . . ?
    Has the child learned that . . . ?
    Does the child understand that . . . ?
    Can the child explain why . . . ?

3   What applications of understanding will I be looking for?

In developing understanding, the target objectives may include some references to applying knowledge and understanding in new and different ways and these can be translated into assessment criteria. For example,

Can the child apply what he has learned about . . . to . . . ?

Does the child understand that . . . is the same as . . . ?

Does the child relate the cause of . . . to the effect/pattern of . . . ?

4   What attitudes will I expect the children to show?

The target objectives might include some reference to personal qualities or attributes to be developed or reinforced through the science experience. Again, these can become assessment criteria. For example,

Does the child show a sense of responsibility during . . . ?

Does the child accept/value the ideas of others about . . . ?

Does the child persist with the task until . . . ?

Can the child co-operate with . . . ?

Can the child work independently on . . . ?

It is important to remember that not all target objectives are equally important, and therefore you may have to weight or emphasize particular ones for assessment purposes. Applying the assessment criteria when observing a child or a group of children is made easier by using an observation grid, as shown in Figure 13.3.

Discussing activities with the children

Eavesdropping on the dialogue between pupils as they work can provide you with useful insights into pupils' thinking, motivation and levels of understanding. Teachers often do not have time to do this and thereby lose valuable opportunities to look into the children's minds. Such opportunities can then be built upon through subsequent discussion and questioning. This allows pupils' ideas and understandings to be explored and extended. With young children in particular, such discussion is an important way to collect evidence about what they are doing and thinking, since their recording skills may be limited. Such dialogue not only allows you to determine progress. It also allows you an opportunity to give praise, positive reinforcement and feedback to the pupils.

It is important that the dialogue is relaxed, and pupils feel free to express their ideas and feelings. The questioning style should be open-ended, with the children being prompted to explain what they think, give reasons why they think it and not simply recall facts and procedures and give the answer which they think you want. You must also ensure you give children enough time to respond to questions. They need absorption and thinking time as well as answering time. Often the two or three seconds waiting time which teachers allow is insufficient for the child to take in the question, retrieve the relevant information or ideas, process them, construct a response, evaluate it and respond. Questions that ask *Which . . . ?, What . . . ?, When . . . ?* and *Where . . . ?* are generally closed and can be answered quickly. More open questions,

writing true or false beside it. The demand can be increased by asking the children to give correct answers for those which they identify as wrong. For example,

Water freezes at 0°C...........TRUE or FALSE (Circle one of them)
Water is needed for rusting............._____(Tick or Cross)
A person could last for four days without water. . . . RIGHT or WRONG
The sun is a planet. TRUE or FALSE _____

Multiple choice questioning

Multiple choice questions are commonly used with older primary school pupils, yet their use as an assessment strategy is weakened by the element of chance brought to the task by 'guessing by recognition'. With only three choices to select from, the pupil has a one in three chance of guessing correctly rather than having to know or understand what he is working on. Therefore, if multiple choice questions are used, the strategy should be used only occasionally and the questions should be carefully designed to make the children do more than guess. All of the alternatives should seem feasible and there should be enough selection so that over a number of questions the acceptable answer is unlikely to be guessed by chance alone a significant number of times. The response can be usefully extended by simply adding the word *Why?* at the end of each question choice. For example,

Which of the following materials would be the best to make a bag for carrying frozen foods from the suppermarket?
[a] Newspaper   [b] Polythene
[c] Cooking foil   [d] Leather
[e] Cotton cloth
Why?_____
_____

Multiple choice options can also be used successfully with tasks where the children have to make inferences and deductions from the evidence presented in pictorial form.

Extended writing

This is a useful strategy to explore children's abilities to translate ideas into practical investigations. The children are presented with a short scenario, an idea to test or a problem to solve. They then have to write an account of how they would tackle the investigation. When using the account for assessment purposes, the teacher would look for evidence of the use of a range of appropriate skills needed for planning experimental work and obtaining and considering evidence. For example,

1   *Tom and Mary planted some sunflower seeds at home. They grew them on their bedroom windowsills. Mary's did not seem to be growing as well as Tom's. Their mother said it was because Mary watered hers with cold tea. Their father said it was*

because Tom's window faced south. What could Tom and Mary do to see who was right?

2   *You have some wires and crocodile clips, some bulbs in bulb holders and two 1.5V batteries. When you connected two wires, a bulb and a battery together to make a circuit, nothing happened. Describe three things which you could do to find out why the bulb did not light. Use drawings to help you to explain.*

Concept mapping

A concept map is a diagrammatic way of representing ideas and showing how, if at all, those ideas are connected. With very young children it is best to work on a one-to-one basis, with the key ideas – about six of them – presented to the children on separate cards, like flashcards. The child has to choose pairs of cards (pairs of ideas) and explain to the teacher how they are connected. For example, the cards might say:

| water   cold   winter   snow   ice   hands   freeze   snowman |

The child might pick up 'winter' and 'snow' first and say, *In winter it snows*. Next, the child might say, *The water freezes because it is cold*. The various combinations of ideas and how they are connected can be drawn by the teacher as the child expresses them. This can become a permanent record of the child's ideas at that particular time. With slightly older children, a variation of this is to give them cards with ideas and a pile of paper arrows. The arrows not only express that there is a connection between ideas but also the direction of the relationship. The children arrange the words on the table and put arrows between the ones they want to connect. They can have as many arrows as they want coming from or going into an idea card. They write on the arrow the nature of the connection. The cards and arrows can be glued onto a large sheet of paper to make a more permanent record. Finally with older Key Stage 2 children, they can be given about ten ideas or concepts as a list on the chalkboard or on a task sheet. The children then draw in their own connecting arrows and write along them how they are connected.

Concept mapping can be used as a specific task in science to elicit children's ideas and the connections between those ideas. It can also be used as part of the general development of science topics, particularly when the children are asked to draw a concept map at the beginning and at the end of the topic. You can compare the maps to determine the development and changes in their ideas.

Involving children in their own assessment

In the past, self-assessment has been thought of as only suitable for use with older pupils but now it is also seen as appropriate for primary age pupils as well. If children are to take greater responsibility for their own learning, then they should be allowed to take some of the responsibility for the assessment of their learning. However, the skills to do this need to be developed slowly and carefully. If children are encouraged to believe that their opinions matter and their reasons are listened to seriously, then they will put their beliefs to good use when participating in self-assessment. A starting point for this is a science Plan-Do-Review sheet. Children of all ages, from nursery classes onwards, are capable of completing these sheets and usually do so with a remarkable degree of honesty and self-criticism. With older children, asking them to keep a learning log or diary is another way to encourage reflection and self-evaluation. Initially, questions can be used to support their self-assessment, for example,

> What was I trying to find out?
> What did I actually do?
> What do I think I have learned?
> What did I enjoy doing? Why?
> What do I think I could do next? Why?

If the child is working as part of a team, then questions would need to focus on her or his contribution to the group effort. For example,

> What were we trying to find out?
> What ideas did I suggest?
> What part of the work did I do?
> Did I work well with my group?

The teacher can also use these questions to analyse events when observing the group.

COMPARING ASSESSMENT METHODS

When different formal assessment methods are compared there are a number of features they all share. Any formal method of assessment usually has an element of:

> (a) presentation;
> (b) response;
> (c) judgement;
> and, (d) feedback.

These features are also inherent in most informal assessment methods.

(a) Presentation

This is the form in which the assessment task, activity or problem is presented. It can:

(i)   *be a pencil and paper task* – using words/as a picture or diagram/using numbers . . .
(ii)   *use another medium* – on an audio or video tape recording/as a model . . .
(iii) *use a practical activity* – as a demonstration/practical task to carry out . . .

(b) Response

This is the way in which the pupils can respond to the assessment task. They can:

(i)   *select from alternatives presented* – tick or cross – yes or no – right or wrong . . .

(ii)   *write an answer* – provide a missing word – complete a sentence – write a short account . . .

(iii) *use another medium* – draw or paint a picture – make a model – take a photograph – record on audio or video tape . . .

(iv)   *manipulate practical resources* – design and/or set up and/or carry out an investigation . . .

(c) Judgement

There will be standards or criteria against which the response will be judged. They can be by reference to:

(i)   *norms* – what is judged to be the standard or average for that particular group or class;

(ii)   *criteria* – statements which indicate level of performance (behaviour, skill, knowledge, understanding) has been reached and against which individuals can be compared, irrespective of how others perform;

(iii) *expectations* – comparisons with previous personal best performances, and the expectations of self and others.

(d) Feedback

This is the form in which the results of the assessment will be acknowledged by you. It can be in the form of:

Task 13.3 Marking children's work	Find out from your class teacher whether or not the school has a marking policy. If so, discuss the policy with him or her and how it was achieved.

With your class teacher's permission, look at the children's science work to see how they have been marked. What kinds of comments and feedback does your teacher give? Is a rating scale used? Does your teacher use positive reinforcement? How do they record the evidence gathered from marking the work? How is it used to inform subsequent planning?

Write a short summary about marking children's work in science. To what extent do you feel that children's exercise books can reflect what they know, understand and can do?

(i) *marking* – literally putting positive marks (ticks) and negative marks (crosses) on the pupil's response to indicate its success, worth or value; other marks (underlining, stars in margins, etc.) convey similar messages;

(ii) *rating or grading* – expressing judgements in terms of a scale, a grade of A to E, a mark out of ten, a qualitative rating from Very Good through to Unsatisfactory;

(iii) *qualitative statement* – using descriptive responses, often carrying an affective message and each purely personal to the individual. For example, *I enjoyed reading your interesting account of . . . Have you thought about doing . . . ?*

WHAT IS TO BE ASSESSED IN SCIENCE?

As far as the National Curriculum Orders for Science are concerned, assessment is based upon a combination of Teacher Assessment (TA) and SAT Assessment. The former relies on your professional judgement as the teacher about each pupil's level of attainment during the period the children are with you. The latter uses the results from the annual Standard Assessment Tasks given to 11-year-olds and 13-year-olds at the end of the key stages. TA is intended to be based on an accumulated record and is meant to be confirmed by the SATs.

Science education is both process and product oriented. It would be easy to look only for the facts that the children recall. But facts without understanding do not explain the world. Similarly, an ability to apply knowledge and understanding in different contexts and use it to solve problems will be advantageous. Thus, since children must not only acquire the concepts (Sc2, Sc3 and Sc4) but also the ability to think and work scientifically (Sc1), both of these must be assessed.

Finally, what children are *able* to do can often be very different from what they are *willing* to do. The former is determined by level of skill, knowledge and understanding. The latter reflects personal qualities such as curiosity, interest and motivation. You need, therefore to bear this in mind when collecting assessment evidence and when considering the *What?* and the *How?* as well as the *How well?*

Assessing skills and Sc1

In science, pupils will develop and use a range of skills, processes and strategies as they carry out their science activities. Few of these skills will be unique to science. At the most basic level, children use a range of *fine* and *gross motor skills* when using equipment. Their general level of manual dexterity and hand–eye co-ordination will be important in practical activities. Science investigation will also require skills acquired in other areas of experience, such as *estimation and measurement* from mathematics. From English, the *language skills* of reading, writing, talking and listening will be used as children discuss, record and report their ideas and findings and communicate these to others in a variety of ways. *Information technology skills* will help them seek information, use games and simulations, word process findings and store evidence in databases.

From their design and technology work, children will learn how to develop strategies for meeting challenges and solving problems. These include planning and sequencing activities, observing accurately, evaluating ideas and choosing appropriate ways forward, and rethinking evidence in the light of success or failure.

Scientific investigations may also foster desirable personal qualities and attitudes. Children can be observed to see what behaviours they are exhibiting. Such observation is, of course, informal but it helps to have a checklist against which to note the development of these qualities. For science investigations, the list might include:

- co-operation
- imagination
- independence
- initiative
- leadership

- organization
- perseverance
- reliability
- responsiveness to others' ideas
- safety consciousness

Development of such attributes is reflected not only in academic performance but also in the non-academic aspects of school life and out-of-school activities.

Assessing knowledge and understanding and Sc2, Sc3 and Sc4

You will need to know what specific scientific facts, laws, principles and generalizations children have acquired. The ability to recall such knowledge is relatively easy to check through oral and written questions. However, the acquisition of knowledge is not sufficient. The aim is for children to understand the scientific ideas and be able to apply them in new contexts. Assessment needs to be able to show what understandings the children have constructed and what science-specific language they understand.

RECORDING AND RECORD KEEPING IN SCIENCE

Recording and record keeping is an aspect of communication which has an important role to play in your teaching of science. It operates at several different levels in the primary classroom. At one level, children need to record their experiences in science. This was discussed earlier. At a different level, teachers need to record the science experiences offered and the consequences of those experiences for the children's development in science. There are a number of questions to guide you here.

1   Should children's progress in science be recorded?
2   How should formal records be kept?
3   What types of records can be maintained?
4   Should records be reviewed and updated?

Should children's progress in science be recorded?

You will need to maintain some sort of record of each child's progress in science for several reasons. First, in a busy classroom so much is happening that it is not possible for you to remember everything about each child's achievements in all subjects. Second, by bringing together various pieces of information collected over time you can begin to see any pattern in the pupil's progress and build a profile of their development. Third, the record allows you to spot areas of strengths and weaknesses. Finally, such records provide support in discussions between yourself, other teachers and parents.

An efficient and informative system of recording and record keeping is needed to achieve these goals. It is likely that the science co-ordinator will have designed such a system to fit in with the broader school record keeping policy. However, it must be remembered that any record keeping system is not an end in itself, but a stage in the evaluation cycle, working in conjunction with planning and assessment.

How should formal records be kept?

The 3Ms principle identified by Harlen (1983) is a good one to follow. Records should be:

- Minimal
- Manageable
- Meaningful

Minimal

Ideally, formal records should provide only the information needed. Different records serve different purposes and should be kept in different formats. For example, general records (personal details, health, school transfers, etc.) are likely to be stored in the school office, accessible to certain people. Science records, on the other hand are likely to be kept by you for different purposes. They will need to indicate:

1   the science experiences offered to the pupils (an activity record which is likely to apply to the whole class, perhaps the detailed class planning sheets would serve this purpose);
2   the children's reactions to the various experiences offered (a personal record applying to each child with the supporting evidence to substantiate judgements, perhaps in the form of observation checklists or examples of pupils' work collected as a portfolio); and,
3   the achievements of each child over time (a summative record, perhaps one which is completed at the end of each topic, term or year and passed on to the next teacher to continue).

Manageable

Formal records should be neither arduous nor time-consuming to maintain. Most teachers have little time to spare. Time spent filling in records is time taken from planning, producing resources, marking work and thinking about the needs of the pupils. While good record keeping can support all of these activities, they should not be at their expense.

Meaningful

The maintenance of formal records should not be seen as a chore but as a part of the teaching-learning process in which they contribute something to that process. Such records should contribute to planning and decision making at all levels and show progression and continuity in science throughout the school.

What types of records can be maintained?

A number of options are available to you according to the purpose of the record. If the record is intended to support the day-to-day routines of the classroom and the formative judgements that you have to make, then the record keeping format is likely to support the assessment strategy being used. You might use any or all from activity lists, criterion-based checklists, rating scales, test scores and free comments.

Activity lists

Most teachers record the general experiences offered to pupils as part of their general planning documentation. A record for each topic of the tasks and activities offered and completed provides a quick check on progression and continuity throughout the school. Such a record does not have to be produced separately for every child, but can be a summative class record. With older pupils it is possible to produce the record in the form of a chart that the pupils complete themselves. This not only encourages pupils to be more independent; it saves you time. The chart can be one kept by each child in her or his work folder, or maintained as a class chart on the wall. The latter, of course, allows an individual's progress to be seen by all and there may be reasons for not doing this. However, some modern commercial schemes do supply charts for this purpose.

Criterion checklists

The National Curriculum level descriptors provide an excellent example of a criterion-based checklist. You may also devise your own lists of suitable descriptors more attuned to the topics under study and drawn from your planning targets and assessment criteria. Completing the checklists builds a profile of pupils' development of skills, knowledge and understanding, and personal qualities. An example of a criterion-based checklist was shown in the observation grid earlier (Figure 13.3).

Rating scales

Marks of 1 to 10, grades of A to E, or comments such as Very Good, Good, Satisfactory, Poor and Very Poor, are all examples of different kinds of rating scales which teachers tend to use in different contexts. Implicit in such scales is the notion of the 'average' child, against which the individual in question is being compared. As such, the recording system builds into it comparisons of pupils' performances with an expected normal or average performance. (This does, of course, parallel the model provided by the National Curriculum when describing the 'average' 7 or 11-year-old who is working at a particular level.)

Test scores

When science content knowledge is being assessed and marks are being awarded, the marks can be recorded for future reference. Copies of such tests, whether teacher-designed or commercially produced (as with SATs) should be retained in the child's portfolio along with other evidence, such as concept maps.

Free comments

Observing children as they work on practical investigations and discussing their work with them provides information for the record. A notebook with a double page allocated to each child allows space for free comments about progress. These should reflect how the children are reacting to the practical activities and should include reference to their own comments and evaluations. Brief entries, made regularly, build into a detailed picture of how the child is progressing and serve as a useful *aide-memoire*. Such notes, which can be in the teacher's own 'shorthand', can be transformed into more permanent records, if necessary.

The final stage is to turn the information into a *summative record* of each child's progress. Again, by necessity, such a record needs to be as informative as possible but economical on time and effort. Recording charts are provided with the National Curriculum guidance materials. Alternatively, you could design your own. Recording wheels which relate directly to the National Curriculum Orders for Science can be used for this purpose. There could be a separate wheel for each child for each Programme of Study. It is, of course, possible to design the wheels to cover all programmes at once or any other particular dimension of science education preferred.

The wheel comprises concentric rings that reflect the levels of attainment in the Science Orders and cover the full range of levels the most able child is likely to achieve during their time in school. For a primary school, the circles would normally expand to level 6. Each concentric ring is subdivided to represent the different sub-statements for each level descriptor. A coding bar runs from the Reception class to Year 6, and a different colour is allocated to each year group. As children in each class show repeated evidence of competence in certain skills and processes or acquisition of particular ideas and understandings, the relevant block is completed in the colour for that class. The strength of this system is that it enables a teacher to see quickly where children's strengths and weakness lie. It also allows you to check whether or not experimental and investigative science skills are being developed in a coherent and progressive way and whether there are any imbalances or biases in the coverage of living things, materials, forces and energy across the school.

Reviewing and improving records

It is essential that the form and content of records be reviewed regularly and, if necessary, revised in the light of other changes and developments in the school. The most obvious source of change is that imposed from outside as curriculum orders change. However, there are also internal changes that affect the record keeping policy and format, such as changes in approaches and ideas, resources and reporting mechanisms. Reviewing and revising the record keeping system for science is likely to follow from a review of the school's general record keeping policy and is very much a whole staff activity. Since all teachers are to use the records, you should be given the opportunity to contribute to their form.

REPORTING TO DIFFERENT AUDIENCES

Effective reporting is not a simple process. It needs to be part of a broader school policy, agreed and implemented by all staff, but each subject area may contribute unique interpretations and solutions to the process of reporting. In the context of science, good reporting requires a shared understanding of the basis on which assessments are made and the terms used.

For all involved to gain maximum benefit from it, reporting must be carefully planned. Effective reporting is, in essence the passing on to other relevant people necessary information on progress in a way which is usable by that person. You should consider:

- who is being reported to;
- why the report is given;
- when reporting should take place;
- how the reporting should be carried out.

Who do you need to give reports to?

Teachers often give informal feedback to children as they work or to parents when they call into the school. However, you need to report more formally on children's progress to a variety of audiences and for a variety of purposes. These include:

- parents or guardians on children's report forms;
- other teachers taking the class (for example, subject specialists who take the class, a supply teacher during an absence; a student working with a class);

- teachers in the school (for example, the subsequent class teacher);
- teachers in other schools (for example, if the family moves to a new area, or when the class transfers to the subsequent school);
- specialist personnel (for example, an educational psychologist or counsellor);
- the children themselves at the end of a unit of work.

Each of these recipients has different needs. Reporting to parents in a form which does not meet their needs and interests, will affect the quality of the relationships. Similarly, giving colleagues information for which they have little need or use will devalue the process. Since the reports are about the children they should, as far as is reasonable, be involved.

Why do you need to give reports?

A cynical response to this question might be because teachers have to produce school reports; they are a legal requirement. However, there are better reasons for viewing reporting more broadly. First, reports can motivate. Constructive and positive feedback, both to the children themselves and to their parents, can encourage children to achieve (socially and emotionally, as well as intellectually) and help to strengthen relationships between pupils and teacher. Second, reporting to parents can help clarify needs and involve them more in the teaching and learning enterprise. Involvement again may contribute to the child's motivation. Third, if the children's learning is not to be wasted, effective reporting is necessary when children transfer to the next class or a new school. This is obviously closely tied to matters of continuity and progression. Fourth, in order to report effectively, you must evaluate the learning experiences that have been offered and the progress the pupils have made, bearing in mind that the children may have different starting and finishing points. Such evaluation should not be simply reflective, but also projective, aiding the teacher in decisions about where to go from here. Fifth, progress reports may be required by the headteacher on particular pupils, perhaps those who have some learning difficulties, who are being monitored for other reasons, or who are receiving additional support. This will aid the headteacher in providing support. Finally, reporting to an educational psychologist on any assessment of pupils who have special needs or learning and behavioural difficulties will be necessary for the purpose of Statementing.

When is reporting necessary?

There is no hard and fast rule as to when reporting should take place. It should be determined by need. The minimalist rule of, *If it's not needed, don't do it!* should be applied. So the first question you should ask is, *Do I need to give this information to Child X, Mrs Y or Mr Z?* This should be followed by the question, *Why?*

Informal reporting can take place anywhere at any time and whenever the opportunity arises to both pupils and parents. However, with more formal reporting to parents the time, place and frequency of such reporting should be planned more carefully. As a general rule, a time should be chosen when there are fewer pressures or distractions so that you and the parent(s) can feel unhurried. A teacher constantly glancing at a clock seldom encourages useful discussion. Similarly, the place where such a meeting occurs is important. Sitting side by side on comfortable chairs is much more conducive to discussion. A very different form of interaction takes place when you and parents face one another across a desk or tables, especially when seated on classroom chairs. While time seldom allows such formal parents' meetings to occur more than once a year, the process can be greatly enhanced by regular contact with parents in other ways.

With written reports, the occasion should be selected to ensure that sufficient evidence is available for making judgements, producing the reports in an appropriate form and giving the recipients time to think and respond.

How should reporting be carried out?

For the reporting to be effective, it is important that it takes place in a way that is meaningful for those who are receiving the information. Reporting often depends on the methods used to record the progress. The latter can be made a lot easier if high quality record keeping is in place, since methods of recording can also be used as methods of reporting. The basis on which the assessment was made and the justifications for judgements and decisions will need to be explored and records and appropriate pieces of evidence will need to be collected for discussion. This is one reason why annotated portfolios of children's work and achievements are proving successful. They provide a concrete, visual starting point for a discussion.

When planning how reporting takes place, you will need to take into account a number of factors. These include:

Timing

Any informal opportunities which arise to report on progress should be taken, as these help to establish good relationships with pupils and parents as well as making interaction easier when the less frequent, formal meetings occur.

Format

Both oral and written reporting are important. The former can occur both formally and informally at any time. The latter occurs either in response to a need (as with the educational psychologist) or as an end-of-year requirement. In both cases the quantity and nature of information written and the language used must be carefully considered.

Quantity

Different audiences will need different amounts of information. The reports should contain only as much detail as is necessary. Reporting to a parent might focus only on the child's achievement now compared to his or her previous achievements, and this would be related to the National Curriculum with language chosen for the non-expert. However, reporting to the educational psychologist is a different matter. The detail has more meaning and comparisons with other pupils might be essential.

Language used

As with the quantity of information given, the language used must be carefully selected to suit the audience. Clarity should be the rule and avoid jargon. Simple, clear, concise language is appropriate for everyone.

Context

Although not directly concerned with reporting to parents, but related to it, is the presentation of information for open days and parents' evenings. Displays can greatly support the sharing of meanings, give opportunities for clarifying language and terminology, and ensure that there is a clear understanding of what the process of education in science and assessment is about.

Task 13.4 Recording and reporting achievement	When you have monitored children's progress and maintained records of their achievements, you often need to pass this information to others. Make a list of the various people who may need the information and the reasons they might need it.

How does your class teacher report information on children's progress to:
- the pupils themselves?
- their parents?
- the teacher in their next class?
- the staff at their next school?

Discuss with your class teacher or mentor the different forms of record keeping and procedures for reporting achievment that are used in the school.

SUGGESTIONS FOR FURTHER READING

If you would like to explore further some of the issues touched upon in this chapter, the following books should be of some interest to you.

ASE (1990) *Teachers' Assessment – Making It Work in the Primary School*, Hatfield: ASE
This short volume is a joint production of the various associations for English, mathematics and science educations and aims to give teachers clear and succinct guidelines on how to handle the process of assessment in a busy primary classroom.

Davis, A. (1998) *The Limits of Educational Assessment*, Oxford: Blackwell
Andrew Davis's book provides an overview of assessment issues generally and raises a number of important questions about why and how we assess. It provides a useful springboard for a deeper exploration of assessment.

PART 3

Your Continuing
Professional Development

Introduction

Your initial teacher training course is just the first rung of a professional ladder. It lays the foundation for your teaching career, preparing you for your first teaching post and your first year of teaching. It does not, however, equip you for the rest of your life as a teacher, it simply starts you off on that life. When you enter the teaching profession, you will begin the process of *Continuing Professional Development*. You will soon ask: *How can I improve as a teacher? How can I progress in my career?* Annex A of Circular 4/98 contains a section relating to *Other Professional Requirements* (Section D). This section describes some of the more generic, non-subject specific criteria you must satisfy before being awarded your Qualified Teacher Status. They are likely to have been covered in the professional studies elements of your training course and during work in school. One particular requirement is that:

> *For all courses, those to be awarded Qualified Teacher Status should, when assessed, demonstrate that they:*
> e. understand the need to take responsibility for their own professional development and to keep up to date with research and developments in pedagogy and in the subjects they teach;
>
> (Circular 4/98, p. 16)

In this final section we shall look at your continuing professional development in the context of science. We shall consider your needs once you have completed your teacher training course and, in particular, we will examine:

- applying for teaching posts and what to expect at interview, particularly relating to science;
- the requirements relating to your continuing professional development and becoming a reflective practitioner in primary science education; and,
- developing yourself and moving on, perhaps by becoming a primary science co-ordinator or curriculum area leader.

14 Applying for Jobs and Interviews

Your initial teacher training programme will help make secure your confidence and competence as far as science subject knowledge and subject application are concerned. Your next challenge is ahead. You will begin to apply for teaching posts around the January or February of your final year. This means that you have to think about your future before you have finished the training programme. Although applying for teaching posts is not an element of Circular 4/98, everything that you do in terms of meeting the standards can be seen as part of your preparation for this next stage in your professional development, and Section D of Annex A does refer to it obliquely. In this chapter, we will consider what you should think about and expect when you apply for your first teaching post.

APPLYING FOR TEACHING POSTS

Good classroom practitioners who have performed well during their training programme, both professionally and academically, are not necessarily good at 'selling themselves'. Yet that is what the interview game is all about. There are a few basic rules that can help you.

First, in the autumn begin to think about where you want to teach: do you want to stay where you are training, go back to your home area or go somewhere completely new? Begin scanning various newspapers and publications (like the *Times Educational Supplement* or the National Union of Teachers' *The Teacher*) to get a feel for the way posts are advertised. You will find that at the primary level there are likely to be two ways of doing things. In the first, schools will advertise directly: these are likely to be larger primary schools that are controlling their own budgets under the Local Management of Schools (LMS) arrangements, perhaps offering posts for one year in the first instance. Do not be put off by this. It is a way to ensure the school is recruiting the right person. At the end of the year, if you have proven yourself an effective teacher you could become a permanent member of staff. This is something you could explore with the headteacher if called for interview. Alternatively, many primary schools are still under the financial control of the LEA. Here, a pool system may be in operation. The LEA would have a rough idea of how many primary teachers will be needed in the following September and organize blocks of interviewing over several days. Successful interviewees would then be placed in the LEA pool. Headteachers would look through the application forms, *curriculum vitae* and interview reports held by the LEA and choose someone from the pool for their school. You would then be offered a post at that school.

Task 14.1 Applying for jobs	Look in a recent issue of an education newspaper like the *Times Educational Supplement* for the posts available in the key stage for which you are training.

Choose one of the posts that attracts you. Draft a letter of application and a *curriculum vitae* (CV) as if you intended to apply for the post.

Show your application to your tutor or mentor for comment and advice on how to improve it.

Once you have spotted the post or the LEA pool you wish to apply for, you should write to the address provided (either the school or the LEA office) for the details and an application form. Take care, even with this preliminary letter, to make a good impression. What exactly is asked of you varies, but usually you are asked to include three things in an application:

A letter of application

Some schools or LEAs will ask you to include a short letter of application. Even if not asked to do so, it is always wise to include one. This should be a short, personal statement about your interest in the post/LEA, your suitability for it (identify two or three strengths that you would bring to the situation) and your potential (again, two or three points). Normally, a letter of application should not run over one, or at the most two, sides. In a way, it is pulling out the key points you want to emphasize from the formal application form or *curriculum vitae*. Try to put something of yourself in it by showing how much you enjoy teaching.

Sometimes you are asked explicitly to write your letter of application in your own handwriting. It is important to comply with this, as it will be used in the decision making procedure. Take care with presentation, spelling, grammar and punctuation. If you are not asked to write it freehand, and your handwriting is good, then it is worth doing so. On the other hand, if your writing is poor, use a word-processor.

A curriculum vitae (CV) or a completed application form

This usually includes brief biographical details to provide a personal and academic context, qualifications and experience before and during your training programmes and your different and varied experiences teaching in schools. With respect to the latter, remember that if you decide to identify the schools where you have had placements, the headteachers of those schools may be contacted. It is polite to check with them first that they do not mind you identifying the school.

Application forms commonly have an open section which asks you for a personal statement. You can also include such a personal statement with your CV. Link your personal statement to what you know about the school. Write confidently about your experience and expertise, your strengths and developing interests in terms of primary teaching and learning. Finally, indicate how you would fit in with the philosophy of the school and help to meet the needs of the children. This might include reference to a *portfolio* which you would take to the interview, if invited to attend (see below).

Names of people who will provide references

Never give people's names without first contacting them for permission. One referee should be someone from your training course (usually your course director or personal tutor – you might use both). This person can comment on your academic and professional profile. A second person should be able to comment on you as a person. This may be a tutor, but could also be someone who has known you in other contexts, for example, someone associated with your religious affiliation. Finally, whoever you use, give them some information about the post you are applying for and some brief points about any specific things you would like them to refer to in their reference. This helps them tailor the reference to suit the post.

You should have been sent some general information about the school with the details of the post and the application form. Do your homework. At the very least, look up the school's most recent Ofsted report on the Internet. This will give you a feel for the 'official' face of the school. If the school is local, try to visit it one evening or weekend, to get a feel for the area and the environment. If you like what you see then go ahead and apply for the post. If you are invited to go on a visit prior to an interview, try to do so. It not only gives you a chance to look around the school and meet staff and children but also to ask some informal questions. It enables you to go into the inteview feeling confident that you like what you see and would like to teach there. On very rare occasions, the reverse can happen. You find this is not the right school for you. You can save everyone time and effort by withdrawing before the interview. This really is better than going through an interview and possibly being offered the post, just to turn it down. That creates ill feeling and if you are applying for other posts in the same area you can put yourself at a disadvantage if it becomes known.

Completing forms and writing letters is a time-consuming, tedious task. Do not underestimate how long it will take. Start early and give yourself plenty of time to do the job well, to gather information, contact referees and prepare the materials you must send. The professional way you do this will show. When shortlisting is being carried out, the quality of the application itself can make the difference between you and someone else with similar expriences and qualifications being called for interview. Information technology has made the task of writing personal statements and letters of application and CVs easier. It is possible to change them and adapt them to school-specific contexts relatively easily so take advantage of that.

Another advantage you can give yourself is to prepare a *personal portfolio*. Refer to this in your letter of application and/or personal statement and take it along for interview.

Task 14.2 Creating a portfolio

In order to 'sell yourself' well, you need to be thoroughly prepared for your interview. This includes preparing a personal portfolio to show to the interview panel so they can gain a feel for you in the school and classroom context. It is also a chance to show off your ICT skills.

Use a file with plastic wallets and collect positive, high-quality evidence to show at interview. This could include:

- an attractive front page with brief biograpical information, perhaps even a photograph of yourself;
- a brief CV;
- a synopsis of your experiences in schools and with children;
- some examples of your planning which you feel shows your thoroughness, imagination and professionalism;
- examples of workcards or worksheets you created (particularly some showing evidence of differentiation);
- photocopies of good observation reports by your tutors or mentors;
- photocopies of good report forms from previous school placements;
- photographs of displays you created in schools;
- photocopies of children's work, showing the quality you maintained and how you marked it;
- examples of some good lesson evaluations.

There are more things you could include. It is up to you to choose what will show you at your best. Remember to label your samples.

Good personal portfolios take time to prepare. They are not something that can be left to the weekend before the interview. This is something you can begin at the start of your course to show progression in your skills, knowledge and understanding as a teacher as well as your best qualities. Most importantly, make sure you bring it to the attention of the interviewing panel. Offer it to the chairperson when you go in to the interview and suggest you leave it with them and collect it later.

ATTENDING FOR INTERVIEW

Far more people tend to apply for posts than can possibly be interviewed and so a shortlisting panel is set up. In school, this is usually the headteacher and the chair of the governing body and perhaps a local primary adviser. For the LEA pool interview it may be a primary adviser with one or two headteachers. The task is to select from those who are thought suitable a manageable number for interviewing.

If you are called for an interview and you are on school placement, arrange with your class teacher what she or he will do while you are away. Try to plan, prepare and mark so that you are up-to-date. Allow the night before the interview to concentrate on preparing yourself. This does not mean just reading through what you said in your application and rehearsing your answers to possible questions. You need to plan your route to the school and the times of local transport. Think about your physical appearance, decide what to wear and make sure everything is ready. While you may not be able to afford a smart, new suit, you can look well-groomed in a cared for existing outfit. Remember that outlandish fashion can reflect your personality but could also count against you in a professional context. Try to relax and have a reasonable night's sleep and a decent breakfast. Give yourself plenty of time so that you do not have to rush.

| **Task 14.3 Interviews** | At interview you are likely to be asked questions which will help the interview panel make comparisons between you and other candidates. Remember, they want the right person for the post. |

In the context of science, how might you answer the following questions? They are in no particular order but are typical of the kinds of questions asked at interviews.

1   How do you feel science contributes to the all-round education of primary school pupils?
2   What methods of organizing and managing children and classrooms have you experienced?
3   Use specific examples from your school placements to give us a feel for how you would plan for, teach and assess science.
4   Do you think there should be more time for science in the primary school curriculum? Give your reasons for your answer.
5   How will you manage science experiences with a class of 35 pupils, all with very different needs and abilities?
6   How would you assess children's learning in science?
7   How could you link science to other areas of the curriculum?
8   What do you feel is the most serious problem facing you when teaching primary school science?
9   How would you make the science education you provide explicitly relevant to the needs of the pupils in this school?
10   What are your main strengths and weaknesses as a teacher of primary science? How will you address the latter?

Which questions would you find difficult? Draft responses to them.

The focus at interview could be on:

- *You as an individual:*
  Are you an interesting person? What are your personal interests? What do you do outside school? Will you fit in with the existing team of teachers? Where do you see yourself in five or ten years' time?
- *You as a potential primary teacher:*
  What attracts you to teaching as a career? Why do you want to work in that area, school, and with that age range? What is your philosophy of education? How do you see yourself in the classroom? How would you organize, manage and assess the teaching and learning situation? How would you deal with specific situations (for example, bullying or bad behaviour)? What extra-curricular experiences could you bring to the school?
- *You as a potential subject co-ordinator:*
  If you were asked to lead an area of the curriculum, what would it be? Why? What sorts of things would you need to think about? (This is looked at in more detail in Chapter 16.)

A final point: do not become disheartened if you do not succeed immediately. This is not unusual and it may take several interviews before you are successful. This reflects the current economic situation in education and the level of competition. Learn from the experience. Take opportunities offered to you to be given feedback on your performance at interview and act on the advice given. It pays to do so.

HAVING GOT THE JOB – INDUCTION

The old probationary year for new entrants to teaching was abolished in 1992. In March 1999, the government announced details of the new induction arrangements for newly qualified teachers (NQTs). NQTs should spend 10 per cent less of their time teaching than their experienced colleagues. This is to allow more time for planning, preparation and marking. On completion of the first year, headteachers will judge the NQT's performance against induction standards set by the Secretary of State and then recommend to the LEA whether or not the NQT should pass, fail or have the induction year extended. The regulations state that:

1   All NQTs should complete a one-year *induction period* in a qualifying school. Part-time teachers must do an equivalent period (for example, two years for those working 2.5 days per week).
2   *Qualifying schools* for induction are all state schools except those on special measures and pupil-referral units; independent schools which meet national curriculum requirements are also included.
3   *Assessment* of NQTs is the responsibility of the LEA on the recommendations of the headteacher and in line with the government's guidelines.
4   Teachers who fail or who have their induction period extended have a right to *appeal* and appeal bodies can reverse a decision.

SUGGESTIONS FOR FURTHER READING

If you would like to explore further some of the issues touched upon in this chapter, the following books should be of interest to you.

Moyles, J. (1995) *Beginning Teaching, Beginning Learning in Primary Education*, Buckingham: Open University Press.
This book covers the main educational issues you need to think about as a teacher in chapters that are clearly organized and well illustrated with examples. Particularly useful is Chapter 15, 'Don't make a drama out of a crisis! Primary teachers and the law' (p. 244 *et seq.*).

Proctor, A., Entwistle, M., Judge, B. and McKenzie-Murdoch, S. (1995) *Learning to Teach in the Primary Classroom*, London: Routledge.
Like Janet Moyles's book, this book covers most of the main educational topics relating to classroom practice and pedagogy. It is one which can be dipped into to refresh your memory of things covered on your training programme.

The Times Educational Supplement
This weekly newsapaper is a useful source of information about teaching posts around England, Wales and Scotland. In addition, occasional special interviews are aimed directly at students applying for their first teaching posts, and focusing on how to apply, what to expect at interview, what to expect in your first year, and so on.

15 Becoming a Reflective Practitioner

Task 15.1 Why do I want to teach?	Think of the reasons why you want to become a primary teacher.
	Jot down the first three that you thought of.

Classify your responses as:
- focused on children;
- focused on yourself;
- focused on teaching subjects/content;
- other reasons.

When you were interviewed for your place on your initial teacher training course you may have been asked why you wanted to teach. Your answer probably included reference to liking children and gaining pleasure from helping them to learn. By now you will know that nothing in education is so simple. If all that was needed to be a teacher was to like children and have pleasure in helping them, most people could teach. As Pollard (1997) explains, teaching is:

> . . . a complex and highly skilled activity which, above all, requires classroom teachers to exercise judgement in deciding how to act.

> (p. 4)

Your course will have raised your awareness of the complexity of your role as a teacher. You will have had opportunities to practise all of these but you will not be an expert yet. You have begun the process of *Professional Development*. Once you start teaching you should ask yourself: How can I improve as a teacher? How can I progress in my career? How do I continue my professional development? Pollard goes on to say that you need to develop the skills of reflecting on practice, that is, to become a reflective teacher.

> Reflective teaching is seen as a process through which the capacity to make such professional judgements can be developed and maintained.
>
> (p. 4)

He has introduced the concept of the reflective practitioner. So what does this mean?

MOVING ON IN YOUR TEACHING

You will not pass on your school placements and gain Qualified Teacher Status if you cannot teach, so QTS indicates that you can do the job. You have reached at least a minimal level of competence. Is this enough? Those of us who have been teachers for a long time know that there are some teachers who have been teaching for many years but can be descibed as having one year of experience many times over. They are competent teachers but they have stood still in their thinking and practice. On the other hand, other teachers have moved on. Many years of experience really does mean many years of thought, learning, change, adaptation and personal development.

The notion of the reflective practitioner is not new. Dewey (1933) contrasted *routine action* with *reflective action*. Routine actions are guided by factors such as tradition and habit (*I do it like this because I have always done it like this . . .*) and authority (*. . . and it works.*). This is the teacher with one year of experience twenty times over. Reflective action, on the other hand, indicates a social and educational awareness and a willingness to carry out self-evaluation and to develop necessary skills to develop and be flexible. As Pollard suggests,

> . . . teaching concerns values, aims, attitudes and consequences as well as skills, knowledge and competence . . . there is a constructive relationship between the state of classroom competence and the processes of reflection through which competence is developed and maintained.
>
> (p. 4)

Task 15.2 Reflecting on teaching primary science	Think through your preparation to teach primary science. Try to make explicit:

[a] your own values, aims, attitudes about science and science education and the possible consequences of these;

[b] the skills, knowledge and competences you are acquiring that will help you to be effective in teaching science to primary children.

How do you feel [a] will influence [b], if at all?

DEVELOPING COMPETENCE

The competence mentioned by Pollard develops with time, opportunity and experience. In your teaching career you will exhibit different levels of competence as you travel along the road from *novice* (the student teacher at the beginning of your training), through *competent* to *expert* (the teacher who is thoughtful, adaptable, searching for ways to move the teaching and learning forward). When you finish your course, you take with you your career entry profile. This identifies your experiences during training, your particular strengths and areas for further development. During your induction year you will be supported both within the school (by the headteacher or a designated mentor) and by the LEA with a programme aimed at meeting your personal development needs. This support should help you deal with the challenges of classroom life. A number of challenges face you as a teacher. These are to do with:

- *organization:* of children, resources, tasks, space, time, . . .
- *interaction:* relating to children, other staff, other adults, . . .
- *delegation/control:* how much freedom to give, flexibility, . . .
- *motivation:* children's involvement, relevance, expectations, . . .
- *standards:* quality control, breadth, balance, progression, . . .
- *individual needs:* differentiation, individual programmes, special needs, . . .
- *national curriculum:* integration, subject teaching, time on each area, . . .
- *whole curriculum issues:* personal/social/moral development, equality, . . .

Pollard (1997) sums these up as challenges relating to:

- practicalities;
- teaching competences;
- personal ideals; and
- wider educational concerns.

This means that as a teacher, to prove your competence, you must rise to the challenge, reconcile numerous demands and make numerous decisions. To resolve the dilemmas, you must use your professional judgement to assess the situation, make decisions on how to act and have the skills to carry out those actions. If you do so effectively, you will be exhibiting the characterstics of the next level of competent practitioner – the experienced and reflective teacher. As such, you go through a cycle of reflective teaching: planning action, organizing for action, carrying it out, collecting evidence of the consequences, analyzing and evaluating evidence, reflecting upon it and feeding that reflection into the next planning cycle.

For any teacher, the aim is to show evidence of being able to:

- recognize issues;
- identify which of those issues are important;
- understand the situation as a whole; and,
- make appropriate decisions.

With these four abilities in mind, you can see that a *novice* teacher, a student teacher and a teacher in his or her first few years of teaching, would tend to recognize issues out of context (having no real experience to work from). As a consequence they would be unable to select the important ones (all tend to loom large and be seen as important). He or she will probably be analytical in understanding the whole situation (breaking it into individual components) and make decisions rationally (using logic and reasoning).

A *competent* teacher, on the other hand, after a few years of teaching experience, would tend to recognize issues in context (drawing on prior experiences of similar events) and select only the important ones (knowing which are minor and can be ignored). He or she would still tend to understand the whole situation analytically and make decisions rationally.

Finally, an *expert* teacher, who has both experience and has done some further reading, research and training, will tend to recognize issues in context, select the important ones, understand the whole situation holistically (viewing the integrated whole rather than the individual component parts) and make decisions through a finely developed intuition (drawing on experience and practice).

Task 15.3 A competence action plan	Think of your own development as a teacher of primary science.

[a] What level of competence do you bring to the start of your teaching career?
[b] What are your weaknesses as far as teaching primary science is concerned?
[c] If given a free choice in your first three years of teaching, what continuing professional development support or courses would you like to participate in to address your weaknesses or develop your competence further?
[d] Draw up a personal action plan, listing a timescale for what you would like to achieve and how you might achieve it.

As with any model, this is simplified and there are always exceptions, but you should be able to see that your professional development as a teacher is a continuous process. Remember that you cannot stand still. Children, curricula, environments all change. You must be flexible and adapt to change. Eventually you will want promotion. The first stage may be to become a subject leader or curriculum co-ordinator. This is what the final chapter is about.

SUGGESTIONS FOR FURTHER READING

If you would like to explore further some of the issues touched upon in this chapter, the following books should be of interest to you.

Pollard, A. (1996) *Readings for Reflective Teaching in the Primary School*, London: Cassell Education
   In this weighty book, Andrew Pollard brings together readings from experts in education across the whole spectrum of educational pedagogy. He does not limit himself to contemporary writers, but includes writings from the past to show how ideas in education have

changed and developed. The whole is intended to support the primary teacher in the process of reflecting on his or her own practice.

Pollard, A. (1997) *Reflective Teaching in the Primary School: A Handbook for the Classroom,* London: Cassell Education
This is a companion volume to the *Readings* . . . above, but is much more focused on actual classroom practice, supporting the student teacher and the new practitioner. Again, it is a large volume that covers a wide range of educational skills and ideas.

16 Becoming a Science Co-ordinator

Having taught for a while you will reach the stage where you begin to feel you would like to take on more responsibility (and the salary enhancements which usually go with it). If science is your specialism, the next step could be to apply for a post of responsibility in science. There are a number of titles given to teachers who take on such responsibility, each reflecting a slightly different focus to the role.

- *The science specialist teacher:* someone who has some subject expertise in an aspect of science and who may be asked to teach science to several classes in the school. There may be a number of teachers in the school with this expertise.
- *The science curriculum leader:* someone who usually has a subject specialism in science and who can provide advice on the subject, guide colleagues on how to teach it and perhaps teaches science to several classes. The addition here is involvement in working with and supporting other colleagues who are not experts in science.
- *The science curriculum manager:* someone with good administrative skills and perhaps (though not always) some subject expertise, who takes responsibility for the structure, form and direction of the science programme throughout the school. Sometimes, someone who is an excellent manager and administrator takes on the administrative side of the school's science work and works with the curriculum specialist.
- *The science curriculum co-ordinator:* someone who is likely to have science expertise and can co-ordinate the teaching and learning of science throughout the school, manage the programme and support and guide colleagues. In reality, the science co-ordinator's role tends to be an amalgam of the other three roles. It is also in line with the definition of a co-ordinator as given in the Ofsted *Handbook for the Inspection of Schools* (1993):

> . . . a teacher responsible for leading and co-ordinating the teaching and
> learning within a subject, curricular area or key stage . . .
>
> (p. 29)

At an interview, you are likely to be asked about the personal qualities you would
bring to the school as a subject co-ordinator, how you see the role of the science co-
ordinator and the extent to which you are prepared for that role. The remainder of
this chapter will look at these three elements. A fuller account of your role as a
science co-ordinator can be found in Newton and Newton (1998b).

THE QUALITIES OF A CURRICULUM CO-ORDINATOR

As a co-ordinator, you would be expected to have a number of personal qualities.
You would need to have proven your abilities as an effective class teacher and be a
good organizer, manager and communicator. Interpersonal skills are also important.
A command of the subject knowledge that underpins the primary school National
Curriculum Order for Science is also essential as is a knowledge of how to implement
it effectively from Reception to Year 6.

THE SCIENCE CO-ORDINATOR'S ROLE

Ofsted inspection reports consistently emphasize that well-trained and knowledgeable
co-ordinators are essential for a school to be successful. What is a science co-ordinator
and what might you be expected to do?

Task 16.1 The science co-ordinator's role

During your time in school, on one of your placements,
talk with the science co-ordinator about his or her role.
Try to find out about the following:

- the administrative responsibilities;
- involvement with other colleagues;
- involvement with children other than her/his own class;
- resource responsibilities; and,
- other responsibilities to do with the role.

How does she or he keep up to date and informed about what is happening in
science education?

Morrison (1985) explored the role of a subject co-ordinator and produced a list,
ranking the characteristics according to perceived importance. He suggested that co-
ordinators should:

- communicate with the headteacher;
- exercise curriculum leadership;
- communicate with staff;
- organize resources;
- establish continuity throughout the school;
- organize in-service training;
- liaise between head and staff;
- establish record systems;
- motivate staff; and,
- promote curriculum development.

A later study by Bell (1992), while generally endorsing Morrison's list, added the warning that:

> . . . there are some specific demands made on individual co-ordinators which are closely related to the nature of their particular curriculum area. Science perhaps makes greater demands than other areas.
>
> (p. 96)

Bell identified the demands as arising from:

- the essential practical nature of science education which requires the use of resources and equipment;
- the safety considerations which practical activity in science necessitates;
- the need for the development of teachers' personal scientific skills, knowledge and understanding; and,
- the fact that many teachers lack confidence and training in science.

The official job description for a science co-ordinator is given by Ofsted in the discussion document, *Primary Matters* (1994). The role involves:

1   developing a clear view of the nature of science and how it contributes to the wider curriculum;
2   providing advice and documentation to help colleagues teach science and interrelate its constituent elements; and,
3   playing a major part in organizing the teaching of science and the resources available for science, so that the statutory requirements of the National Curriculum Order for Science are covered.

Newton and Newton (1998b) identify two central aspects to a science co-ordinator's role which you need to think about. First, you need to think about supporting what is currently happening in your school. This is the static aspect. Second, you need to plan the development of science in your school. This is more dynamic. These can be summarized as shown in Figure 16.1.

Support: maintaining science	Development: promoting science
Advising colleagues: about science (know what) about teaching science (know how)	**Keeping yourself informed:** awareness of new publications attending courses professional development
Managing resources: storage stock taking and ordering maintenance and repair safety audits	**Disseminating information to others:** to staff to governors to parents staff development
Liaising with others: your headteacher staff in your school staff in other schools advisory teachers LEA inspectors and HMI others, e.g. parents	**Preparing and reviewing working documentation:** policy statement for science action plans scheme of work assessment and record keeping evaluation of learning

Figure 16.1   The role of the science co-ordinator (from Newton and Newton, 1998b, p. 14)

In the support role you will be expected to maintain the school's day-to-day science teaching. This will involve you in advising and supporting your colleagues, managing the science resources and liaising with other people. As a curriculum developer, you will be expected to identify needs and promote change in science education. This means you need to keep yourself up to date and informed about developments in science education, disseminate relevant information to colleagues and others in an appropriate way, and prepare and review the range of working documents associated with the teaching and learning of science throughout the school.

Many aspects of your role as a science co-ordinator will take time to achieve. You must not expect to do everything at once. Nor will you necessarily be successful at everything you attempt to do. You should work out a programme for your role, which includes a strand focusing on your own personal development as a co-ordinator.

Also remember that even though you are a co-ordinator, you are not alone. Work cooperatively with other co-ordinators in your school. Find out how they approach their task. Seek advice from the head teacher, from colleagues and from advisers. Establish links with science co-ordinators in other schools. Finally, consult books and journals where much of the hard work has already been done for you. You do not need to reinvent the wheel.

YOUR OWN PERSONAL DEVELOPMENT AS A SCIENCE CO-ORDINATOR

In recent years, the government has carried out a review of continuing professional development of primary teachers and introduced a new national qualification – the *National Professional Qualification for Subject Leaders* (NPQSL) (TTA, 1996). The standards of skill, knowledge and understanding are clearly specified and are in four groups:

- The co-ordinator's core role in the school.
- The main areas for development and assessment:
  - (a) teaching, learning and curriculum;
  - (b) monitoring, evaluating and improving;
  - (c) people and relationships;
  - (d) resource management; and,
  - (e) accountability.
- The co-ordinator's own professional knowledge and understanding.
- The co-ordinator's own skills and abilities.

You could use these to plan ahead and set your own targets, particularly for the third and fourth in the list above. Start from where you are. If you are thinking about applying for a science co-ordinator's post, the first thing to do is to check your own level of professional knowledge and understanding of science.

Task 16.2 Audit of professional knowledge and understanding in science	Carry out an audit of your own professional knowledge and understanding. For each of the following questions, ask yourself how confident you feel in this respect and justify your response.

1. Am I up to date on science and science-related pedagogy?
2. Do I have a broad understanding of the key issues in science?
3. Am I aware of recent research in science education?
4. Do I know what national inspection evidence tells us about science education?
5. How does the achievement of pupils in my school compare with national standards in science?
6. Are the methods I am using to monitor, develop and improve science teaching in my school the most appropriate?
7. Do I understand how children with different needs learn most effectively in science?
8. Am I up to date with health and safety requirements?
9. Have I a broad overview of science in the curriculum as a whole?
10. Have I read the recent, relevant publications from government and other national bodies?

If you feel you are able to answer all or most of these questions positively, then you should feel fairly confident about your professional knowledge and understanding. If you also feel you have appropriate subject expertise and personal qualities, then you are probably well-suited for a post of responsibility in science. To check this, try responding to the following scenarios.

- Imagine that you have applied for a teaching post as a science co-ordinator in a local primary school and have been called for interview. How thorough is your grasp of the National Curriculum Order for Science for the primary school and your role as a science co-ordinator?

  Either: As well as being the science co-ordinator, the post is as a Key Stage 1 teacher, working with a Year 2 (6–7 year old) class. You are asked the following questions:

  What science are the pupils in your class likely to have covered before they come to you?
  What are the children likely to cover in Key Stage 2, for which their time with you is a preparation?

  Or: As well as being the science co-ordinator, the post is as a Key Stage 2 teacher, working with a Year 4 (8–9 year old) class. You are asked the following questions:

  What science are the pupils in your class likely to have covered before they come to you, in both Key Stage 1 and Year 3?
  What are the children likely to cover in upper Key Stage 2, for which their time with you is a preparation?

- One of your colleagues is considerably older than you – near to retirement – and is not teaching science to his class very effectively. It is your task as the science co-ordinator to sort this out. How would you go about it?
- The school (an infant school) is amalgamating with the adjacent junior school in September. You will need a new policy document, scheme of work and so on. What does the 'and so on' include? How will you go about the task?
- If you had £500 to spend on resources for primary science, what would you do with it?

How well you answer these questions should give you a feeling for how ready you are for a leadership role in science.

SUGGESTIONS FOR FURTHER READING

If you would like to explore further some of the issues touched upon in this chapter, the following books should be of interest to you.

Harrison, M. (ed.) (1995) *Developing a Leadership Role in Key Stage 2 Curriculum*, London: Falmer Press

Although Mike Harrison's book focuses on the role of the co-ordinator in Key Stage 2, the principles can easily be translated to Key Stage 1. It is of particular relevance for anyone interested in a phase as well as a subject responsibility.

Newton. L.D. and Newton, D.P. (1998) *Coordinating Science Across the Primary School*, London: Falmer Press

This is one of 16 books published by RoutledgeFalmer in their **Subject Leader's Handbook Series**. If science is going to be your subject specialism, then you should explore in some depth what would be expected of you as a subject leader. This book covers the role of the science co-ordinator, what you need to know, how to develop whole school policies and schemes of work for science, monitoring for quality and resources for learning. If science is not your specialism, all other subjects of the National Curriculum, plus Religious Education and other specialist co-ordinator roles (for example, SENCO – the Special Educational Needs Coordinator) are included in the series.

PART 4
Further Information

Appendix
Addresses and Sources of
Information and Support

As you begin your teaching career, there are various materials and resources to help you teach primary science. What follows is a summary of those most readily available but, inevitably, the list cannot be complete. Commercially produced schemes, for example, have not been included although it is important to recognize that some provide very good support materials which you can use to plan, organize, manage and assess science. This list includes:

1   associations which provide support for teaching primary science;
2   journals published by these associations;
3   some suppliers' addresses;
4   sources of industry/enterprise links;
5   interactive science and technology centres; and,
6   websites.

You may also come across free resources in unusual places which might help you. For example, many of the large superstores produce leaflets for customers which describe how they are being environmentally friendly. Some building societies produce advice leaflets on buildings and structures. Electricity and gas board shops often have leaflets on energy efficiency in the home. Post offices sometimes have posters and materials on aspects of communication. Ask for copies for yourself or even class-size sets. You will usually find the business or store very helpful.

[1] ASSOCIATIONS

While you do not have to be a member of a science group or association, you will find that it is a good way to keep informed and share ideas. For example,

Association for Science Education (ASE)

The ASE has a long history of support for science teaching, initially in secondary schools but now in primary schools as well. They publish the *Primary Science Review*. This has been a major source of ideas and information for primary teachers since 1986. The ASE produces a range of books and guidance materials for teachers, which are advertised in *PSR* and can be purchased at a 10 per cent discount by members. The association also organizes local and national meetings, and runs an advice and support system. There are different categories of membership; teachers can subscribe as individuals or schools can take out a group subscription.

Membership: The Membership Manager,
                  Freepost,
                  The Association for Science Education
                  College Lane,
                  Hatfield,
                  Herts. AL10 9BR
Telephone: 01707–267411

British Association for the Advancement of Science (BAAS)

The British Association aims to support and promote science at all levels. It holds an annual festival of science, open to schools, other institutions and the general public and produces *SCAN*, a science awareness newsletter. At the primary school level, the BA supports the BAYS club scheme (*British Association for Young Scientists*) for 8 to 18-year-olds, organizing science challenges and awarding bronze, silver and gold level certificates. The BA also holds a national database of speakers on science and technology, called *Talking Science Plus*.

Membership: The British Association for the
                  Advancement of Science,
                  Fortress House,
                  23, Savile Row,
                  London W1X 1AB
Telephone: 020–74943326

Earth Science Teachers' Association (ESTA)

ESTA publishes journals for teachers at both primary and secondary school levels, containing ideas and information related particularly to aspects of geology and organizes in-service meetings and conferences (see *Teaching Primary Earth Science*, below). There are special rates for members buying rock and mineral samples, books, maps and postcards.

Membership: Mrs K. York,
                  ESTA Primary Committee,
                  346, Middlewood Road North,
                  Oughtibridge,
                  Sheffield S30 3HF

[2] JOURNALS AND PROFESSIONAL MAGAZINES

There are a number of journals and professional magazines which you should try to look at on a regular basis, both for ideas and to keep yourself informed. Most should be available through your local university library. For example,

Primary Science Review (PSR)

First issued in Summer 1986, *PSR* is now published five times a year by the ASE, and is the primary science journal for the association. It includes articles and information on science, D&T and IT, as well as having a research round-up section, book reviews and information about conferences and meetings. For details of the address and membership, see under ASE (above).

Primary Maths and Science (PMS)

First published in October 1988 as *Questions: Exploring Science and Technology 3–13*, this professional publication for teachers combined with its mathematics equivalent, *Strategies*, and is now known as *PMS*. Published nine times a year, it provides articles and information for teachers covering subject knowledge and application, new books and resources, support organizations and meetings and conferences. It also includes pull-out teaching packs, usually topic focused, containing ideas and materials for immediate use in the classroom.

Order from: Questions Publishing Company,
                27, Frederick Street,
                Birmingham,
                B1 3HH
Contact: Fran Stevens
Telephone: 0121–2120919
Fax: 0121–2120959

Teaching Primary Earth Science (TPES)

This is a journal for primary teachers produced by the Earth Science Teachers' Association four times a year. It provides ideas, activities and information on Earth

Science topics based on NC Science and Geography; it also provides details of in-service conferences and materials and resources useful for teaching in the primary school. For details of the address and membership, see under ESTA (above).

The Young Detectives Magazine

This is a new magazine produced by BNFL in summer 1996. It contains news, ideas and resources for Primary Science and Technology, and is issued free, three times a year.

> *Contact:*   The Young Detectives Magazine,
> Resources for Learning,
> 19, Park Drive,
> Bradford,
> West Yorkshire
> BD9 4DS
> *Telephone:*   01274–544155

[3] SOME SUPPLIERS

The list of possible suppliers of science resources and equipment is enormous, and some schools are restricted by their LEAs to purchasing from particular ones. However, if you are given a budget for primary science and have a choice it is worth shopping around, because prices can vary tremendously. Some you might look at include:

Heron Educational Ltd

Heron provide a range of resources from furniture and workstations to tools and equipment. They publish different catalogues for Primary Science, Primary Technology and Early Years.

> *Contact:*   Heron Educational Ltd.,
> Carrwood House,
> Carrwood Road,
> Chesterfield S41 9QB
> *Telephone:*   0800–373249 (free)

NES Arnold Educational Supplier

Although a general educational supplier, NES Arnold offer a range of resources to support primary science teaching. As well as the large general catalogue, a Primary Science catalogue is available.

Contact: NES Arnold Ltd.,
            Ludlow Hill Road,
            West Bridgford,
            Nottingham NG2 6HD
Telephone: 0115–9452200

NIAS – Northamptonshire Inspection and Advisory Service

The science centre provides to schools a range of resources, both kits and textual materials, to support the teaching of primary science in schools. Produced by their advisory teams for their own schools, the materials are closely tied to the needs of schools and have often been prepared in consultation with school staff. The resources are often advertised in the *Primary Science Review*.

Contact: NIAS,
            The Science Centre,
            Spencer Centre,
            Lewis Road,
            Northants NN5 7BJ

Technology Teaching Systems (TTS)

Despite its misleading name, TTS provides a full range of resources for teaching primary science. A catalogue is available giving full details.

Contact: TTS,
            Unit 4, Holmewood Fields Business Park,
            Park Road,
            Holmewood,
            Chesterfield S42 5UY

[4] INDUSTRY, ENTERPRISE AND OTHER LINKS

The DFE (1993) published a booklet, *Building Effective School-Business Links*, about ways in which schools can enhance their links with industry and business, and maximize the value of such links.

British Kidney Patient Association

A teaching resources pack is available which includes a 10-minute video, classroom poster, teacher's guide and photocopiable sheets for use in the classroom and at home.

It is aimed a 9–14 year olds. The pack is free but a charge of £4.45 is made to cover package and postage.

Contact: The British Kidney Patient Association,
Bordon,
Hampshire GU35 9JZ
Telephone: 01420–472021

British Nuclear Fuels Ltd

BNFL produce video materials, booklets and posters, resource packs and other resources to support school science teaching at the primary as well as secondary school levels. Visits to power stations and energy centres can also be arranged with the education officers. A free catalogue is available.

Contact: BNFL,
Community Affairs,
Risley,
Warrington,
Cheshire WA3 9AS
Telephone: 01925–832826

The Chemical Industry Education Centre

The CIEC at the University of York works with teachers and industrialists to write teaching materials which make science and technology experiences explicitly relevant to primary and secondary pupils. For primary school use, over 20 theme-related units are available, for example, *Tidy and Sort* (for 5–7 year olds) and *Plastics Playtime* (for 8–10 year olds). Each unit contains teachers' notes, background information and photocopiable activity sheets. A catalogue is available on request.

Contact: CIEC,
Department of Chemistry,
University of York,
York YO1 5DD
Telephone: 01904–432523

Royal Society for the Protection of Birds (RSPB)

The RSPB have a network of education officers around the country who will visit schools and give talks on topics related to birds. Teaching resource materials are also available and schools as well as individuals can apply for membership.

Contact: The RSPB Education Office,
The Lodge,
Sandy,
Beds SG19 2DL

[5] INTERACTIVE SCIENCE AND TECHNOLOGY CENTRES

ISTCs are fashionable, being one way to take science and technology to the wider public and aimed at changing people's perceptions of and attitudes towards science and technology. Their essence is their hands-on approach, which enables sensory interaction and interests and motivates all involved. As with museums, a preliminary visit by the science co-ordinator is advisable to assess how it might be used, make contacts and see what kind of support is available during visits. There are ISTCs spread nationally in most of our large cities, and some of the more well-known are listed here.

- **Discovery Dome**
  c/o Science Projects,
  Turnham Green,
  Terrace Mews,
  London W1 1QU
- **Glasgow Dome of Discovery**
  South Rotunda,
  100 Govan Road,
  Glasgow G51 1JS
- **Light on Science**
  Birmingham Museum
  of Science and Industry,
  Newhall Street,
  Birmingham B3 1RX
- **Technology Testbed**
  National Museums and Galleries
  on Merseyside,
  Large Objects Collection,
  Princes Dock,
  Pier Head,
  Liverpool L3 0AA

- **The Exploratory**
  The Old Station,
  Temple Meads,
  Bristol BS8 1QU
- **Launch Pad**
  Science Museum,
  Exhibition Road,
  London SW7 2DD
- **Science Factory**
  Newcastle Museum of
  Science and Engineering,
  Blandford Street,
  Newcastle upon Tyne NE1 4JA
- **Xperiment!**
  Greater Manchester Museum of
  Science and Industry,
  Castlefield,
  Manchester M3 4JP

[6] WEBSITES

Association for Science
Education: http://www.ase.org.uk
BBC Education: http://www.bbc.co.uk/education/schools/science.html

British Association:	http://www.britassoc.org.uk
British Library:	http://www.portico.bl.uk
Channel Four:	http://www.channel4.com/schools
Meteorological Office:	http://www.meto.govt.uk
NCET's Science Curriculum IT Support Project:	http://www.ncet.org.uk/science/scindex.html
Natural History Museum:	http://www.nhm.ac.uk
Schools Online Science:	http://www.shu.ac.uk/schools/sci/sol/contents.html
Science and Plants for Schools at Homerton College:	http://www-saps.plantsci.cam.ac.uk
Students' and Teachers' Educational Materials (STEM) Project at the Science Museum:	http://www.nmsi.ac.uk/education/stem
Wellcome Trust:	http://www.wellcome.ac.uk

References

Association for Science Education (1990) *Be Safe! Some Aspects of Safety in School Science and Technology for Key Stages 1 and 2* (2nd edition), Hatfield: ASE

Association for Science Education (1990) *Teachers' Assessment – Making it Work in the Primary School*, Hatfield: ASE

Association for Science Education (1997) *Learning and Teaching: Policy Statement*, Hatfield: ASE

Association for Science Education (1998) *IT in Primary Science*, Hatfield: ASE

Bell, D. (1992) 'Co-ordinating science in primary schools: A role model?', in Newton, L.D. *Primary Science: The Challenge of the 1990s*, Clevedon: Multilingual Matters, pp. 93–109

Berlak, A. and Berlak, H. (1981) *Dilemmas of Schooling*, London: Methuen

Blyth, A. (1998) 'English Primary Education: Looking backward to look forward' in Richards C. and Taylor P.H. (eds) *How Shall We School Our Children? Primary Education and Its Future*, London: Falmer Press, pp. 3–16

Bradley, L.S. (1996) *Children Learning Science*, Oxford: Nash Pollock Publishing

Carey, J. (1995) *The Faber Book of Science*, London: Faber & Faber

Cashdan, A. and Overall, L. (eds) (1998) *Teaching in Primary Schools*, London: Cassell

Central Advisory Council for England (1967) *Children and Their Primary Schools (The Plowden Report)* Volumes 1 and 2, London: HMSO

Conner, C. (1999) 'Two steps forward, one step back: progression in children's learning', *Primary File*, 36, pp. 141–4

Cullingford, C. (ed.) (1989) *The Primary Teacher: The Role of the Educator and the Purpose of Primary Education*, London: Cassell

Davies, J. (1998) 'The Standards Debate' in Richards, C. and Taylor, P.H. *How Shall We School Our Children? Primary Education and Its Future*, London: Falmer Press, pp. 160–172

Davis, A. (1998) *The Limits of Educational Assessment*, Oxford: Blackwell

Department for Education (DFE) (1995) *Science in the National Curriculum*, London: HMSO

Department for Education and Employment (DfEE) (1997) *Excellence in Education (White Paper)*, London: DfEE/HMSO

Department for Education and Employment (DfEE) (1998) *National Literacy Strategy: Framework for Teaching*, London: DfEE/HMSO

Department for Education and Employment (DfEE) (1998) *Teaching: High Status, High Standards – Requirements for Courses of Initial Teacher Training* (Circular number 4/98), London: TTA Publications

Department for Education and Employment (DfEE) (1998) *The National Numeracy Project*, London: DfEE/HMSO

Department for Education and Employment (DfEE) (1999) *Science: The National Curriculum for England, Key Stages 1–4.* London: DfEE/HMSO

Department of Education and Science (DES) (1978) *Primary Education: An HMI Report*, London: HMSO

Department of Education and Science (DES) (1982) *Mathematics Counts (The Cockcroft Report)*, London: HMSO

Department of Education and Science (DES) (1985) *Science 5–16: A Statement of Policy*, London: HMSO

Department of Education and Science (DES) (1989) *Science Non-Statutory Guidance*, London: HMSO

Department of Education and Science (DES) (1991) *Science: Key Stages 1 and 3. A Report by Her Majesty's Inspectorate on the First Year, 1989–1990*, London: HMSO

Desforges, C. (1985) 'Matching tasks to children' in Bennett, N. and Desforges, C. (eds) *Recent Advances in Classroom Research*, Edinburgh: Scottish Academic Press

Dewey, J. (1933) *How We Think*, New York: D.C. Heath, revised edition

Driver, R., Leach, J., Scott, P. and Wood-Robinson, C. (1995) 'Young people's understanding of science concepts' in Murphy, P., Selinger, M., Bourne, J. and Briggs, M., (eds) *Subject Learning in the Primary Curriculum: Issues in English, science and mathematics*, London: Routledge, Chapter 14, pp. 158–183

Dunbar, R. (1995) *The Trouble with Science*, London: Faber and Faber

Edwards, A. and Collison, J. (1996) *Mentoring and Developing Practice in Primary Schools: Supporting Student Teachers Learning in Schools*, Milton Keynes: Open University Press

Edwards, D. and Mercer, N. (1987) *Common Knowledge: The Development of Understanding in the Classroom*, London: Routledge

Eisner, E. (1979) *The Educational Imagination*, New York: Macmillan

Farrow, S. (1999) *The Really Useful Science Book: A framework of knowledge for primary teachers*, London: Falmer Press (2nd ed.)

Feasey, R. and Siraj-Blatchford, J. (1998) *Key Skills: Communication in Science*, Durham: University of Durham/Tyneside Training and Enterprise Council

Fitz-Gibbon, C.T. (1995) *Monitoring Education: Indicators, Quality and Effectiveness*, London: Cassell

Fowler, H.W. and Fowler, F.G. (eds) (1964) *The Concise Oxford Dictionary of Current English*, Oxford: Clarendon Press, 5th edition

Fuller, S. (1997) *Science*, Buckingham: Open Unviesity Press

Goldsworthy, A. (1998) 'Learning to Investigate' in Sherrington, R. (ed.) *ASE Guide to Primary Science Education*, Hatfield: ASE, pp. 63–70

Gott, R. and Duggan, S. (1998) 'Understanding Scientific Evidence – Why It Matters and How It Can Be Taught', in Ratcliffe, M. (ed.) *ASE Guide to Secondary Science Education*, Hatfield: ASE, pp. 92–99

Harlen, W. (1983) *Guides to Assessment in Education*: Science, London: Macmillan

Harlen, W. (1992) *The Teaching of Science*, London: David Fulton

Harlen, W. and Jelly, S. (1989) *Developing Science in the Primary Classroom*, Edinburgh: Oliver and Boyd

Harrison, M. (ed.) (1995) *Developing a Leadership Role in Key Stage 2 Curriculum*, London: Falmer Press

Hatano, G. and Inagaki, K. (1992) 'Desituating cognition through the construction of conceptual knowledge', in Light, P. and Butterworth, G. (eds) *Content and Cognition: Ways of Learning and Knowing*, London: Harvester-Wheatsheaf, pp. 115–133

Her Majesty's Inspectorate (HMI) (1985) *Science 5–16: A Statement of Policy*, London: HMSO

Her Majesty's Stationery Office (1989) *COSHH: Guidance for Schools*, London: HMSO

Higgins, S. and Miller, J. (in press) *Meeting the Standards in . . . Primary ICT*, London: RoutledgeFalmer

Hughes, M. (ed.) (1996) *Progression in Learning*, Clevedon: Multilingual Matters

Humberside Local Education Authority (1991) 'Whole Curriculum Planning in the Primary School', Paper presented by staff from Humberside County Council Education Department at the National Curriculum Council's Northern Associates' Conference, York, 12/11/98

John, P.D. (1994) 'Academic tasks in history classrooms', *Research in Education*, **51**, pp. 11–22

Juniper, D.F. (1989) *Successful Problem Solving*, Slough: W. Foulsham

Keogh, B. and Naylor, S. (1993) 'Progression and continuity in science' in Sherrington, R. (ed.) *The ASE Primary Science Teachers' Handbook*, Hemel Hempstead: Simon and Schuster

Kerry, T. and Eggleston, J. (1988) *Topic Work in the Primary School*, London: Routledge

Kuhn, T. (1970) *The Structure of Scientific Revolutions*, Chicago, IL: University of Chicago Press, (2nd edition)

Lakatos, I. (1975) *The Methodology of Scientific Research Programmes (Vol.1)*, Cambridge: Cambridge University Press

Lock, R. and Ratcliffe, M. (1998) 'Learning about Social and Ethical Applications of Science' in Ratcliffe, M. (ed.) (1998) *ASE Guide to Secondary Science Education*, Hatfield: ASE, pp. 109–117

Logan, A. (1998) 'Get connected', *Child Education*, September 1998, p. 25

Millar, R., Gott, R., Luben, F. and Duggan, S. (1996) 'Children's performance of investigative tasks in science: A framework for considering progression', in Hughes, M. *Progression in Learning*, Clevedon: Multilingual matters, pp. 82–108

Mills, R.W. (1988) *Observing Children in the Primary Classroom*, London: Unwin Hyman

Moon, B. (1996) *A Guide to the National Curriculum*, Oxford: Oxford University Press

Morrison, K. (1985) 'Tensions in subject-specialist teaching in the primary school', *Curriculum*, **6**, 3, pp. 24–9

Moyles, J. (1995) *Beginning Teaching, Beginning Learning in Primary Education*, Buckingham: Open University Press

National Curriculum Council (1989) *Science Non-Statutory Guidance*, York: NCC

Newton, D.P. (1989) *Making Science Education Relevant*, London: Kogan Page

Newton, D.P. (1992) 'Children Doing Science: Observation, investigation and the National Curriculum for England and Wales', in Newton, L.D. (ed.), *Primary Science: The Challenge of the 1990s*, Clevedon: Multilingual Matters, pp. 8–19

Newton, D.P. (2000) *Teaching for Understanding*, London: RoutledgeFalmer

Newton, D.P. and Newton, L.D. (1987) *Footsteps into Science*, London: Harcourt Brace Jovanovich

Newton, L.D. (ed.) (1992) *Primary Science: The Challenge of the 1990s*, Clevedon: Multilingual Matters, pp. 8–19

Newton, L.D. and Newton, D.P. (1993) 'Investigation in National Curriculum science: Some definitions', *Primary Science Review*, **30**, December, pp. 15–17

Newton, L.D. and Newton, D.P. (1998a) 'Primary children's conceptions of science and the scientist: is the impact of a National Curriculum breaking down the stereotype?', *International Journal of Science Education*, **20**, 9, pp. 1137–49

Newton, L.D. and Newton, D.P. (1998b) *Coordinating Science Across the Primary School*, London: Falmer Press

Nissani, M. (1996) 'Dancing flies: A guided discovery illustration of the nature of science', *The American Biology Teacher*, **58**, 3, March, pp. 166–171

Office for Standards in Education (OFSTED) (1993) *Handbook for the Inspection of Schools*, London: HMSO/OFSTED

Office for Standards in Education (OFSTED) (1994) *Primary Matters: A Discussion on Teaching and Learning in Primary Schools*, London: HMSO/OFSTED

Office for Standards in Education (OFSTED) (1996) *Subjects and Standards*, London: HMSO/ OFSTED

Office for Standards in Education (OFSTED) (1998) *Inspection '98 Supplement to the Inspection Handbooks Containing New Requirements and Guidance*, London: HMSO/OFSTED

Office for Standards in Education (OFSTED) (1998) *Standards in Primary Science*, London: HMSO/OFSTED

Ogborn, J., Kress, G., Martins, I. and McGillicuddy, K. (1996) *Explaining Science in the Classroom*, Buckingham: Open University Press

Osborne, J. (1998) 'Learning and Teaching about the Nature of Science' in Ratcliffe, M. (ed.) (1998) *ASE Guide to Secondary Science Education*, Hatfield: ASE, pp. 100–108

Osborne, R.J. (1985) 'Children's own concepts' in Harlen, W. (ed.) *Primary Science: Taking the Plunge*, London: Heinemann

Osborne, R. and Freyaberg, P. (1985) *Children's Learning in Science*, London: Heinemann

Parkin, T. and Lewis, M. (1998) *Science and Literacy: A Guide for Primary Teachers*, Nuffield Primary Science Series – Glasgow: Collins Educational

Pennell, A. and Alexander, R. (1990) *The Management of Change in the Primary School – Implementing the National Curriculum in Science and Design Technology*, London: Falmer Press

Pollard, A. (1990) *Learning in Primary Schools*, London: Cassell

Pollard, A. (1996) *Readings for Reflective Teaching in the Primary School*, London: Cassell Education

Pollard, A. (1997) *Reflective Teaching in the Primary School: A Handbook for the Classroom*, London: Cassell Education

Popper, K.R. (1959) *The Logic of Scientific Discovery*, London: Hutchinson

Primary Science Review (1998) *Literacy and Numeracy Through Science*, Special Issue **53**, May/June 1998, Hatfield: ASE

Proctor, A., Entwistle, M., Judge, B. and McKenzie-Murdoch, S. (1995) *Learning to Teach in the Primary Classroom*, London: Routledge

Qualifications and Curriculum Authority (QCA) (1998) *Science: A Scheme of Work for Key Stages 1 and 2*, London: DfEE Raising Standards Unit

Qualifications and Curriculum Authority (QCA) (1999) 'New television series about key skills', *ONQ*, Issue 5, April 1999, p. 8

Qualter, A. (1996) *Differentiated Primary Science*, Buckingham: Open University Press

Ratcliffe, M. (ed.) (1998) *ASE Guide to Secondary Science Education*, Hatfield: ASE

Science Processes and Concepts Exploration (SPACE) Project, *SPACE Project Research Reports*, Liverpool: Liverpool University Press

Sherrington, R. (ed.) (1998) *ASE Guide to Primary Science Education*, Hatfield: ASE, pp. 63–70

Simon, S., Brown, M., Black, P. and Blondel, E. (1996) 'Progression in learning mathematics and science', in Hughes, M. (ed.) *Progression in Learning*, Clevedon: Multilingual Matters, pp. 24–49

Sperber, D. (1994) 'The modularity of thought and the epidemiology of representation', in Hirschfield L.A. and Gelman S.A. (eds.) *Mapping the Mind*, Cambridge: Cambridge University Press, pp. 39–67

Task Group on Assessment and Testing (1987) *Report of the Task Group on Assessment and Testing* (Chair: Prof. P. Black), London: HMSO

Teacher Training Agency (TTA) (1996) *Consultation Paper on Standards and A National Professional Qualification for Subject Leaders*, London: TTA

Teacher Training Agency (TTA) (1998) *Teaching – A Guide to Becoming a Teacher*, London: TTA Publications

Watson, R. (1997) 'ASE-King's Science Investigations in Schools (AKSIS) Project: Investigations at Key Stages 2 and 3', *Education in Science*, **171**, pp. 22–3

Watson, R. and Wood-Robinson, V. (1998) 'Learning to Investigate', in Ratcliffe, M. (ed.) *ASE Guide to Secondary Science Education*, Hatfield: ASE, pp. 84–91

Wenham, M. (1995) *Understanding Primary Science: Ideas, Concepts and Explanations*, London: Paul Chapman Publishing

White, R.T. (1988) *Learning Science*, Oxford: Basil Blackwell

White, R. and Gunstone, R. (1992) *Probing Understanding*, London: Falmer Press

Wolpert, L. (1993) *The Unnatural Nature of Science*, London: Faber & Faber

Wynn, C.M. and Wiggins, A.C. (1997) *The Five Biggest Ideas in Science*, New York: John Wiley & Sons, Inc.

Index